THE THEORY AND PRACTICE OF INTERNATIONAL LAW

Responses to a Variety of International Legal Issues

Editor
Abdul Ghafur Hamid @ Khin Maung Sein

SERIALS PUBLICATIONS
NEW DELHI (INDIA)

Edition: 2009

ISBN: 978-81-8387-292-8

Published by
SERIALS PUBLICATIONS
4830/24, Prahlad Street, Ansari Road
Darya Ganj, New Delhi-110002 (India)
Phone : 23245225. Fax : 91-11-23272135
E-mail: serials@sify.com

CONTENTS

PREFACE

We have to admit that international law is not a perfect system and that there are weaknesses in the international legal system, in particular in terms of enforcement. Still the overwhelming majority of States normally comply with international law. There is indeed one exceptional area where States tend to flout the law, that is, the regulation of the use of force. This is due to the fact that the use of force is the one area where national interests are at stake and where power matters. Apart from this, the general trend is that States observe rules of international law.

To have a clearer picture of the current trend of the international legal order, we need to evaluate both the theoretical as well as the practice aspect of international law. This is the main objective of the book, which is a collection of research papers ranging from the basic conception of the international legal personality to *jus ad bellum*, *jus in bello*, software piracy, the regulation of international trade, and the protection of human rights.

The first Chapter of the book showcases an illuminating article of *Abdul Ghafur Hamid @ Khin Maung Sein* on the "Defence of Superior Orders", a hotly debated issue affecting both international criminal law and international law of armed conflict. The writer strongly supports the compromised formula, as enshrined in Article 33 of the Rome Statute establishing the International Criminal Court, acknowledging the partial acceptance of the defence only in the exceptional situation where the order of the superior is not manifestly illegal.

Bryan C. Bank's article is on "The Security Council as Global Legislator: Using Chapter VII Authority to Redefine the United Nations Role in Developing International Legal Norms". The writer argues that the Security Council has the competence to act as a global legislator, and that it is simply a matter of acceptance by the Member States. Admitting that the character of the Security Council, with the power located in the hands of the permanent members, has caused some hesitation on the part of the international community, the writer emphasizes some distinct advantages of the Security council, namely, its flexibility and ability to take a swift response to addressing situations of international concern, compared to either the process of custom formation or treaty negotiation.

The article by *Mohammad Monirul Azam and Abdul Hamid Chowdhury* outlines the socio-economic impact of "software piracy" and the effectiveness of international and national legal measures to combat it. The main thrust of the article is an analysis of the measures enshrined in the TRIPS agreement, the most comprehensive IP agreement adopted at the international level, which imposed upon all the member countries of the WTO to ensure effective enforcement mechanisms. The article concludes with recommendations to deter software piracy and thereby to exploit the benefits of IP.

Mohammad Naqib Ishan Jan, in his fascinating article, first of all admits the fact that international trade law and international human rights law are closely intertwined. The writer then explores the areas where the two laws conflict with each other. One question raised by the writer is why international trade law should prevail in case of conflict with international human right law. The writer suggests that the WTO Member States should make sure that whatever trade policy they agree upon must not in any way compromise their capacity to respect their international human rights obligations and that the trade rules that they adopt must be just and must not, in any way, undermine the protection of human rights.

Myint Zan, in his thought-provoking revisit to the Security Council Resolution 678 (1990), critically analyzes the Resolution in light of the power situations at the time of the Gulf War and of later developments like the United States invasion of Iraq in 2003. The writer concludes that in the matrix of power politics and of international relations, international law is not always irrelevant and what one believes to be a politico-legal analysis of one of the most significant UN Security Council resolutions in recent history is a worthwhile task.

Hamiff Ahamat's article entitled "The WTO Trade Policy Regimes and the Welfare Discourse: Searching for the Symbiosis", discusses the implications of welfare on the use of trade policy measures which are `sanctioned' by the World Trade Organization. It also analyses how the notion of economic welfare interacts with other competing notions that justify the use of such measures, such as `social welfare'. Such dichotomy explains the gap between the legal and economic aspects of the WTO trade policy regimes. The paper investigates whether the gap can be reduced through the symbiosis of economic and social welfare of such regimes and proposes mechanisms to institutionalize such symbiosis.

Last but not least, the philosophical piece of *Christopher Barbara*, entitled "A Back-To-Basics Approach to International Legal personality: New Thinking about the Individual, the State and the Era of Globalization", argues that law is a social phenomenon which finds its genesis in helping to assure the survival of Mankind, and seeks to explore the future of international law-via the fundamental concept of international legal personality–in the contemporary context of globalization. The writer's main thrust is to move away from the state-centric international legal system and towards one built upon Man and his wellbeing. The writer, nevertheless, admits that instigating this type of change is the true challenge here.

The Editor is greatly indebted to all those who readily agreed to contribute to this book with their articles. Without their contributions and support, the book would never come out. The Editor would also like to express his special thanks to Mr. Vijay Kumar and Serials Publications for their hard work in publishing the book.

Abdul Ghafur Hamid @ Khin Maung Sein
April 2009
Kuala Lumpur

ABOUT THE CONTRIBUTORS

Christopher G. Barbara is a Canadian jurist specializing in international law. He holds an LLM in Public International Law from Leiden University (The Netherlands) and a BA Honours degree in Law from Carleton University (Canada).

Myint Zan, B.A., LL.B. (Rangon), LL.M. (Michigan), M. Int. Law (Australian National University), Ph.D. (Griffith), is currently Principal Lecturer in the School of Law, Multimedia University, Malacca, Malaysia. His specialized areas include International law, human right law, international trade and commercial law. He has published over 50 academic journal articles and Chapters in Books published in Australia, India, Italy, Malaysia, New Zealand, Singapore, the United Kingdom and the United States. He has been a judge at Jessup international law moot competitions and the international humanitarian law moot competitions, held in Malaysia, Australia and the United States and Hong Kong, and an arbitrator, the Vis International Arbitration moot held in Austria. He recently authored the moot problem based on international legal issues for all the competed teams from Malaysia and abroad for the 2008 Law Asia Moot competition.

Muhammad Monirul Azam, LL.B. (Hons.), LL.M. (Uni. of Chittagong), LL.M. in Intellectual Property (jointly awarded by the University of Turin and ITC-ILO, Italy and WIPO Academy, Geneva, Switzerland), is Assistant Professor of law at the University of Chittagong, Bangladesh. His area of expertise includes Public Law, Intellectual Property Law, Labour and Industrial Law, WTO and International Trade Law and Human Rights Law. One of his recent publications is the "Establishment of the WTO and Impacts on the Legal System of Bangladesh," *Macquaire Journal of Business Law* (October, 2006, Vol. 3), Australia. *Abdul Hamid Chowdhury* is Assistant Professor at the

Department of Business Administration, International Islamic University Chittagong (IIUC), Bangladesh.

Haniff Ahamat holds an LLB (Hons) from International Islamic University, Malaysia (IIUM) and an LLM from National University of Malaysia (UKM). He also did his PhD in Law at Essex University, the UK, specialising in intersections of consumer interests and anti-dumping policy. He is currently Assistant Professor at Ahmad Ibrahim Faculty of Laws, International Islamic University Malaysia (IIUM). His recent publications include "Addressing Competition Concerns in the Use of EC Anti-Dumping Regime", *Manchester Journal of International Economic Law*, 5(3) (2008) 39-71.

Mohammad Naqib Ishan Jan, LL.B., MCL., Ph.D. (IIUM), is Associate Professor of law at the International Islamic University Malaysia. He is specialized in international law of armed conflict, international humanitarian law and refugee law. His recent publications are: *Principles of Public International Law : A Modern Approach*, [Kuala Lumpur: Research Management Centre, IIUM, 2008]; *Family and Succession Law, International Encyclopedia of Laws - Suppl. 38 [*The Netherlands: Kluwer Law International BV, May 2008] (Co-author); The United Nations Security Council's Sanctions against Iran : A Nuclear Apartheid" [2007] 7 *MLJ* , cxlii; "International Law Issues Arising out of Israel's Military Attack Against Lebanon in 2006" [2007] Vol. 2, Issue 1 - 2, Jan - Dec2007 *Asian Journal International Law*, 29 – 68; "War Crimes with Impunity: The Case of Abu Ghraib Prisoners", [2006] 4 *Malayan Law Journal* (MLJ) clxxiv.

Abdul Ghafur Hamid @ Khin Maung Sein, LL.B., LL.M. in International Law (Yangon), Ph.D. (IIUM), is Professor of Law and Coordinator of the International Law and Maritime Affairs (ILMA) Research Unit of the International Islamic University Malaysia. His specialized areas are international law of the sea, international trade law and international law of armed conflict. He has published 12 books, written over 30 articles, and presented a number of papers at local as well as international conferences. His recent publications include: "The WTO Rules versus Multilateral Environmental Agreements: The Search for Reconciliation", [2008] Vol. 5, *Macquarie Journal of International and Comparative*

*Environmental Law (JICEL)*57-79; "Legality of Anticipatory Self-Defence in the 21st Century World Order: A Reappraisal", [2007] Vol. 54, Issue 3, *Netherlands International Law Review* (NILR), 441-490; "Maritime Terrorism, the Straits of Malacca, and the Issue of State Responsibility", [2006] Vol. 15, No. 1, *Tulane Journal of International and Comparative Law*, 155-179; "Immunity versus International Crimes: the Impact of Pinochet and Arrest Warrant Cases" [2006] vol. 46, No. 4, *Indian Journal of International Law* (IJIL), 495-516; "A New Carriage of goods by Sea Act for Malaysia: A Holistic Approach on the Basis of International Practice", [2006] Vol. 12, No. 3, *The Journal of International Maritime Law* (JIML), 206-216.

THE DEFENCE OF SUPERIOR ORDERS, MANIFEST ILLEGALITY PRINCIPLE AND THE STATUTE OF THE INTERNATIONAL CRIMINAL COURT

Abdul Ghafur Hamid @ Khin Maung Sein*

The defence of superior orders has a long and controversial history. Once it was thought that only superiors who gave the illegal orders should be liable and soldiers should be absolutely free from liability. But such an approach has rarely been approved by national and international courts. The Nuremberg Charter, followed by the statutes of the ad hoc *international criminal tribunals adopted four decades later, affirms absolute liability theory and denies superior orders as a defence though it can be a mitigating factor. On the other hand, the Rome Statute establishing the International Criminal Court recognizes limited liability approach and accepts superior orders as a defence if the soldier did not know that the order was illegal and it was not manifestly illegal (manifest illegality principle). The present paper casts doubt on the argument that the manifest illegality principle as enshrined in the Rome Statute is contrary to customary international law. The paper argues that the absolute liability principle as adopted by the Nuremberg Charter do not reflect customary international law of the time because State practice is divided and decisions of domestic courts in most countries are not in favour of it. The paper concludes that incorporation of manifest illegality principle in a multilateral treaty like the Rome Statute has the potential of generating the principle to be a rule of customary international law in future.*

I. INTRODUCTION

International criminal law has borrowed extensively from domestic criminal law, in particular in its infancy. However, due to the desirability of impunity for horrendous crimes that shock the international community, international criminal law has rapidly developed into a full-fledged specialized subject of international law. Very much similar to domestic criminal law,

* LL.B. (Yangon), LL.M. in International Law (Yangon), Ph.D. (IIUM), Professor of Law and Coordinator of the International Law and Maritime Affairs (ILMA) Research Unit of the International Islamic University Malaysia

certain defences are available to the defendants in international criminal proceedings.[1] Among the factors that preclude international criminal liability, 'defence of superior orders' is quite controversial and widely debated.

According to military discipline and under military law a soldier is bound to obey the orders of his superiors without hesitation and without any question. At the same time, it is quite possible that some orders will be illegal and will be a crime under either domestic law or international law. In such cases, the soldier's duty to obey will clash with his duty not to commit a criminal act. He is therefore placed in a very difficult position and caught on the horns of a dilemma. The crucial question is whether he should be exempted from criminal liability even though what he did amounts to a heinous crime.

The present paper traces the history of the defence of superior orders and identifies the three main approaches, namely: (1) the notion of *absolute defence* or *respondeat superior*; (2) the notion of *absolute liability*; and (3) the concept of *limited liability* for following manifestly illegal order. The paper finds that neither of the first two approaches deals with the soldier's dilemma well and they both fail to give a practical solution to the problem. The absolute defence approach has rarely been approved by national or international courts and the absolute liability approach is inconsistent with the demands of military discipline. The paper suggests that the limited liability approach or the '*manifest illegality principle*', which aims at adjusting the conflicting demands of military discipline and the supremacy of the law, is the correct solution to the dilemma.

Although the Nuremberg Charter and the statutes establishing *ad hoc* international criminal tribunals stick to the absolute liability approach, the Rome Statute of the International Criminal Court incorporates the limited liability approach (manifest illegality principle) in its Article 33. The present paper concludes that such incorporation in a multilateral treaty like the Rome Statute has the potential of generating this principle to be a rule of customary international law in future.

II. THE THREE MAIN APPROACHES TO THE DEFENCE OF SUPERIOR ORDERS

The issue of pleading superior order as a defence has been a particularly controversial and debatable one and there has been a lack of consistency regarding its applicability under international law. One of the reasons why the defence causes problems is that it demonstrates a tension between national and international law. That is, while soldiers have a legal obligation under national law to obey superior orders without ever questioning them, they also have a corresponding legal obligation under international law to refuse to commit international crimes. Therefore, soldiers can often be placed in an extremely awkward dilemma. The intensity of the dilemma can clearly be seen in the following remarks: "The soldier who refuses to obey an order which is legal from the standpoint of national law may well find himself before a firing squad after being court martialled by his own state."[2]

If we look into the history of the defence of superior orders, we can clearly find that the legal thinking has been developed into three main approaches: (1) the notion of *absolute defence* or *respondeat superior*; (2) the notion of *absolute liability*; and (3) the concept of *limited liability* for following manifestly illegal orders.

(A) Absolute Defence Approach: Respondeat Superior

Professor Oppenheim was the staunchest supporter of the idea of absolute defence of superior orders. This approach is also known as the doctrine of *respondeat superior*. According to this doctrine, a soldier who commits an offence whilst following an order should be entirely exempted from responsibility and it is the superior who has to take all the blame for issuing an illegal order.[3] The rationale behind this approach of course is the utmost upholding of military discipline. There are, however, some shortcomings in this approach. It, for example, fails to assign responsibility in cases where the soldier is aware of the illegality of the order, but nevertheless agrees with it.[4] It favors the principle of military efficiency to the complete neglect of personal criminal accountability. Fortunately, absolute defence approach has rarely been approved by national and international courts.[5]

However, the unprecedented brutality of World War I gave rise to an opposite theory of 'absolute liability' in which individual combatants who commit atrocities should be tried for their crimes without having any recourse whatsoever to the defence of superior orders.

(B) Absolute Liability Approach

This approach absolutely prohibits the defence of superior orders. Obedience to superior orders may only serve as a mitigating factor for sentencing purposes. According to this doctrine, soldiers are not required to obey illegal orders. It is, therefore, diametrically opposed to the absolute defence because its main purpose is to safeguard the supremacy of the law, at the expense of military discipline, ignoring that a successful military is built on a foundation of discipline that demands "total and unqualified obedience [to orders] without any hesitation or doubt."[6] The absolute liability approach asserts that soldiers are legally bound to follow only lawful orders. Thus, it denies that obedience to superior orders creates a defense *per se* when a soldier follows an illegal order.[7]

This absolute liability approach requires the subordinate to scrutinize and understand the practical and legal implications of all his superior's orders. If the subordinate determines the orders are illegal, he must refuse to follow them. Otherwise, the subordinate assumes responsibility for the consequences of his or her actions. The main weakness of this approach is that it is entirely based on the false assumption that the legality of an order is easily discernable to the subordinate. There will be situations where the impropriety of an order is not clear, especially to a subordinate who does not have the same access to material information as his superior. A high-ranking U.S. Army officer recently commented that "I know that if I ever go to war again, the first person I'm taking is my lawyer."[8] This suggests that even high ranking commanders have difficulty discerning all the legal implications of wartime acts and the difficulty is only amplified at lower levels where subordinates have less access to the intelligence and overall command strategy upon which their orders are based.

Another weakness of the absolute liability approach is that it fails to address the dilemma of how to promote military discipline while maintaining the supremacy of the law.[9] Under such a strict liability regime, it is likely that hesitation in carrying out orders will increase, there will be more instances of insubordination, and in volunteer armed forces, recruiting may be adversely affected. Indeed, as soldiers begin questioning every order, military preparedness erodes, which has devastating effects for a nation's security. This is the main reason why national laws and military manuals in most of the countries do not acknowledge the absolute liability approach.

It was with the Nuremberg Charter that the absolute liability approach gained international recognition and approval. However, the Nuremberg and Tokyo Charters are seen by many as somewhat of an overreaction by the Allied Powers to the horrific events that took place during the war. It is for that reason that many scholars now question the legitimacy of the two Charters, as well as the trials, as valid precedents in the context of the superior orders defence.[10]

(C) Limited Liability Approach: Liability for Manifestly Illegal Orders (Manifest illegality principle)

Neither of the two approaches stated above deals with the soldier's dilemma well. They both fail in practical application. The absolute defence approach is not in accord with national or international law and the absolute liability approach is inconsistent with the demands of military discipline. As a result, courts have developed a compromise whereby a soldier may rely on the superior orders defence in the event of an order which is manifestly illegal. This solution is usually referred to as the "*manifest illegality principle*" and is aimed at adjusting the conflicting demands of military discipline and the supremacy of the law.

The doctrines of 'respondeat superior' and 'absolute liability' represent two polar extreme positions towards an issue that, in fact, requires a much more nuanced approach. Such a nuanced, 'middle-of-the-road' approach first appeared in the very beginning of the 20th century in the case of *Regina v. Smith.*[11] Smith was a soldier who, acting on the orders of his superior during the Boer War, killed a native. Solomon J held that:

> It is monstrous to suppose that a soldier would be protected where the order is grossly illegal... I think it is a safe rule to lay down that if a soldier honestly believes that he is doing his duty in obeying the command of his superior, and if the orders are not so *manifestly iilegal* that he must or ought to have known that they were unlawful, the private soldier would be protected by the orders of his superior.[12]

This judgment marks the introduction of what is known as the 'manifest illegality principle' whereby, for the defence to succeed, the accused must demonstrate (1) absence of subjective knowledge of the illegality of the order and (2) that the order was not 'manifestly illegal' in the objective sense that a reasonable person in the same position would not have known the order to be illegal. However, this approach of superior orders did not gain real prominence until the Leipzig Trials following World War I. In the *Llandovery Castle Case,*[13] in which the accused had torpedoed a British hospital ship under superior orders, the court stated:

> It is certainly to be urged in favor of the military subordinates that they are under no obligation to question the order of their superior officer, and they can count upon its legality. But no such confidence can be held to exist, if such an order is universally known to everybody, including the accused, to be without any doubt whatever against the law.[14]

The limited defense of superior orders or the 'manifest illegality principle' is a compromise that balances the competing aims by promoting discipline in the military while not entirely subverting the supremacy of the law.[15] The principle has a number of merits. First of all, it allows the subordinate to presume that his orders are legal, and obedience to those orders is a defense unless the illegality of the orders is obvious to any person of ordinary understanding.[16] The presumption that orders are legal helps maintain and promote good order and discipline. Since subordinates do not risk incurring liability in most situations, the presumption effectively compensates for the subordinate's lack of information and eliminates the possibility of hesitation and delay in carrying out orders. Thus, the defense of obedience maintains the supremacy of the law by assigning culpability where "moral choice" was in fact possible.[17] Indeed the defense holds commanders responsible for their orders, rather than subordinates.

Assigning the superior presumptive knowledge of the law, and thus liability under the law, should create an incentive for the superior to learn the law and a disincentive to deliver illegal orders. While the defendant can raise the defense in this situation, a prosecutor can attempt to prove that the subordinate did know the law. Just as a subordinate may argue that he subjectively believed an illegal order he obeyed was lawful, the prosecution may introduce evidence about a defendant's subjective knowledge to demonstrate that he in fact knew the illegality of the order. If the prosecutor succeeds in establishing that the subordinate knew his order was illegal, but followed the order nonetheless, the defense will not succeed in negating the *mens rea* element of the criminal act. It is even possible that a court-martial or military commission could determine that the order was manifestly illegal to a reasonable person in the defendant's subjective situation. It thus seems likely that the defendant who knowingly follows an illegal order will be subject to criminal liability.

The supremacy of the law is upheld with the manifest illegality defense of superior orders, because the defense serves to establish that the defendant does not possess the *mens rea* required for the criminal act for which he is charged. Thus the manifest illegality principle results in a defense, which guides jurists between the conflicting demands of military discipline and the supremacy of the law. The defense promotes military discipline while maintaining the supremacy of the law by focusing on those with the requisite *mens rea.*

III. 'MANIFEST ILLEGALITY PRINCIPLE' AS ILLUSTRATED BY THE DECISIONS OF DOMESTIC COURTS

According to the "*manifest illegality principle,*" military orders must be obeyed unless they are manifestly unlawful. The crucial question here is: what is meant by '*manifest illegality*'?[18] The nature and meaning of the 'manifest illegality principle,' can be gathered from the following leading decisions decided by courts of various countries.

A leading case in English legal history is that of *Regina v. Smith.*[19] During the Boer War a patrol of British soldiers, sent out on a dangerous mission, had an argument with a native who hesitated to find a bridle for them. Smith, one of the soldiers, under orders of his superiors, killed the native on the spot. After the war, a special court tried Smith for murder and acquitted him. The court said, "I think it is a safe rule to lay down that if a soldier believes he is doing his duty in obeying commands of his superior, and *if the orders are not so manifestly illegal that he must or ought to have known they were unlawful,* the private soldier would be protected by the orders of his superior officer."

In *Llandovery Castle* Case,[20] the soldiers, following the orders of their U-boat commander, not only sank the hospital ship but also machine-gunned the survivors in the water. The German Supreme Court held:

> However, the subordinate obeying an order is liable to punishment, if it was known to him that the order of the superior involved the

> infringement of civil or military law... *if such an order is universally known to everybody, including the accused, to be without any doubt whatsoever against the law.* As naval officers by profession [the accused] were well aware... that one is not legally authorized to kill defenceless people... They should therefore be refused to obey.[21]

In *Border Guards Prosecution Case,*[22] two former German Democratic Republic (East Germany) border guards were convicted of unlawful homicide by a Regional Court of the Federal Republic of Germany. The two shot and killed S, a twenty year old citizen of the GDR as he ascended a ladder and placed his hand on the top of a wall separating East from West Berlin. The two guards were under orders to prevent escape and, if necessary, to kill escapees.[23] The admonition regularly repeated to guards was that "in no event are breaches of the border to be permitted. A person violating the border is to be caught or destroyed." [24]

The Supreme Court noted that the defense of superior orders under East German law was inapplicable in those instances in which the command *"represents a manifestly gross violation of fundamental concepts of justice and humanity."* East as well as West Germany had acceded to the International Covenant on Civil and Political Rights. In the view of the Supreme Court, East Germany's harsh policy towards escapees contravened the Covenant's provisions pertaining to freedom of movement across borders and the arbitrary deprivation of life.[25] The Court determined that the defendants were guilty of unlawful homicide while acting under orders.[26] *The fact that the defendants were not aware of the manifestly illegal nature of the order was not controlling.*[27]

In *US v Kinder,*[28] the defendant, Thomas Kinder, was convicted of killing a captured Korean civilian who was not violent or attempting to escape. Kinder argued that he was ordered to kill so as to scare other locals and to boost troop morale.[29] Kinder further conceded that he knew the order was illegal. He was convicted and it was held that no defence if the crime is a result of *an order manifestly unlawful and no reasonable doubt could exist on the part of a man of ordinary sense and understanding.*[30]

My Lai Massacre: The ruling in *US v Kinder* was followed in the famous case of US v *Calley.*[31] In 1968, Lieutenant Calley's platoon swept through the village of My Lai, shooting at everything that moved. The civilians were rounded up and murdered in cold blood. The estimated number of dead

Vietnamese was 347.[32] At trial, Calley argued that he lacked *mens rea* because he acted in accordance with orders issued by Captain Ernest Medina. It was proven that no such order was given. In any event, the Court held that even if it existed, Calley could not rely on the superior orders defence if the jury determined that *he knew the order was illegal and that a man of ordinary sense and understanding would have known the orders to be unlawful.*

The most prominent Israeli case involving superior orders was the *Eichmann* case.[33] Eichmann's principal defense was that he was trained and obligated to serve as an obedient and unquestioning subordinate who was expected to carry out every command, regardless of whether the order required repression or murder.[34] The District Court determined that Eichmann knowingly and enthusiastically pursued a clearly criminal course of conduct.[35] The Supreme Court judgment contains a particularly useful discussion of superior orders.[36]

The counsel for the Appellant in the Supreme Court of Israel proposed the defense of obedience to superior orders claiming that Eichmann took the oath of allegiance when he joined the SS and thus Hitler's compulsion to destroy the Jews completely was the order he received by his superior. The court rejects such contention declaring in particular that "the defense that the act was done in obedience to superior orders means...that the person who performed it had no alternative – either by law or virtue of the regulations of the disciplinary body (army, etc.) of which he was a member–but to carry out the order he received from his superior." The Judge stated that the accused acted independently and even exceeded the tasks that were assigned to him through the official chain of command.

The court in *Eichmann* case says that the question whether to allow superior order defense depends on the mental state of the accused at the time of the offense and in particular *whether the offender knew about the unlawful nature of the order*. The court establishes in accordance with the tendency from the English law that *"such defense is admissible where there was obedience to an order not manifestly unlawful."* Following the suggested criteria the court then declares that the superior orders defense will be rejected for the accused because:

(i) The order for extermination of the Jews was manifestly unlawful and contrary to the "basic ideas of law and justice", and

(ii) The accused was well aware at the time of committing his crimes that he was a party to the perpetration of the most grave and horrible crimes.

To prove such knowledge the court cites Eichmann's own statements where he himself declares that in the extermination of the Jews he sees "one of the gravest crimes in the history of the mankind" also admitting that he had such realization when he committed the crimes: "I already at that time realized that this...was something illegal, something terrible..."

In the *Malinki* case,[37] an Israeli Military Court of Appeal affirmed, in part, a district military court's conviction of eight policemen charged with killing forty-three Arab residents of Israel. These killings arose during a curfew imposed on the village of Kafr Qassem.[38] The Court of Appeal ruled that an order to kill peaceful and innocent citizens who were returning home from work on the grounds that this was required to maintain a curfew "is an order to commit a crime of murder".[39] Israeli law significantly recognized that an individual was not criminally responsible for an act or omission carried out in accordance with a superior's orders *unless the command was manifestly unlawful.*[40] The Court observed that the values of discipline and the rule of law collided when a soldier was required to obey an illegal order and that this "creates an excruciatingly difficult dilemma" for both the legislature which was charged with creating standards and for the combatant compelled to choose between insubordination and contravention of criminal law.[41]

The Court noted three possible solutions to this dilemma. The imposition of strict liability had the disadvantage of compelling subordinates to examine and explore every command and undermined order and discipline.[42] The recognition of superior orders as a justification would insulate every excess from legal sanction and limit liability to those in command.[43] The preferable position recognized the difficulty of reconciling these competing considerations and struck an intelligent balance by affirming the *obligation of soldiers to obey all but manifestly unlawful orders.*[44] The Court noted that the illegal character of these clearly criminal commands do not require the subtle and nuanced judgment of the trained legal expert.[45] *This was an objective standard based on the perception of a reasonable combatant; the subjective belief of the defendant as well as the belief of other witnesses as to the legality of an order is not strictly relevant.*[46] In applying this test, a court should consider evidence concerning the circumstances under which a defendant carried out an order, including his knowledge, beliefs, and honest and reasonable mistakes which might have influenced his behavior.[47]

The case of *Malinki* contributed to the jurisprudence of obedience to superior orders by clarifying that *the manifest illegality of an order was to be evaluated in light of the reactions of a reasonable person under the circumstances and context of the command.*

In the Canadian case of *Regina v Finta,*[48] Finta served as a captain in the Royal Hungarian Gendarmerie and was posted to Szeged by the Nazi controlled regime.[49] Finta was charged with carrying out the so-called "Baky Order" and allegedly supervised the deportation of 8,617 Hungarian Jews to Auschwitz where they were subjected to forced labor and extermination. Finta eventually emigrated to Canada where he was charged and acquitted of crimes against humanity and war crimes.[50]

The Supreme Court recognized that military organizations depend upon immediate, instantaneous and unhesitating obedience to superior orders.[51] This has "through the centuries led to the concept that acts done in obedience to military orders will exonerate those who carry them out."[52] Judge Peter Cory, however, noted that this rule has been disregarded in the case of *manifestly illegal orders.*[53] These are *commands which offend the conscience of "any reasonable, right-thinking person; it is an order which is obviously and flagrantly wrong."*[54] *The order cannot be in a "grey area or be merely questionable; rather it must patently and obviously be wrong."*[55]

The following conclusions can be drawn from the above discussions. First, although knowledge of the accused is taken into consideration by some courts, the jurisprudence of the overwhelming majority of courts is that if an order is manifestly illegal, the defence is not available even though the accused does not know about the illegality of the order. Secondly, whether an order is manifestly illegal or not is to be determined objectively. A manifestly illegal order is an order which is obviously and flagrantly wrong. It must be a gross violation of fundamental concepts of justice and humanity. The test is that of a 'reasonable man'. The manifest illegality of an order is to be evaluated in light of the reactions of any *reasonable* or *right-thinking person* under the circumstances and context of the order.

IV. IS THERE AN ESTABLISHED RULE OF CUSTOMARY INTERNATIONAL LAW ON THE DEFENCE OF SUPERIOR ORDERS?

Before the World War I, the weight of scholarly opinion was in favour of the *'absolute defence'* approach and English, French and American law insulated a subordinate officer who acted in accordance with superior orders from criminal prosecution. The leading treatise on international law authored by Professor Oppenheim pronounced to that effect.[56] Article 443 of the British Manual of Military Law on superior orders of 1914, drafted by Oppenheim, followed the same idea. Article 443 further provided that individuals issuing illegal orders (superiors) were subject to criminal punishment.[57] This provision was adopted, with only slight modification, as Article 336 of the Rules of Land Warfare approved by the United States Army and issued in April 1914.[58] However, judicial decisions rarely approved the absolute defence approach and as illustrated by the early common law case of *Regina v Smith*[59] decided in 1900, Courts generally preferred the limited defence or 'manifest illegality' principle.

The Period between World War I and World War II

The unprecedented brutality of World War I gave rise to the *'absolute liability'* theory. This theory squarely opposes the 'absolute defence' approach and denies superior orders as a defence. Thus, the period between World War I and World War II witnessed competing perspectives on the superior orders defense.

The Penal Senate of the German Supreme Court at Leipzig in *Dover Castle* held that a subordinate generally was not culpable for carrying out a superior order. The subordinate was liable in only those instances in which he or she went beyond the parameters of the order or carried out a command which he was aware contravened civil or criminal law.[60]

In *Llandovery Castle*, The Penal Senate stressed that a superior officer issuing an order violative of international law was solely responsible.[61] A combatant obeying such an order only was liable "if it was known to him that the order of superior involved an infringement of civil or military law." The subordinate may assume that a superior order is consistent with international standards and is not obliged to question a facially legal command. Subordinates, however, may incur liability in those instances in which "an order is universally known to everybody ... to be without any doubt whatever against the law." The Penal Senate stressed that the order to fire at defenseless individuals in lifeboats was one of those "rare" and "exceptional" instances in which it was perfectly clear that an order constituted a breach of the law. The command was "universally known" to be contrary to the law of nations. The defendants, as professional naval officers, were well-aware of the relevant law and were obligated to refuse to carry out the command.[62]

These German decisions appeared to balance the desirability of military discipline with recognition that subordinates possessed the responsibility to resist clearly and conspicuously illegal demands and directives. The conclusion then is that before the World War I, the prevailing view on the defence of superior orders was that of the absolute defence and that the practice of domestic courts before and after the World War I inclined more on the 'manifest illegality' principle. Schabas even went so far as to say that prior to World War II, customary international law held that a crime committed as a result of superior orders was excusable to the extent that it fell under the rubric of the 'manifestly illegal' principle.[63]

The World War II and the Nuremberg Charter

During the World War II, the Allies learned of the atrocities being committed by the Nazis and realized that they could not continue to support the absolute defence if they were going to deny it to prospective German defendants in the upcoming trials. In 1944, both the American and British armies modified their respective war manuals. Other countries followed this trend and introduced similar legislation–all in order to ensure that no potential defendant would be able to avoid responsibility by arguing that he was acting under superior orders.

The Charter of the International Military Tribunal at Nuremberg, after extensive negotiations, came into being in 1945. The superior orders defence was addressed in Article 8, which provides:

> The fact that the Defendant acted pursuant to order of his Government or of a superior shall not free him from responsibility, but may be considered in mitigation of punishment if the Tribunal determines that justice so requires."

The Article in effect abrogated the defence completely and thus imposing *'absolute liability'*. Accordingly, no prospective defendant could be exempted from responsibility on the basis of obedience to orders.[64] In fact, the Allies were fully aware of the fact that, from 1906 to 1945, obedience to superior orders was an absolute defence in several countries. However, for fear of the fact that the recognition of an absolute defence approach would have led to acquittals rather than convictions, the Allies went from one extreme to another. That is the reason why some scholars argue that the defence of obedience to superior orders was not abolished as a result of the Nuremberg trials but merely excluded due to very unusual circumstances of the aftermath of the World War II. In other words, there was no shift in international legal doctrine after the Nuremberg trials.[65]

The Nuremberg Charter restricts the use of "superior orders" to mitigating punishment only in instances where justice so requires.[66] In trials before the tribunal, defence counsel repeatedly asserted that their clients were following orders, and they did not confine such assertions to the mitigation of punishment. Thus, lawyers for Field Marshal Wilhelm Keitel and Colonel General Alfred Jodl argued that the defendants were following orders and thus not only should have mitigated punishment but also should have no criminal liability.[67] The tribunal explicitly rejected all of these claims and announced that the law of all nations rejected a defence based on superior orders to kill or torture in violation of international law.[68] Some judges at Nuremberg wanted to go further. They urged holding defendants responsible unless they lacked a "moral choice"—a personal capacity to act differently without risking one's own life or the safety of one's family.[69] This concept in contemporary terms has more in common with the defence of duress, and indeed, duress has sometimes been confused with the defence of superior orders.[70]

Yet, after the Nuremberg trials, diplomatic efforts to establish a permanent international criminal court and to codify the rejection of the superior orders defence failed as Western powers and the Soviet Union approached each negotiation in light of Cold War tensions.[71] Despite long meetings with expert committees, the United Nations could not secure agreement on proposed codifications of the laws of war, peace, and security; efforts to formulate principles from Nuremberg failed.[72] Nor could the International Red Cross summon sufficient support to include the superior orders provision in the 1949 Geneva Conventions or the 1977 Additional Protocols.[73] National representatives disagreed over whether soldiers should ever be expected to think for themselves and decide whether or not to obey orders.[74]

Some experts conclude that this failure by any international group to adopt a formal statement rejecting the defence of superior orders means that the defence is now available.[75] One scholar argues that because international law has not clearly rejected the superior orders defence, defence counsel in war crimes trials who do not assert a defence of superior orders would be "professionally derelict."[76] Others emphasize that even the Nuremberg formulation preserved the defence in connection with coercion or lack of moral choice, or in limited circumstances.[77]

Most experts, in contrast, emphasize that even though efforts to codify the rejection of the superior orders defence failed, developing international law eliminates the defence in the case of orders that are manifestly illegal.[78] This leaves the defence available to soldiers who can show that the orders they followed were not clearly and obviously illegal.

We can draw two conclusions from the above discussions. First, the approach of the Nuremberg Charter on the defence of superior orders did not have the effect of codifying the pre-existing customary international law because from 1906 to 1945 obedience to superior orders was an absolute defence in several countries. Second, the approach of the Charter has not crystallized or generated a new customary international law because State practice is divided and decisions of domestic courts in most countries are not in favour of the absolute liability theory.

The Impact of the *ad hoc* International Criminal Tribunals

Four decades later, the United Nations Security Council followed the Nuremberg Tribunal's rejection of superior orders when it authorized the ad hoc International Criminal Tribunal for the Former Yugoslavia ("ICTY").[79] Article 7(4) of the *ICTY Statute* directly mirrored Article 8 of the Nuremberg Charter in entirely excluding superior orders as a full defence. It reads: "The fact that an accused person acted pursuant to an order of a government or of a superior shall not relieve him or her of criminal responsibility, but may be considered in mitigation of punishment if the Tribunal determines that justice so requires."

The United Nations authorizations for the ad hoc *International Criminal Tribunal for Rwanda* (ICTR) and the *Special Court for Sierra Leone* each omit superior orders as a defence but permit the use of superior orders to mitigate punishment.[80] After some initial ambiguity, the *Special Panels to hear Serious Crimes in East Timor*[81] and the *Statute of the Iraqi Special Tribunal,* signed by the administrator of the Coalition Provision Authority also follow the lead of the Nuremberg Charter.[82] Yet while each uses the same approach, denying a defence based on superior orders but permitting mitigation if justice so requires, there are complications. Superior orders did supply a defence at the time the mass violence in East Timor was committed, so the tribunal's elimination of the defence raises the danger of punishment under a retroactive law.[83] In addition, an illegal order may still give rise to a defence without any assessment of whether it was manifestly illegal.[84]

Accordingly, "the jurisprudence of the courts set up after 1945 to punish war criminals was...strongly leaning towards the absolute liability principle."[85] Nevertheless, even at the time of the adoption of the ICTY Statute, US Permanent Representative, Madeleine Albright, curiously declared the 'manifestly illegal' principle to be the guiding standard: "It is, of course, a defence that the accused was acting pursuant to orders where he or she did not know the orders were unlawful and a person of ordinary sense and understanding would not have known the orders to be unlawful."[86] Seemingly then, Scaliotti is correct in asserting that the "answer to the question regarding the rule applicable to superior orders under international law before the Rome Statute is... far from clear."[87]

Furthermore, it is certainly questionable whether strict adherence to the Nuremberg standard is appropriate given the nature of modern international criminal tribunals. The following observation by Rowe is particularly relevant:

> "It is no real answer to argue that the Nuremberg principles will supply the answer to the scope of defences under international law. The defendants at the International Military Tribunals at Nuremberg and Tokyo were the senior directors of war crimes committed by others. The Hague Tribunal, by way of contrast, is, for the most part, having to deal with the 'small fish' who, in 'armies' with disciplinary

> systems that would hardly be recognized by senior officers of established state armies and with inadequate training *were often as much victims of their own side as were their enemies.*" [88]

This conception of the 'small fish' war criminal as 'victim' is an interesting one. Surely a military disciplinary system in which a superior can, for example, threaten to kill a subordinate and/or his or her family for failure to obey an order is one that would hardly be recognized by senior officers of established state armies. If the accused can be perceived as victimized in this way by the military hierarchy to which he or she belongs then perhaps the more accommodating manifestly illegal' principle is the more appropriate standard. However, the question remains, as in the above example, what happens when the order to kill innocent human beings is accompanied by a threat to life or limb? The psychologically coercive effects are now fundamentally different in that the accused no longer merely feels a conflict between competing duties under national and international law - instead the conflict is between the competing interests of self-preservation and protecting the lives of others. The issue no longer becomes one of superior orders, but becomes one of duress.

The International Criminal Court and the 'Manifest Illegality' Principle

The drafters of the Rome Statute establishing the International Criminal Court departed from the stand of the other international tribunals by permitting the defence where the order, given by a superior to a subordinate, was not manifestly unlawful and where the soldier did not know the order was unlawful. A soldier charged with war crimes - though not genocide or crimes against humanity - can defend himself or herself from criminal liability by satisfying three conditions: that he or she was legally obligated to follow the orders to commit the war crimes, that he or she did not know the orders were illegal, and that the orders were not on their face manifestly illegal. Some countries that are parties to the ICC have already amended their domestic law to be in accord with the ICC approach of superior orders. It can be expected to generate a rule of customary international law in future.

Due to divergence in State practice and differences in the approaches of the ICC and other international tribunals, the conclusion that can be made for the time being is that no customary international law on the defence of superior orders has been established and that no single international norm governing the defence of superior orders currently exists.

V. AN ANALYSIS OF ARTICLE 33 OF THE STATUTE OF THE ICC

In 1994, the International Law Commission adopted a Draft Statute for an International Criminal Court and submitted it to the General Assembly.[89] On 11 December, 1995 the General Assembly established the Preparatory Committee on the Establishment of an International Criminal Court to prepare and develop its own draft statute, building upon the International Law Commission's text.[90] Finally, the General Assembly convened a diplomatic conference in Rome, Italy, from 15 June to 17 July, 1998, for the adoption of a convention, in the form of a Statute, to establish a permanent international criminal court. The participants at the Rome Conference included 160 states, 33 international organisations and a group of 236 non-governmental organisations (NGOs).

The Rome Statute of the International Criminal Court was adopted by the Conference on 17 July, 1998, by a vote of 120 states in favour, 7 against and 21 abstentions. While France, the United Kingdom and Russia supported the Statute, the United States declared publicly that it opposed it. China, Israel, Iraq, Libya, Quarter and Yemen joined the United States to form the 7 states that voted against the Statute. The Rome Statute entered into force on 1 July 2002. As of 18 July 2008, there are 139 signatories and 108 States Parties to the Rome Statute.[91]

The Rome Statute creates the International Criminal Court (ICC).[92] The jurisdiction of the Court is limited to the most serious crimes of concern to the international community as a whole. The Court has jurisdiction with respect to the following crimes:

(a) The crime of genocide;

(b) Crimes against humanity;

(c) War crimes; and

(d) The crime of aggression.[93]

(A) Drafting History of Article 33

During the Rome Conference which drafted the Statute of the ICC, two main opposing schools of thought emerged. One school of thought was advocated by the group of like-minded countries, particularly Germany, and argued for an 'absolute liability' approach to the superior orders. They argued that 'superior orders' must never be a defence against criminal responsibility for international crimes. It is very clear that this approach strictly followed the guidelines of the Nuremberg Charter and the Statutes of the ICTY and ICTR.

On the other hand, there are States, in particular the United States, which advocated for the 'manifest illegality approach', arguing that a soldier obeying orders of his superiors would not be criminally responsible unless he knew the order to be unlawful or if the order had been manifestly unlawful. The negotiations were quite difficult and finally the Conference drafted the present Article 33 as a compromised formula. Article 33 of the Statute of the International Criminal Court provides:

Article 33
Superior orders and Prescription of Law

1. The fact that a crime within the jurisdiction of the Court has been committed by a person pursuant to an order of a Government or of a superior, whether a military or civilian, shall not relieve that person of criminal responsibility unless:
   (a) The person was under a legal obligation to obey orders of the government or the superior in question;
   (b) The person did not know that the order was unlawful; and
   (c) The order was not manifestly unlawful.
2. For the purposes of this article, orders to commit genocide or crimes against humanity are manifestly unlawful.

When we make a careful analysis of Article 33, the very first thing we can take note is that the Statute of the ICC acknowledges 'superior orders' as a defence *per se*, rather than a sub-category of the defence of mistake. Nevertheless, Article 33 clearly states the principle that superior orders shall not relieve a person of his or her criminal responsibility unless certain specific requirements are satisfied. Therefore, we can say that Article 33 upholds the general principle of the irrelevance of superior orders. Thus any reference to the defence of superior orders under Article 33 would constitute an exception and the defence will, therefore, have to be interpreted narrowly in accordance with rules of interpretation.

The Meaning of Superior Order

According to Article 33(1), the superior order must come from either a government or a superior. Therefore, the order might have emanated from a government, for example, in the form of legislation or a regulation that would amount to an international crime under the Statute. That is why the heading of Article 33 reads: 'Superior orders and prescription of law". Alternatively, the order might have come from a superior who stands higher in the hierarch of the chain of command.

(B) The Three Requirements for a Lawful Defence of Superior Orders

The general rule under Article 33 is that there is no defence of superior orders. Therefore, as an exceptional situation, it is for the defendant to prove the existence of the three requirements. These requirements are cumulative in the sense that all the three must be satisfied in order for the defence to be successful.

(i) The Offender was under a 'Legal Obligation' to Obey the Order

The first requirement is that the person claiming the defence was *under a legal obligation to obey the said order*. The Statute thereby refers back to the domestic legal system within which both the superior or the government as the case may be, and the offender were acting. The Court will have to appraise the binding effect of such orders according to that domestic legal system.

(ii) The Offender did not know that the order was Unlawful

An offender may only rely on the defence of superior orders if he or she did not know that the order was unlawful. Whether unlawful or not depends on whether it is a punishable crime under the Statute (whether it is a recognized international crime) or not. Therefore, whether the act was a punishable offence under the domestic legal system of the offender is not relevant.

This requirement is a purely subjective test as the main concern here is with the accused's actual knowledge. It is a lower threshold because it is quite easy for the accused to claim his lack of such knowledge. Like any other fact, knowledge on the part of the accused can be proved by circumstantial evidence, that is, facts from which it may be inferred that the accused had such knowledge. But this lower threshold is raised by the third requirement that the order must not be 'manifestly unlawful'.

(iii) The order was not 'Manifestly Unlawful'

This is the objective requirement, introduced to limit the scope of the purely subjective second requirement. An order must be considered to be manifestly unlawful if the illegality was 'obvious to a person of ordinary understanding'.[94] The question to be asked here is whether an ordinary person in the situation of the accused would have seen that the order was unlawful. When determining the unlawfulness of the order, the domestic legal system is irrelevance. The decisive factor is whether the order was manifestly unlawful under international law. Therefore, the test is whether even a layman (not necessary to be a legal expert) with only a basic knowledge of international humanitarian law should have considered the action to be unlawful.

(C) The Defence Not Available to Genocide and Crimes Against Humanity

According to Article 33(2), orders to commit genocide or crimes against humanity are considered to be manifestly unlawful and therefore, the defence of superior orders is not applicable to these cases. In other words, the defence is only applicable to orders to commit 'war crimes'. In fact, this provision was inserted in Article 33 in order to appease those States that advocated absolute liability approach and opposed the inclusion of the defence in the Rome Statute[95] and its main purpose was to limit as far as possible the scope of the application of the defence.

However, many scholars are critical of Article 33(2). It is stated in the Commentary to the Rome Statute of the ICC:

> This distinction drawn between war crimes, on one hand, and crimes against humanity and genocide on the other, is a novelty of the Rome Statute. It is deplorable in the sense that it sets up two different standards with regard to, on the one hand, acts of genocide and crimes against humanity, and on the other, war crimes. This distinction is not based in customary international law, nor does it exist in any domestic law.[96]

Furthermore, Article 33(2) appears to give a wrong signal that the commission of war crimes creates lesser injury to the humanity than acts of genocide or crimes against humanity, which is not the case. Because of the distinction made in Article 33(2) people might think that victims of war crimes are granted a lesser degree of protection than victims of genocide or crimes against humanity.

(D) The Nexus between Superior orders and Command Responsibility

Apart from Article 33, the Rome Statute contains other provisions that are relevant to the superior orders debate. The most relevant among them is Article 28 which deals with *"command responsibility"*.

Article 28
Responsibility of Commanders and other Superiors

In addition to other grounds of criminal responsibility under this Statute for crimes within the jurisdiction of the Court:

(a) A military commander or person effectively acting as a military commander shall be criminally responsible for crimes within the jurisdiction of the Court committed by forces under his or her effective command and control, or effective authority and control as the case may be, as a result of his or her failure to exercise control properly over such forces, where:

  (i) That military commander or person either knew or, owing to the circumstances at the time, should have known that the forces were committing or about to commit such crimes; and

  (ii) That military commander or person failed to take all necessary and reasonable measures within his or her power to prevent or repress their commission or to submit the matter to the competent authorities for investigation and prosecution.

This Article allows for the individual liability of those issuing illegal orders. Accordingly, the liability is shared between the superior and the soldier[97] so that the latter is not made a scapegoat.

(E) Defence of Superior orders under the Rome Statute: Shortcomings and Merits

The Rome Statute establishing the International Criminal Court is the first ever international convention which codifies the principle of superior orders and the first attempt of the international community to formulate the principle in the form of treaty law. Although there are other international instruments dealing with superior orders, such as the Nuremberg Charter and the Statutes of the ICTY and the ICTR, they do not create treaty law which is based on the consent of States, but instead they were either established by the victorious powers or the Security Council of the United Nations, as the case may be.

One criticism made by Professor Cassese and others is that they would prefer a clear confirmation of the absolute liability principle as contained in the Nuremberg Charter and later affirmed by the Statutes of the ICTY and the ICTR, that is, that superior order is no defence, but may be considered in mitigation of punishment if justice so requires. In this way, according to them, the Rome Statute could have paved the way towards a clear customary international standard.[98] It is submitted that since the Rome Statute was the result of thorough negotiations among the participating States it is quite foreseeable that a delicate balance had to be struck between the need to punish those committing heinous crimes, on the one hand, and the need to protect persons who unknowingly commit war crimes, on the other.

Another criticism is that Article 33 has departed from pre-existing rules of customary international law because it does not abide by the absolute liability principle.[99] However, it has been shown above that there is no uniform and consistent state practice and thus it is very much doubtful that there has already been established customary international law on the defence of superior orders. One of the merits of the successful codification of the defence of superior orders in the Rome Statute is that we can at least say that an agreement could finally be reached and that this will surely influence the development of customary international law in future on this subject.

Several countries committed to the ICC have already amended their domestic law to match the ICC standard on superior orders.[100] If many come to do so, this could change the status of the defence in customary international law, i.e. the approach of the ICC could well be accepted by the international community. In the meantime, without having endorsed the ICC, the United States has indicated room for the defence under limited circumstances. Thus, the United States *Manual for Courts-Martial* (MCM) currently permits the defence as follows: "It is a defense to any offense that the accused was acting pursuant to orders unless the accused knew the orders to be unlawful or a person of ordinary sense and understanding would have known the orders to be unlawful."[101] This provision not only permits superior orders as a defence but does so when a person of ordinary sense and understanding would not realize that the order is unlawful. By pegging the standard to the person of ordinary sense and understanding, this version extends the defence beyond an objective test of illegality to a standard considering ordinary persons' knowledge of the law. Moreover, the manual indicates that doubts about the legality of an order are to be resolved in favour of its legality.[102]

The Canadian version permits the defence except if the order was manifestly unlawful to a reasonable soldier under the circumstances.[103] It adopts a definition of manifest illegality as that which is "obviously and flagrantly wrong."[104] Variations over time, across nations, and among tribunals render doubtful the assertion that the Nuremberg Tribunal rejected the superior orders defence as a matter of international law.

Despite some of the criticism directed against Article 33, it is the view of the present writer that the Article is very carefully phrased and it reflects a clear proposition of the law in this respect. It correctly adopts the manifest illegality approach which can be found in much of the case law, both before and after the Nuremberg trials. Another advantage is that it is extremely limited in its scope as it contains a high threshold that many defendants will find very difficult to satisfy.

VI. CONCLUSION

Article 33 of the Rome Statute correctly adopts the compromised formula by means of acknowledging the *'manifest illegality principle'*. It is the humble opinion of the present writer that this approach is more flexible and hence more amenable to justice. Moreover, this is the first time that the international community has actually reached an agreement with respect to the defence of obedience to superior orders. This is in itself a significant advance in view of the fact that there is no treaty law dealing with the topic. The writer believes that the inclusion of Article 33 in the Rome statute will result in long-term benefits to the international community. It is hoped that it will also contribute to the standardization of national laws and martial laws in respect of the defence of superior orders in various countries of the world. Finally it will contribute to the development of customary international law in future.

Notes

1. The following defences are available under the Rome Statute Establishing the International Criminal Court: (1) Mistake of fact or law (Art. 32, the Rome Statute); (2) Superior orders (Art. 33); (3) Mental disorder (Art. 31(1)(a); (4) Intoxication (Art. 31(1)(b); (5) Self-defence (Art. 31(1)(c); (6) Duress (Art. 31(1)(d).
2. P. Gaeta, "The Defence of Superior Orders: The Statute of the International Criminal Court versus Customary International Law" (1999) 10 EJIL 172 at 173.
3. L. Oppenheim, *International Law: a Treatise*, 2nd ed. (London: Longmans, Green, 1912) at 264.
4. J. Insco, "Defence of Superior Orders before Military Commissions" (2003) 13 *Duke J Comp. & Int'l Law*, 389, at 393.
5. R. Jonassen, "The Defence of Superior Orders in New Zealand Law: A Soldier's Dilemma?" (2002) *AULR* 643, at 654.
6. Yoram Dinstein, *The Defence of 'Obedience to Superior Orders' in International Law*, (Leyden: A.W. Sijthoff, 1965), 5.
7. *Ibid.* at 69.
8. Col. Patrick Finnegan, "*Operational Law: Plan and Execute*", *MIL. L. REV.* (Mar.-Apr. 1996) 29-30.
9. Dinstein, above note 6, at 9.
10. See, for example, Ian Bownlie, "Superior Orders – Time for a New Realism?", (1989) *Crim L R* 396, at 403.
11. (1900) 17 SC 161 (Cape of Good Hope).
12. *Ibid.* at 567-8 [emphasis added].
13. *Annual Digest* 1923-1924, Case No. 235, Full Report, 1921 (CMD. 1450).
14. *Ibid.* at 45.
15. Dinstein, at 8.
16. *Ibid.* 34.
17. *US v Hermann Goring et. al*, XXII Trials of the Major War Criminals Before the International Military Tribunals, 411, 465 (1948); Principles of International Law Recognized in the Charter of the Nuremberg Tribunal and in the Judgment of the Tribunal, princ. IV, [1950] 2 Y.B. Int'l L. Comm'n 374.
18. Jordan Paust Leila Sadat , M. Cherif Bassiouni (eds.), *International Criminal Law: Cases and Materials*, (Carolina Academic Press, 2000) 120.
19. (1900) 17 SC 561 (Cape of Good Hope).

20. Judgment in Case of Lieutenants Dithmar and Boldt, Hospital Ship "Llandovery Castle", (1922) 16 *AJIL* 708.
21. *Ibid.*, at 722.
22. *Border Guards Prosecution Case* (Fed. Sup. Ct., Fed. Repub. Germany, Nov. 3, 1992), 100 ILR 366 (1997).
23. *Ibid.*
24. *Ibid.* at 366.
25. *Ibid.* at 380-383.
26. *Ibid.* 391.
27. Ibid. 366.
28. *US v Kinder*, 14 CMR 742 (1954).
29. See L C Green, "Fifteenth Valdemar A Solf Lecture in International Law" (2003) 175 *Mil L Rev* 309, at 336.
30. *Ibid.*
31. *US v Calley*, U.S. Court of Military Appeals (1973) 22 USCMA 534, 48 CMR 19.
32. M. Lippman, "War Crimes: The My Lai Massacre and the Vietnam War", (1993) 1 *San Diego Justice Journal* 295, at 309.
33. *Israel v. Eichmann* (Dist. Ct., Dec. 12, 1961), 36 I.L.R. 18 (1961); 36 I.L.R. 277 (Sup. Ct., May 29, 1962).
34. *Ibid.* at 254.
35. *Ibid.* at 258, 270.
36. *Ibid.* at 313-14.
37. *Chief Military Prosecutor v. Malinki* (Military Court of Appeal, 1959), II *Palestine Y.B. Int'l L.* 69, 77 (1985).
38. *Ibid.* at 78.
39. *Ibid.* 105-06.
40. *Ibid.* 103.
41. *Ibid.* 106.
42. *Ibid.* 107.
43. *Ibid.* 107-08.
44. *Ibid.* 108.
45. Among the factors a court should take into account in deciding whether an order is manifestly illegal are: the difference in rank between the issuer and recipient of the order; whether the receiver had grounds for believing that the issuer had access to facts unknown to the receiver; whether the receiver had time to clarify to himself whether the order was lawful; was the order issued in times of normality or emergency; did the receiver have a reasonable basis for believing that he would suffer death or great bodily harm in the event that he refused to execute

the order. In addition, a defendant is to be provided with the benefit of the doubt as to any honest and reasonable mistake as to the facts which led him to execute the order. *Ibid.* at 109-10.

46. *Ibid.* at 111. The defendant must demonstrate that he acted in accordance with an order issued by an authorized authority and the prosecution then bears the burden of proof in establishing manifest illegality. Ibid. at 112.
47. *Ibid.*
48. *Regina v. Finta* [1994] 1 S.C.R. 701
49. *Ibid.* at 725.
50. *Ibid.* at 726.
51. *Ibid.* at 828-29.
52. *Ibid.* at 829.
53. *Ibid.* at 829, 834.
54. *Ibid.* at 824.
55. *Ibid.*
56. Lasa Oppenheim, II *International Law, A Treatise: War and Neutrality* (2nd ed. 1912) 310.
57. George A. Finch, "Superior Orders and War Crimes", (192115 *AJIL* 440, 441.
58. *Ibid.*
59. (1900) 17 SC 561 (Cape of Good Hope).
60. Judgment In Case of Commander Karl Neumann Hospital Ship "Dover Castle" (1921), 16 *AJIL* 704 (1922).
61. Judgment In Case Of Lieutenants Dithmar And Boldt, (1921) 16 *AJIL* 708, 709-10 (1922).
62. *Ibid.* at 721-722.
63. William A. Schabas, *Genocide in International Law—The Crime of Crimes* (Cambridge: Cambridge University Press, 2000) at 325.
64. Dinstein, above note 6, at 18.
65. See H McCoubery, "From Nuremberg to Rome: Restoring the Defence of Superior Orders" (2001) 50 *Int'l & Comp L Q* 386, at 391.
66. Art. 8, Charter of the IMT, 8 August 1945, 82 U.N.T.S. 280, art. 8, 59 U.S. Stat. 1544.
67. See *United States v. Karl Brandt (Medical Case)* (1947), 1 Trials of War Criminals at 290-91, 325.
68. U. K., H. C., "Judgment of the International Military Tribunal for the Trial of German Major War Criminals (With the Dissenting Opinion of the Soviet Member)", Cmd 6964 in *Sessional Papers*, vol. 25 (1946-47) 511 at 556.
69. See Charles Garraway, "Superior Orders and the International Criminal Court: Justice Delivered or Justice Denied" (1999) 81 Int'l Rev. Red Cross

785. Article 6 of the *Charter of the International Military Tribunal for the Far East,* 19 January 1946, T.I.A.S. No. 1589, echoes article 8 of *Charter of the IMT*.

70. See Suzannah Linton & Caitlin Reiger, "The Evolving Jurisprudence and Practice of East Timor's Special Panels for Serious Crimes on Admissions of Guilt, Duress and Superior Orders" (2001) 4 Y.B. Int'l Human. L. 167 at 169-78.
71. See Matthew Lippman, "The Convention on the Prevention and Punishment of the Crime of Genocide: Fifty Years Later" (1998) 15 Ariz. J. Int'l & Comp. L. 415 at 459.
72. See Howard S. Levie, "The Rise and Fall of an Internationally Codified Denial of the Defense of Superior Orders" (1991) 30 *The Military Law and Law of War Review* 183 at 199.
73. See *ibid.* at 199-203; Garraway, above note 69 at 785-94.
74. See International Committee of the Red Cross, *Report on the Work of the Conference of Government Experts on the Reaffirmation and Development of International Humanitarian Law Applicable in Armed Conflicts, Second Session, Geneva, July 1972,* Vol. 1, at 188.
75. In his August 2002 memorandum explaining why the *Convention Against Torture* would not prevent the use of coercive practices in interrogation, then–US Assistant Attorney General Jay Bybee indicated that superior orders could be a defence in an international prosecution for violations of the *Convention Against Torture.* See Memorandum re: Standards of Conduct for Interrogation from Jay S. Bybee, Assistant Attorney General, Office of Legal Counsel, U.S. Department of Justice to Alberto R. Gonzales, Counsel to the President (1 August 2002) at 45, online: FindLaw *<http://fl1.findlaw.com/news.findlaw.com/hdocs/docs/doj/bybee80102mem.pdf*
76. Levie, above note 73, at 204.
77. See *Report of the Secretary-General pursuant to paragraph 2 of Security Council Resolution 808 (1993),* UN SCOR, 48th Sess., Supp. April, May and June 1993, UN Doc. S/25704, 117 at para. 57; Theodore Meron, *War Crimes Comes of Age: Essays* (New York: Oxford University Press, 1998) at 224; *Report of the International Law Commission on the Work of its Thirty-Ninth Session,* UN GAOR, 42d Sess., Supp. No. 10, UN Doc. A/42/10 (1987) at 16-20. Cherif Bassiouni, *Crimes Against Humanity in International Criminal Law,* 2nd ed. (The Hague: Kluwer Law International, 1999) at 483 (stating that obedience to superior orders is not a defence under customary international law to an international crime when the order is manifestly illegal, but "[i]f the subordinate is coerced or compelled to carry out the order, the norms for the defense of coercion (compulsion) should apply" as mitigation).
78. The resolution by the United Nations General Assembly at its first session in 1946 affirmed "the principles of international law recognized by the Charter of the N rnberg Tribunal and the judgment of the Tribunal" *(Affirmation of the Principles of International Law Recognized by the Charter of*

the N rnberg Tribunal, GA Res. 95(1), UN GAOR, 1st Sess., UN Doc. A/RES/95(1) (1946) 188). For an example of analysis using this resolution to presume continuity in international law, absent the explicit contrary authority in the authorization of new tribunals, see Christopher Staker, "Defence of Superior Orders Revisited" (2005) 79 Austl. L.J. 431 at 431-32.

79. *Statute of the International Tribunal for the Prosecution of Persons Responsible for Serious Violations of International Humanitarian Law Committed in the Territory of the Former Yugoslavia since 1991 (1993),* Annex to *Report of the Secretary-General pursuant to paragraph 2 of Security Council Resolution 808 (1993), supra* note 72, 134.
80. For Rwanda, see Article 6(4), *Statute of the International Tribunal for Rwanda,* Annex to SC Res. 955, UN SCOR, 49th Sess., UN Doc. S/RES/955 (1994) 15. For Sierra Leone, see *Statute of the Special Court for Sierra Leone,* Enclosure to UN SC, *Report of the Secretary-General on the establishment of a Special Court for Sierra Leone,* UN Doc. S/2000/915 (October 2000), art. 6(4).
81. *On the Establishment of Panels with Exclusive Jurisdiction over Serious Criminal Offenses,* see TAET Reg. 2000/15, UN Doc. UNTAET/REG/2000/15, s. 21.
82. *The Statute of the Iraqi Special Tribunal,* GC/Law/10 December 2003/1, Al Waqai Al-Iraqiya Official Gazette of Iraq 2003, Vol. 44, No. 3980 at 127, art. 15(e).
83. See Suzannah Linton & Caitlin Reiger, "The Evolving Jurisprudence and Practice of East Timor's Special Panels for Serious Crimes on Admissions of Guilt, Duress and Superior Orders" (2001) 4 Y.B. Int'l Human. L. at 34.
84. See *ibid.* at 44 (considering application of the defence in the East Timor situation). The authors also suggest that the cultural context may make obedience to orders especially compelling there *(ibid.* at 45).
85. A. Zimmerman, "Superior Orders" in A. Cassese, P. Gaeta & J.R.W.D. Jones, eds., *The Rome Statute of the International Criminal Court: A Commentary* (Oxford: Oxford University Press, 2002) at 964.
86. UN SCOR, 48th Year, 3217th Mtg., UN DOC. S/PV.3217(1993) at 15.
87. Massimo Scaliotti, "Defences before the ICC" (2001) 1 Int'l Crim. L. Rev. 111 at 141.
88. P. Rowe, "Duress as a Defence to War Crimes after *Erdemovic:* A Laboratory for Permanent Court?" (1998) 1 Y. B. Int'l Env. L. 210 at 226.
89. (1994) 33 *I.L.M.* 253.
90. General Assembly Resolution 50/46 of 11 December, 1995.
91. *http://www.un.org/law/icc/statute/status.htm*
92. Articles 1, the Rome Statute, 1998.
93. Article 5 (1), the Rome Statute, 1998.
94. See, A. Cassese, P. Gaeta and J. Jones, (eds.) *The Rome Statute of the International Criminal Court: A Commentary,* Vol. I, (Oxford University Press, 2002), 970.

95. See for example, Charles Garraway, "Superior Orders and the International Criminal Court: Justice Delivered or Justice Denied", *International Review of the Red Cross*, (1999) No. 836, 785, at 790.

96. A. Cassese, P. Gaeta and J. Jones, (eds.) *The Rome Statute of the International Criminal Court: A Commentary*, Vol. I, (Oxford University Press, 2002), 971.

97. See Anthony D'Amato, "Superior Orders vs. Command Responsibility", (1986) 80 *American Journal of International Law*, 604, at 605, arguing for the "Split-Responsibility Solution".

98. A. Cassese, P. Gaeta and J. Jones, (eds.) *The Rome Statute of the International Criminal Court: A Commentary*, Vol. I, (Oxford University Press, 2002), 972.

99. Paola Gaeta, "The defence of superior orders: The Statute of the International Criminal Court *versus* customary international law", *European Journal of International Law*, Vol. 10, 1999, pp. 172 ff.

100. Christopher Staker, "Defence of Superior Orders Revisited" (2005) 79 Austl. L.J. 431, at 442-46 (describing efforts by Australia, New Zealand, and the United Kingdom to bring their domestic laws in line with the ICC treatment of superior orders).

101. Art. 90, *Manual for Courts-Martial* (MCM) (2008 Edition), U.S., Department of Defense, *http://www.jag.navy.mil/documents/mcm2008.*

102. See for the practice of states as to the default rule of the presumption of legality of superior orders, Nico Keijzer, *Military Obedience* (Neth.: Sijthoff & Noordhoff, 1978) at 97, 133 (comparing court martial rules in the U.S., U.K., France, the Netherlands, and Israel).

103. "An act is performed in compliance with an order which is manifestly unlawful to a reasonable soldier given the circumstances prevailing at the time does not constitute a defence and cannot be pleaded in mitigation of punishment" (Canada, Department of National Defence, *Law of Armed Conflict at the Operational and Tactical Levels* (Ottawa: Department of National Defence, 2003) [the *JAG Manual*] at para. 1615.2. This rule implies that, absent manifest illegality, following orders can supply a defence in Canada.

104. *Ibid.*, citing *R. v. Finta*, [1994] 1 S.C.R. 701 at 834, 112 D.L.R. (4th) 513, Cory J. The *JAG Manual* further cites Cory J. to the effect that in order for an order to be considered manifestly unlawful, "[i]t must be one that offends the conscience of every reasonable, right thinking person. It must be an order which is obviously and flagrantly wrong" *(ibid.).*

THE SECURITY COUNCIL AS GLOBAL LEGISLATOR: USING CHAPTER VII AUTHORITY TO REDEFINE THE UNITED NATIONS ROLE IN DEVELOPING INTERNATIONAL LEGAL NORMS

Bryan C. Banks

> Mankind's problems can no longer be solved by national governments. What is needed is World Government.
>
> —*Jan Tinbergen*[1], *winner of the first Nobel Prize for Economics in 1969.*

I. INTRODUCTION

International terrorism has become a dangerous phenomenon threatening the peace and security of all nations.[2] Although terrorism has long been part of human history,[3] the last four decades have seen a dramatic increase in the use and scope of terrorist acts.[4] During this time, the phenomenon has not only crossed regional boundaries, but it has acquired an international character, and is spreading throughout the world. The grave consequences of modern terrorism threaten the very foundation of the international community.

Terrorism is a tool, not a political movement.[5] Groups from Ireland, the Philippines, the Korean Peninsula, Japan, Africa, the Middle East, Russia, India, and the United States[6] have used terrorism to advance their political causes and goals precisely because it has proved to be such an effective tool when a small, powerless group confronts a much larger, more powerful adversary. Because terrorism is used for political ends, it has proved very difficult to define.[7] The international community has approached the concept of terrorism from two distinct viewpoints.[8]

* 2150 McCowans Ferry Road, Versaille, Kentucky 40383, USA

Historically, some have considered terrorism to simply be a socio-political phenomenon and are therefore very reluctant to prohibit its use.[9] At the same time, others have long agreed that terrorism is merely a means to a political end and should be prohibited.[10] The divergence in viewpoints was forever altered on one fateful day in September 2001. As the international community responded with sympathy[11] to the events that unfolded in New York City and Washington, D.C., it also united with outrage at the callous disregard for innocent life, instantly refocusing its attention on the issue of international terrorism.

Immediately following the September 11th terrorists attacks on the United States, the United Nations Security Council took a series of steps that would radically transform the fight against international terrorism. First, the Security Council universally condemned global terror.[12] It also recognized the inherent right to self-defence under Article 51 of the United Nations Charter in response to terrorist attacks.[13] Most significantly, through adoption of Resolution 1373 and Resolution 1540, the Security Council used its authority under Chapter VII of the U.N. Charter to impose binding legislative and administrative obligations[14] on individual Member States to fight terrorism.

Adoption of Resolution 1373 and Resolution 1540 represent a radical departure from prior Security Council practice. For the first time, the Security Council was directing Member States to comply with its mandates in a general context and not in a manner directly related to disciplining any individual country or particular non-state actor for specific violations of international law.[15] The long-term implications of the shift in practice from being an international peace guarantor to being an international legislator are yet to be seen, but form the basis for this paper: Does the United Nations Security Council have authority to act as a Global Legislator? This paper will examine the legal framework for the legislative action taken by the Security Council and discuss the political will of the international community to accept the Security Council in this new role as global legislator. The paper will then conclude by providing several suggestions for the Security Council to avoid implosion á la The League of Nations and ensure that it remains the primary guarantor of international peace and security.

Part II of this paper will examine the sources of international law. Beginning with the development of the doctrine of sources, this section of the paper will attempt to explain the origins of this doctrine and then discuss some of the strengths and weaknesses of each recognized source. This discussion will reveal that treaties, like the United Nations Charter, play a significant role in determining the existence of international legal norms. This section will conclude by recognizing that the doctrine of sources is less doctrine and more an agreed upon road map to assist international lawyers as they search for the validity of legal norms.

The United Nations Charter will be analysed in Part III. This section will examine the chapters of the Charter that provide the Security Council with the positive authority to create international legal obligations. Chapter V of the Charter is the foundation of Security Council's authority and is where the Charter confers primary responsibility for maintaining international peace and security on the Security Council. Chapter VI mandates the Security Council to pursue the "pacific settlement of disputes"[16] between parties, where the dispute does not presently, but could potentially, pose a threat to international peace and security. Chapter VII of the Charter authorizes the Security Council to use a range of non-military, and if necessary, military options to take action against any "threat to the peace, breach of peace, or act of aggression."[17] This section of the paper will conclude with a discussion of the negative authority or limitations on Security Council power.

Part IV of this paper will focus in depth on Resolution 1373 and Resolution 1540. The individual obligations created by these resolutions will be articulated primarily for reference in Part V. This section will however demonstrate that these resolutions are legislative actions in disguise because they require sovereign states to reshape domestic law in order to comply with the new obligations.

In Part V, the author will determine whether the legislative character of Resolution 1373 and Resolution 1540 is indeed consistent with the Security Council's authority. The discussion in this section of the paper will reveal both that the Charter authorizes the Security Council to act in the role of global legislator, and in fact, envisaged it.

Part VI will focus on the political will of the international community to accept the Security Council's enhanced role. Both Resolution 1373 and Resolution 1540 have experienced complications during implementation, partly because the paradigm shift has had consequences greater than could be imagined. At issue is the Security Council's demand that sovereign states modify domestic law to incorporate and act on binding obligations that they did not consent to but are required to follow. The doctrine of incorporation of treaties provides the basis to begin discussion since Chapter VII authority is rooted in treaty. How the international community chooses to accept the Security Council's attempts at legislating will surely have a considerable impact on its future work.

Finally, Part VII presents a strategy for the Security Council to move forward. The first step is to develop an operative definition of terrorism that each member of the international community can use as a baseline. This will help clarify the changes necessary to comply with the new obligations as well as prevent mistreatment of domestic political movements. The next step is to develop a consistent capacity building program. If the Security Council is going to demand changes to domestic law and create a reporting committee, the least it can do is help those that are struggling to comply. Finally, the Security Council must develop a program that provides positive reinforcement for those that are compliant, but at the same time, stimulates noncompliant members of the international community without alienating them.

II. SOURCES OF INTERNATIONAL LAW

Debate over the source of international legal norms benefits from the long-standing, but opposing theories propounded by positivists[18] who believe that law is created through the consent of states, and naturalists[19] who feel that international law derives from moral dictates that exist independent of state consent.[20] This section of the paper attempts to explain the development of the source doctrine. Determining the source of international legal norms is necessary to understanding both what the law is and how it developed.

(A) Historical Development of the Source Doctrine: Positivists vs. Naturalists

During the 17th and 18th centuries, the science and study of international law was dominated by naturalist theory. Legal scholars were heavily influenced by theology and natural law (*jus naturae*).[21] Naturalist-influenced scholars begin with the assumption that, according to its nature, the law is a super-sensible valid order and must therefore derive its validity from a heavenly force rather than man.[22] They maintained that the validity of international law was entirely based on the will of the Supreme Being, God-created law, or the law of nature. Sovereigns were consequently subject not only to divine law, but also the laws of nature as established by God. According to naturalists, the individual has some rights which can be deduced directly from nature as created by God[23] and evident in the reason of man.[24] As legal scholars began to search for scientific principles to explain the nature of law, the domination of the naturalist school of thought began to wane.

Beginning in the 19th century, positivism gradually replaced naturalism. The positivist school generally asserted that the ultimate source of all laws, international and domestic, was the will of the State. The basis of the binding force behind international law could, therefore, only be found in a State's consent to be bound by it. In direct opposition to naturalist theories, positivism teaches that international legal norms are the aggregate of rules by which States have consented to be bound, exclusive of any concepts of natural law, such as "reason" and "justice."[25] Simply stated, positivism teaches that nothing between States can be called "law" to which they have not consented.[26] Consequently, the will of the State is absolute and the State alone provides the validity of all law. Even today, consent remains the compelling force behind international law.

(B) The Doctrine of Sources

The doctrine of sources is an amalgamation of trends in legal scholarship that converged during the nineteenth century. Trying to provide an understanding of how and where international legal norms can be found, legal scholars, influenced by positivism, started to emphasize sources that demonstrated state consent. The doctrine of sources merely provides a general understanding of how and where international legal norms can be located; it also provides a methodology to identify valid legal norms.[27] Most international lawyers today rely on the articulation of sources found in Article 38(1) of the Statute of the International Court of Justice which lists four sources of international law rules: treaty, custom, general principles, and academic and judicial writings.[28] This hierarchy forms the doctrine of sources. This section will begin by looking at each of these four sources of international legal norms, discussing the relative strengths and weaknesses of each.

1. *Treaty*

An international treaty,[29] like other legal documents, is simply a textual articulation of legal obligations between parties. Treaties are voluntary agreements.[30] Parties are free to negotiate their legal obligations and the resulting treaty is a codification of their mutual desire.[31] By signing a treaty, a state consents to be bound by the provisions of the treaty.[32] There are thousands of bilateral and multilateral treaties in existence.[33] This paper primarily focuses on the United Nations Charter treaty.[34] The preamble of the Charter proclaims that one of its fundamental goals is "to establish conditions under which justice and respect for the obligations arising from treaties and other sources of international law can be maintained."[35] A treaty[36] derives its authority from custom. For example, the notion of *pacta sunt servanda* developed to mean that every international treaty in force binds the parties to it and requires them to perform in good faith.[37] Treaties should therefore not be seen as a formal source of law. Treaties, however, are a good indication of consent and as such play a significant role in the doctrine of sources.

The body of law that governs the treaty process is referred to as the 'law of treaties'.[38] International efforts to establish a single legal regime to regulate negotiation, interpretation, and termination of treaties culminated with The Vienna Convention on the Law of Treaties.[39] This document codifies the long-standing customary law governing international treaties. The law of treaties recognizes three critical events in the treaty process: signature, ratification, and termination.[40] Negotiators indicate that the text is an authentic expression of their desire[41] through their signature. Simply signing the treaty does not obligate a state to comply with a specific legal obligation. Treaties do not take force until they have been ratified in domestic law by every signatory.[42] Although the question of what constitutes incorporation of treaty obligations into domestic law remains unanswered, it is generally accepted that the consequence is to accord the international norm binding force similar to the one possessed by statute.[43]

Once a treaty is enforceable, its default duration is infinite.[44] The parties may, however, elect to negotiate a date for termination or specify a specific set of circumstances that when present would result in the termination of the treaty and thereby terminate the state's obligations. While a ratified treaty can clearly be considered a source of legal norms between states, the dilemma with turning to a treaty as a source of legal norms is that a treaty is one-dimensional. The "hard" legal norms established by a treaty are fixed in time and place. It represents a static determination of the law between signatories at the moment of ratification and has a limited ability to establish modified, alternative, or new legal norms in the future.[45] The obligations cannot shrink and they cannot expand without renegotiation.

Treaty-based law governing international terrorism has been largely ineffective. There are thirteen international conventions[46] that specifically deal with terrorism. None of them have been universally ratified.[47] Consequently, treaties have failed in two ways to prevent international terrorism: (1) not every member of the international community has signed all thirteen conventions, and (2) not every signatory has ratified all signed conventions. Thus, this patchwork treaty approach to prevent international terrorism is clearly limited in its effectiveness.[48] The only way to deter international terrorism is to establish a universally binding legal norm. The treaty process has failed to do that, and has left the international community vulnerable.

2. *Customary International Law*

Custom is the most important source of international legal norms.[49] Yet, few principles regulate the complicated formation of customary law.[50] In fact, discerning customary international law "is more of an art than a scientific method."[51] Custom[52] is defined as a practice that emerges outside of recognized legal norms, which individuals and organizations instinctively follow in the course of their interactions, based on a sense of legal obligation.[53] Over time, two, or more, individual actors adopt norms they view as essential to their collective interests.[54] There are, however, conflicting theories regarding the source of the obligation that compels a State to abide by international law. On one hand are the naturalist based theories, whereby states follow the law because it is "right" or "just".[55] On the other hand, the positivist tradition says that consent to a rule is required prior to the state becoming bound to follow it.[56] The mainstream view lies somewhere between these positions. In order for a practice to become custom, the international community as a whole must accept the norm, but that does not mean that every State is required to individually consent to the practice in question. Consequently, situations may arise when a practice has gained the status of customary law, even though an individual State may disagree. Once the practice becomes recognized as custom, absent sufficient evidence of a negative practice, the objecting State becomes bound by the legal norms it initially refused to recognize.[57]

Scholars agree that an enforceable custom emerges upon conjunction of two elements: (a) a quantitative element (State practice) consisting of a general or emerging practice and (b) a qualitative element (*opinio juris*) suggested through the belief that a particular norm will generate a desired outcome.[58] Legal scholars, however, disagree on what kind of activity constitutes State practice, as well as the duration and frequency of that activity that is necessary to satisfy the definition.[59]

(a) *The Quantitative Element (State Practice)*

The quantitative requirement in customary law formation has a two-prong analysis. Both the length of time and the universality of the specific practice at issue must be established. However, there is no minimum duration of time required under this prong for the emergence of customary legal norms. They have evolved from both single events and immemorial practice.[60] Legal scholars are somewhat ambivalent about the necessity of universality of the practice. Well-accepted restatements of international law require consistency and generality, not universality, for custom formation.[61] Furthermore, noting the varying pace at which social norms transform suggests that it is impossible to establish a general time or consistency requirement as an across-the-board condition for the validity of a custom. It is clear, however, that when fluctuations in behaviour render it impossible to identify a general practice, the consistency requirement is not met.

(b) *The Qualitative Element (Opinio Juris)*

The concept of *opinio juris* has a relatively short history in the international legal scholarship.[62] Often defined as "the psychological element in the formation of custom,"[63] this concept generally identifies the second essential element of a customary rule.[64] The introduction of this element was meant to refine the concept of custom and solve the numerous problems surrounding its application.[65] Unfortunately, it has caused more controversy than imagined.[66] *Opinio juris* describes both a widespread belief that a specific practice is desirable and the general conviction that the practice represents an essential norm of social conduct. The problem is that the traditional formulation of *opinio juris* "involves the apparent chronological paradox that States creating new customary rules must believe that those rules already exist, and that their practice, therefore, is in accordance with law."[67]

To better understand this requirement, it might be helpful to revisit the basic notions of relationship between international law and consent.[68] It is a general principle that international law cannot bind States without their consent.[69] Further, these notions of consent are often considered to be the basis for customary international law.[70] If this is true, it follows that customary international legal norms bind a State, if and only if, that particular State accepts that norm as a binding obligation. If consent remains the cornerstone of international law, then *opinio juris* requires that there be both a general acceptance throughout the international community that a particular legal norm exists and specific acceptance of that legal norm by the affected State.[71] Therefore, to avoid accidental *opinio juris* by consent, a State must object loudly and often.

Professor Harold Koh's theory of transnational legal process[72] underscores the elusiveness of *opinio juris* and how it can develop in modern international law without intent.[73] A positivist, Koh argues that through a process of "interaction, interpretation, and internalization," States begin to consent to international legal norms.[74] Essentially, a legal norm becomes internalized as international and domestic actors - state and federal officials, state and federal legislators, nongovernmental organizations, courts, bureaucracies, and individual "norm entrepreneurs"[75] force interactions with each other over suggested rules. These interactions lead to interpretations of legal norms that in turn direct future interaction between both the original actors and third parties.[76]

A legislature may pass legislation, a court may make a holding, an executive may issue an order, or a bureaucracy may adopt administrative regulations that domestically internalize international legal norms. As these interactions are repeated, adherence to these rules becomes increasingly commonplace, and the rules become increasingly internalized. "Through this repeated cycle of interaction, interpretation, and internalization . . . international law acquires its 'stickiness,' and nations start to 'obey' out of perceived self-interest that becomes institutional habit."[77] The ultimate thrust of the transnational legal theory is that through the domestication of international law, even unthinkable political principles can gain acceptance.[78] Koh cited the increased recognition of an international ban on landmines as an example of this principle.[79] In a sense, Koh's theory is inevitable in the modern international community. It seems inconceivable that States could close themselves off from the rest of the world in a way that would prevent the communication of legal norms between them.

Frederic Kirgis attempted to provide a solution to the problem created by the indeterminate elements, analyzing the component requirements of State practice and *opinio juris* on a sliding scale.[80] At one end, highly consistent State practice can establish a customary rule without requiring *opinio juris*. However, as the frequency and consistency of State practice decline, a stronger showing of *opinio juris* is necessary to establish the rule. Kirgis argues that the trade-off between State practice and *opinio juris* depends on the importance of the activity in question and the reasonableness of the asserted rule.[81] This approach can be criticised because it permits the strength of one element to outweigh deficiencies in the other.[82] A second criticism is that while State practice can easily be observed through empirical documentation, identifying *opinio juris* remains a nearly impossible task.[83]

Trying to provide an operative definition for custom, legal scholar Bin Cheng introduced the notion of instant custom,[84] which modifies Kirgis' sliding scale. "[I]nternational law is a horizontal legal system in which states are both the law-makers and the subjects of the legal system, *opinio juris* can arise or change instantaneously."[85] According to Cheng's theory, States can advance a new customary international law, either in concert with other States or unilaterally, simply by evincing a new *opinio juris*.[86] If no other State objects, and if in fact other States follow suit, they will share the same *opinio juris*, thus instantly forming a new rule of customary international law.[87] While based on the Kirgis model, it is important to notice that instant custom extends the same authority to overwhelming *opinio juris* and creates a reverse bell curve. Something could be so important to the international community that even without State action, customary legal norms could develop.

Cheng's theory is supported by legal precedent. In the *North Sea Continental Shelf Cases*,[88] the International Court of Justice[89] deviated from the traditional interpretation of customary international law development.[90] In its opinion, the ICJ endorsed a new method for customary international law formation that allowed official recognition of short-term State practice as binding custom, as long as there was sufficient evidence to demonstrate support for the legal norm.[91] In dicta, the justices noted the desirability of rapidly developing customary international law because it is more attuned to the rate of development in the modern global society.[92]

The "instant" customary law theory has also drawn harsh criticism. Scholars insist that the formation of customary international legal norms and the notion of "instantaneousness" are not compatible concepts.[93] Custom as a method of law creation expresses the idea that rules are based on State practice.[94] The theory of instant custom conveys precisely the opposite, suggesting that State practice is irrelevant to customary international law.[95] The requirement of *usage* is eliminated from the equation. Instant custom can appropriately be viewed as an extreme version of customary international law formation. Regardless of which sliding scale of custom is applied by international lawyers, the equation is ultimately not as important as understanding the nature of the elements. Knowing what to look for is the first step in deciphering the complicated structure.

3. *General Principles*

General principles of international law are described as "some proposition of law so fundamental that it will be found in virtually every legal system."[96] While general principles may lead to custom,[97] they are not, and should not be considered a shortcut to custom.[98] It is important not to confuse these general principles with custom. Rather they serve as connectors, filling gaps in international law left between treaty and custom.[99] International tribunals have referenced these general principles when determining issues of *res judicata*,[100] the effect of circumstantial evidence,[101] and various rules governing the judicial process.[102] The legal norms provided by the general principles of law are significantly "softer" than those provided by treaty and custom.

4. *Judicial Decisions and Academic Writings*

Judicial decisions and academic writings can be categorized as secondary sources of international legal norms[103] which are not sources in themselves, but can be used to determine if customary legal norms or general principles exist.[104] Domestic judicial decisions can sometimes become a source of international law, but the more authoritative decisions come from transnational bodies or arise from the acts of sovereign states in international legal forums.[105] While there is much of the former,[106] there seems to be dearth of the later. Therein lays the fundamental problem with judicial decisions and the reason for classification as a secondary source of international legal norms.

Academic writings share this secondary classification as a source of international legal norms. Critics are concerned by the possibility that international lawyers and courts will incorrectly look to legal scholarship to define customary international law.[107] The problem is that no one can be certain of the ambitions, motives or prejudices that motivate an academic text. A law professor may publish an article in a prestigious journal, both boldly and authoritatively declaring X to be a well established rule of customary international law. But a statement by the most highly qualified scholars that international law is X cannot overcome evidence that the treaty practice or customary practices of States is otherwise. This only underscores the point that legal scholars should not make law and it would be profoundly inconsistent with the law-making processes within and between States for courts to permit scholars to do so by relying upon their statements alone.[108] Therefore, similar to judicial holdings, academic writings are a better indicator than source of international legal norms.

There is no easy way to determine the existence of international legal norms. The difficulty in taking up the subject of sources is that scholars and practitioners have not agreed on a definitive list of what sources contain the rules of international law, let alone the grundnorm for such rules.[109] To give effective consent, States must know what constitutes consent, that is, what action or inaction on their part creates a binding principle of law. Thus, when a court analyzes an international legal dispute, it begins by looking to the established methods for creating binding legal principles to determine what the law is and rules to apply it.[110] Article 38(1) of the Statute of the ICJ is the only roadmap that has been universally agreed on. The primary sources are treaty, custom, and general principles of law. Academic writing and judicial decisions are secondary sources. However, all of the sources interact with each other to help establish the validity of international legal norms. The Charter is a treaty, but it is not bound by the limitations of treaty as a source of international legal norms because of its 'constitutional' nature. This notion will be explored more in the following section.

III. BOUNDARIES OF SECURITY COUNCIL AUTHORITY

The world watched helplessly as the League of Nations, established at the conclusion of World War I, imploded and failed to prevent the start of World War II.[111] Planning for a successor organization began the very moment the League of Nations collapsed.[112] The United Nations was born out of the allied conferences in Moscow and Tehran in 1943, and the Dumbarton Oaks Conference.[113] At this last conference, the structure and form of the United Nations[114] was discussed, although the primary issues were the framework of the Security Council, specifically the veto power.[115] The drafters of the Charter recognized that the organization that they were creating would not abolish war for all time.[116] They did, however, believe it was the best system for maintaining international peace and security that the assembled States could devise for the moment. In the aftermath of World War II, most people would have been happy with the prevention or regulation of war or the peaceful settlement of disputes for a decade or two.[117]

It is difficult to reduce the Charter to a one-dimensional treaty.[118] The Charter is organic in that it can create legal obligations from within. It is more than a treaty; it is a super-treaty,[119] "reflect[ing] constitutional principles ... in force long before the Charter was drafted," and incorporates them into a new legal order. Understanding the Charter's constitutional potential is essential to understanding how the Security Council's role as a global legislator has developed.

The word 'constitution' can be used in several different public law contexts. It can be used in a formal sense, to represent an identifiable set of legal norms.[120] It can also be used to refer to the function of an identifiable set of legal norms.[121] Finally, the term 'constitution' can be used to refer to the establishment of legitimate and independent legal authority.[122] The Charter can assert each of these possible uses. It codified customary law as it existed prior to 1944 and in so doing, the Charter clearly identified a set of legal norms. The Charter establishes and organizes creation of the organs of the United Nations, and then imputes them with the authority necessary for the performance of the express powers. The term 'constitution' here refers to the function of the Charter as it relates to the organs. Finally, the Charter is not derived from a higher source of legal norms. In this sense, the Charter is a constitution – a font or source of international legal norms.[123]

The United Nations is in the midst of a constitutional crisis. This crisis is not caused by the historic ineffectiveness that plagued the United Nations during the Cold War, but rather the fear that some of the organs are beginning to evolve beyond the Charter.[124] The end of the Cold War and resulting effectiveness of the Security Council[125] have altered the fundamental approach of the United Nations when dealing with conflicts. This section will scrutinize the Charter to determine the contours of Security Council authority.

(A) Positive Authority

Positive authority for the purpose of this section refers to the authority granted to the Security Council by the Charter. The focus of this section will be Chapters V, VI, and VII. This section will also briefly discuss the Charter interpretation used to develop "Chapter VI ½" authority, a combination of peacekeeping and peace enforcement, which was adopted by the Security Council at the conclusion of the Cold War.

1. *UN Charter Chapter V*

The Security Council is one of the principle organs of the United Nations[126] and was intended to be the main guarantor of peace.[127] Article 24[128] provides the foundation of the Security Council's authority. In order to ensure prompt action when necessary, Member States confer primary responsibility on the Security

Council to maintain international peace and security.[129] Under Article 25,[130] the Member States further agree to "accept and carry out" whatever decisions the Security Council makes. The international community essentially delegated authority for the maintenance or restoration of international peace and security to the Security Council. Article 29[131] permits the Security Council to establish any subsidiary organs that it considers necessary in order to perform its function under the Charter. The Security Council can delegate authority to subsidiary organs for all matters, except the decision to use force. Recall the one-dimensional nature of treaty as a source of legal norms. The ability to delegate underscores the constitutional nature of the Charter, separating it from other treaties.

2. *UN Charter Chapter VI*

Chapter VI requires the Security Council to promote the peaceful settlement of international disputes that do not yet, but may soon, pose a threat to international peace and security. Article 33(2)[132] and Article 36(1)[133] combine to give the Security Council authority to make recommendations on the procedures or methods of dispute resolution. The Security Council can investigate a dispute *sua sponte* to determine if the situation, if allowed to continue, is likely to endanger international peace and security.[134] Finally, Article 37(2)[135] and Article 38[136] give the Security Council authority to make dispute settlement recommendations.

Peacekeeping operations, while not specifically mentioned or expressly authorized, have developed from a broad interpretation of Chapter VI. Authority for these operations has been inferred from Article 1[137] and Article 33.[138] A peacekeeping mission, in accordance with the requirements of Article 33, is a "peaceful means" of resolution chosen and approved by the parties to pursue a peaceful conflict settlement.[139] The Charter did not anticipate military forces, deployed under UN authority, placed between parties in armed conflict. However, the Charter is a flexible political document, like a constitution, with many possible interpretations, depending on the circumstances.[140] Peacekeeping operations are merely a pragmatic realization of one of those possibilities.[141] The United Nations first peacekeeping operation took place in 1948.[142] In The *Certain Expenses Case*, the ICJ held that peacekeeping is not within the Security Council's Chapter VII enforcement authority.[143]

However, the Court went on to say there was little doubt that since the Security Council had enforcement powers; it was clearly within the Security Council's authority to use less forceful measures including peacekeeping.[144]

Two points must be noted. First, the Security Council has used peacekeeping operations since the early days of the United Nations. But, it is unclear if this has created a normative framework.[145] Second, the Charter does not give explicit authorization for peacekeeping operations, yet they exist. This underscores the constitutional qualities of the Charter. If the Charter were a one-dimensional treaty without the ability to adapt to changing situations in the international community, the United Nations would have followed the League of Nations into oblivion.

Chapter VI ½ peacekeeping authority was first used by Secretary-General Dag Hammarskjold in his efforts to insert the General Assembly into the peace keeping process. During the Cold War, Hammarskjöld recognized that the international community should play a role in helping to resolve regional conflicts. At that time, the Security Council was hopelessly locked in stalemate. With the permanent members on opposing sides, they could simply veto resolutions that appeared beneficial to the other side. Hammarskjöld's solution was the creation of classical peacekeeping. Hammarskjöld expressed his belief that classical peacekeeping is authorized by "United Nations Chapter VI and ½."[146] Hammarskjöld's opinion serves to underscore the "organic" nature of the Charter and illuminate the creative interpretive process.

Peacekeepers are positioned between rival parties, providing an international presence, discouraging the parties in conflict from continuing or resuming hostilities.[147] The value of these operations is in the expression of international determination. Peacekeepers wear blue helmets, display the **UN's** blue flag, and remain impartial and neutral towards the parties.[148] The goal is not to resolve the conflict, but rather encourage an environment that permits the parties to hold constructive negotiations that will restore peace.[149]

It is easy to understand why Hammarskjöld termed this middle ground Chapter VI ½. Peacekeeping operations are clearly more than taking non-military measures to force parties to negotiate peace. At the same time, because they are not advocating one side over the other, peacekeepers are just as clearly not used in an enforcement role. This interpretation is yet another indication that the Charter is organic, a living document with the ability to become a source of normative rules. Acceptance by the international community of the Charter interpretation that allows the use of peacekeepers helps illuminate this as an emerging practice.[150] Most importantly, Chapter VI ½ peacekeeping has been adopted by the Security Council as a bridge[151] between its traditional Chapter VI peacekeeping and Chapter VII peace enforcement authority.

3. *UN Charter Chapter VII*

Chapter VII of the Charter gives the Security Council primacy within the United Nations, for "the maintenance of international peace and security."[152] The Security Council can use "such action ... as may be necessary to maintain or restore" international peace and security.[153] Article 39[154] requires the Security Council first identify potential threats, and then make a determination that the threat will breach the peace. Only then is the use of force allowed. Article 40[155] reminds the international community that after a determination has been made that a threat to the peace, breach of the peace, or act of aggression exists, it should refrain from using force whenever possible. Further the Security Council is authorized to develop any provisional measures "necessary and appropriate"[156] to prevent aggravating the situation while working to restore peace. These recommendations are binding on the parties but non-prejudicial to their rights, claims or positions.[157] Under Article 25, Security Council resolutions are also recognized as binding legal obligations on member states.

If the provisional measures do not work, or if the Security Council feels that based on the situation they will not work, Article 41[158] empowers the Security Council to change tactics and use non-military measures designed to put pressure on the parties and terminate the conflict threatening peace. These measures take the form of targeted sanctions[159] against particular countries. These sanctions are intended to focus the impact on political leaders and those believed to be responsible for the objectionable behaviour while reducing the economic collateral damage to the general population.[160] Previous sanctions have included arms embargoes,[161] travel bans,[162] and financial restrictions.[163]

If these non-belligerent measures prove ineffective, the Security Council is authorized to resort to using armed force under Article 42.[164] The authority to resort to force is the most important grant of authority to the Security Council. It represents a fundamental shift from the failed League of Nations.[165] This authority directly contradicts the Article 2(4) prohibition on the use of force and gives the Security Council enough room to use force if absolutely necessary. There is no mechanism in the Charter for review of the Security Council Article 39 determination or the resulting resolution grounded in Article 42. Essentially, the international community can determine that sometimes force must be used in order to keep or restore peace.

The drafters intended to and purposely placed an enormous amount of responsibility on the shoulders of the Security Council. The drafters feared that the United Nations could become an international organization, similar to the failed League of Nations, which could collapse under the weight of interminable strife. They also imagined a scenario where debate in the General Assembly would be stymied by an overwhelming amount of disagreement. Therefore, it can be inferred from the text of the Charter that the drafters placed responsibility on such a small group of members to ensure action would be taken when necessary. The Allies, who would become the permanent members of the Security Council, had won the war and they were not prepared to lose the peace.[166] As such, they were keeping the primary responsibility for international peace and security.

(B) Negative Authority

Negative authority refers to the limitations placed on Security Council power. Since the Security Council was established by the Charter, it follows that most of the negative authority is imposed by the Charter itself. There is, however, a major limitation on Security Council authority which is caused by political structures rather than legal norms. This section of the paper will identify and explain the impact of those limitations placed on the Security Council as it attempts to discharge its mandate.

1. *Limitations Imposed by the Charter*

(a) Purposes and Principles

Article 2(4)[167] prohibits Member States from using armed force against the territorial integrity and political independence of other states. Article 2(4) was intended to create a buffer between international and domestic spheres of authority. This prohibition on the use of force extends to non-Member States as both a matter of customary international law and through the Charter itself.[168] While Article 2(4) does not explicitly refer to actions of terrorist groups and other non-state actors, it includes a prohibition of state sponsored terrorism. Clearly under international legal norms, acts of terrorism are illegal. Article 2 was drafted in the aftermath of two World Wars, as the international community sought to ban war and replace it with a system of dispute resolution. That is why the Security Council is limited from using force until extraordinary threats are recognized. The Security Council is further limited by Article 2(7) of the Charter, the most significant check on its authority, which precludes the United Nations, and by extension, the Security Council from intervening in matters which are essentially within the domestic jurisdiction of any state.[169] It is the application of Article 2(7) that requires the Security Council to make a specific determination under Article 39. Without Article 2(7) there would be no gatekeeper and the Security Council could develop a habit of using force in situations where force is not warranted.

There is an explicit exception to the prohibitions outlines in Article 2. If the Security Council is acting under Chapter VII of the Charter, it may use enforcement measures that contravene the Purposes and Principles of the Charter. This is important in two ways: (1) even though the Charter places a limitation on the Security Council's authority to act, it provides a clear exception to act when necessary and (2) that exception exists early enough in the text of the Charter, the drafters recognized that action under Chapter VII authority would be inevitable as the Security Council fulfilled its mandate.

(b) Functions and Powers of the General Assembly

The Security Council is limited by several provisions in the Charter dealing with the powers and functions of the General Assembly. Pursuant to Article 15(1)[170] and Article 24(3),[171] the Security Council must provide annual and special reports to the General Assembly detailing what the Security Council has decided on or done, in order to maintain or restore international peace and security. This is important when read in conjunction with Article 10.[172] In theory, the General Assembly could discuss issues relating to any matter within the scope of the Charter or relating to the powers and functions of any organs of the United Nations and make necessary recommendations. Critics of the Security Council argue that this could remove debates over contentious international issues from the Security Council and allow the General Assembly to consider solutions. However, Article 12[173] prevents the General Assembly from making any recommendations on issues still under consideration by the Security Council.[174] Since the Security Council consistently remains 'seized of the matter,' there are rarely opportunities for the General Assembly to step in.

Finally, Article 24(2)[175] reminds the Security Council to act in accord with the purposes[176] and principles[177] of the United Nations Charter. Under Article 1(1),[178] the first purpose of the Charter is to maintain peace and security "in conformity with the principles of justice and international law." Viewing the purposes and principles of Article 1(1) of the Charter as fundamental and therefore relevant to all Security Council activities, including the maintenance of international peace and security,[179] Article 24(2) consequently sets significant limitations on Security Council actions. Additionally, the preamble proclaims one of the major goals of the United Nations is "to establish conditions under which justice and respect for the obligations arising from treaties and other sources of international law can be maintained."[180] If the Security Council violates international law that would certainly fail to establish such conditions.

However, if one reads the Charter closely, the duty created by Article 1(1) only requires conformity with "the *principles* of . . . international law," not with "international law" *per se*. Further, the obligation to act "in conformity with the principles of justice and international law" literally refers only to the Security Council's function to settle disputes peacefully, and this qualification is not contained in the first part of Article 1(1).[181] The Security Council's function is to "take effective collective measures for the prevention and removal of threats to the peace, and for the suppression of acts of aggression or other breaches of the peace."[182] It is, therefore, possible to argue that the Security Council is not obliged in any way to act in accordance with international legal norms when maintaining or restoring international peace and security.[183] The limitation in Article 1 is not absolute. Since the Charter gives the Security Council authority to establish its own powers, and because there is no check on power by another organ of the United Nations, this limitation may merely be theoretical.

(c) Veto

Enforcement authority is clearly located in the Security Council. But, the Charter is based on an uneasy compromise between power and law.[184] A fundamental limitation of Security Council authority is implicated by the veto.[185] Several types of veto have emerged through Security Council practice. The first and easiest to discern is the absolute veto where one of the permanent members votes against a resolution. The second type of veto is the 'double veto.' The veto only applies to substantive matters considered by the Security Council. A determination that a particular issue is procedural prevents veto availability.[186] The Soviet Union vetoed a preliminary determination that a matter was procedural three times in the early years of the United Nations, claiming instead that the determination itself was substantive.[187] The initial veto enabled the Soviet Union to veto the main resolution without voting against it. The third and most insidious veto practice is the 'Hidden Veto.' This arises when a permanent member of the Security Council abstains and the resolution does not achieve unanimity. Or, in the alternative, the permanent member supports the resolution but persuades enough non-permanent members to vote no against the resolution.

The liberal use of the Security Council veto during the Cold War mirrors the members 'distrust of each others' political agendas. Cognizant of the veto, non-permanent members of the Security Council developed the 'Consensus Procedure' during the Cold War. Controversial resolutions were not even introduced when the proponent sensed it had lost support of any one of the permanent members.[188] Instead, resolutions were watered down, made more palatable, and shopped around prior to introduction. While this could be positive in building consensus and general acceptance, it continues to cast doubt on Security Council resolve. At the end of the day, the Security Council adopted resolutions that were non-contentious and often did not contain enforcement measures to ensure that the international community would actually comply with the obligations that they agreed to accept on ratification. Such resolutions are so mild they have no real impact. Meanwhile, resolutions that would have impact in maintaining international peace and security are often never considered because they conflict with the self-interest of one of the permanent Members.

(d) Regional Arrangements

Article 52[189] approves the use of "regional" arrangements or agencies to engage in "such matters relating to the maintenance of international peace and security, as are appropriate for regional action, provided that such arrangements or agencies and their activities are consistent with the purposes and principles of the United Nations."[190] The Cold War prevented the successful use of "regional" organizations, and the relationship between them and the United Nations in peacemaking and peacekeeping is unclear. Remember, Article 24(1) gives "primary responsibility" for the maintenance of peace and stability to the Security Council.[191] This provision has been interpreted by some to mean that only the Security Council can authorize the use of force.[192] However, Article 52(2) encourages regional institutions to resolve conflicts before referring them to the Security Council. Therefore, the Charter places a limit on Security Council authority by encouraging the use of regional arrangements to maintain international peace and security[193] before referring the local dispute to the Security Council.[194]

However, this limitation may merely be symbolic. This section of the Charter continues to recognize the Security Council's primacy. Under Article 53(1)[195] the Security Council must authorize any enforcement action.[196] Article 54[197] mandates that the Security Council should be constantly informed of any action taken or contemplated by these regional arrangements. There is no escaping the authority of the Security Council. It is the only actor in international law that can subvert the customary legal norms against the use of force.

(e) ICJ Article 96

Article 96[198] of the Charter authorizes either the General Assembly or the Security Council to request an advisory opinion on any legal question from the International Court of Justice. All three are principle organs of the United Nations.[199] In theory, this could provide a constitutional check, similar to the separation of powers, and limit the Security Council's authority to act. However, authority for the ICJ to review Security Council decisions is not explicitly granted[200] by the Charter. Nor is it specifically denied.[201] Since the question of judicial review seems to be somewhat unsettled,[202] it is necessary to determine if there is any other foundation on which the Court could assert authority to limit Security Council action.

The ICJ has been very reluctant to assert authority to review the legality of Security Council resolutions.[203] The first argument is that under general principles of law, the Court may be entitled to judicial review. There is, however, a major flaw with this argument that has to be overcome. Judicial review is not a universal concept.[204] Thus, the Court's practice of non review effectively eliminates judicial review.

The Court's hands-off practice has developed over the past fifty years. In the Certain Expenses case, the Court appeared to reject the idea of judicial review, asserting that there was no "procedure" in the "United Nations" to determine the validity of actions by other organs, concluding that the organs must "determine [their] own jurisdiction."[205] In Southwest Africa Cases, the Court said "undoubtedly, [we] . . . do . . . not possess powers of judicial review or appeal in respect of decisions taken by the United Nations organs concerned."[206] The Court nevertheless proceeded to use "judicial review" throughout its reasoning. Twenty years later, in the case involving the bombing of Pan Am flight 103, the majority of the Court declined to exercise the power of judicial review over Security Council resolutions, yet suggested that such a power may exist. Several of the concurring and dissenting opinions argued that the ICJ should review the validity of the Council resolution.[207]

Invalidation is the second method the ICJ could use to limit Security Council authority. As the Court noted in the *LaGrand* Case,[208] the statute of the Court "enables the Court to fulfil the functions provided for therein, and in particular, the basic function of judicial settlement of international disputes by binding decisions in accordance with Article 59 of the Statute."[209] Consequently, if the General Assembly or the Security Council sought an advisory opinion, the ICJ could, in the process of resolving a dispute, make a determination that a Security Council action is invalid.[210]

While not strictly judicial review, the Court does have a mechanism to bind the Security Council. There is no prohibition on concurrent consideration of a threat to peace and security between the Security Council and the ICJ.[211] It is therefore possible that the ICJ could decide to hear a matter before the Security Council has taken the opportunity to act. If the Court can act first, the Security Council is indirectly bound to respect the holding. Under Article 94(2), "if any party in the case fails to perform the obligations . . . under a judgement . . . by the Court, the [opposing] party may have recourse to the Security Council."[212] The Security Council must then take a hands-off approach to the holding of the Court, unless it determines it is necessary for the maintenance of international peace and security to take measures to give the judgement effect. The end result is that the Security Council could be indirectly bound by a decision of the ICJ.

To make matters worse, Article 38 of the Statute of the ICJ[213] restricts reliance on international judicial precedent. The Court's decisions are consequently relegated to the status of secondary means for the determination of legal norms, no more significant than the opinion of legal scholars.

So far the ICJ has declined or has been denied[214] the opportunity to exercise a check over Security Council authority when such a check might enhance the legitimacy of the Security Council's decisions.[215] It is a difficult call for the Court to make. Until the ICJ decides legal norm articulation is a legitimate function,[216] the legality of Security Council resolutions will likely remain unquestioned. However, if the Court determines it has the authority for judicial review, it will have to develop meaningful standards of review.[217] Otherwise, the Court might mistakenly undercut the effectiveness of the Security Council, and jeopardize the legitimacy of the United Nations.[218] This issue is not likely to go away any time soon.

2. *Limitation of Legitimacy*

The Security Council's Chapter VII enforcement powers trouble many Member States because the Council is not regarded as an adequately representative body. There are five unelected, permanent members: China, France, Russia, the United Kingdom, and the United States. Each has the ability to veto any substantive measure.[219] The United States has dominated the Security Council in recent years.[220] The 10 non-permanent members are elected to a two-year term.[221] They do not have individual veto authority, but could mount a block veto. To the extent that legal norms find legitimacy in democratic institutions, the Security Council is open and vulnerable to criticism.[222] While the Security Council is in the best position to fill the gaps in international law, broad compliance with Security Council resolutions cannot be achieved if the majority of Member States view the Security Council's action as illegitimate.[223] As a consequence, Council authority is limited by its search for legitimacy.

International Relations scholars claim that legitimate governance is rooted in the collective belief that those who govern have the right to do so: those that must follow rules do so not from fear, but because there is a sense that the rules and the institutions they come from are legitimate.[224] While it may be tempting for the permanent members to consider their domestic priorities, the permanent members should not ignore larger international concerns. The Security Council merely has to use its best judgment as it passes legislative resolutions.[225] The permanent members are cognizant of the Security Council's primacy and ability to quickly react to emerging international threats. They are aware of the potential consequences if the Security Council, and therefore the United Nations, loses the ability to resolve conflicts that threaten international peace and security.[226] The Security Council is therefore unlikely to overreach as it establishes international legal norms.

IV. SECURITY COUNCIL LEGISLATIVE RESOLUTIONS

Until adoption of Resolution 1373,[227] the Security Council passed resolutions that condemned terrorism generally or only addressed specific acts of terrorism, mostly in the context of state sponsored terrorism.[228] Resolutions 1373[229] and 1540[230] represent the Security Council's attempts to address international terrorism committed by non-State actors and terrorist groups. The Resolutions have several common elements. Each responds to a general, not specific threat.[231] Both were adopted under Chapter VII authority. Both establish a committee[232] of the Security Council to monitor implementation efforts and both require member states to report the efforts taken to comply with the obligations of the resolutions to the committee.[233] Finally, both Resolutions were the result of U.S.-led efforts to fill gaps existing in current international law relating to terrorism,[234] thereby deviating from the traditional multi-lateral treaty process to create binding international legal norms. Critics of the Security Council question these legislative actions as improper and beyond the Security Council's authority. This section of the paper will analyze the text of Resolutions 1373 and 1540.

(A) Security Council Resolution 1373

Resolution 1373 was adopted on September 28, 2001, and represents a watershed for the Security Council.[235] It is the first time the Security Council used Chapter VII authority to mandate Member States take or refrain from taking specific actions other than when disciplining a specific country.[236] Resolution 1373 departs from the normal language of "calls upon" and "urges" and instead issues mandatory directions in a style characteristic of legislation, such as "all States shall. . . ."[237] Rather than start from a blank slate, the Security Council picked the best provisions from the existing international terrorism conventions.[238]

Resolution 1373 encourages Member States to take action against international terrorism, by imposing obligations on them to enact domestic legislation. "All States shall . . . criminalize" financing or raising funds for terrorism.[239] In addition, states must freeze funds and other financial assets[240] and also prohibit their nationals and others residing within their borders from making funds available for terrorism.[241] Pursuant to paragraph 2, States are required to "refrain from providing any form of support, active or passive, to entities or persons involved in terrorist acts, including suppressing recruitment of members of terrorist groups and eliminating the supply of weapons to terrorists."[242] States are also required to "ensure that any person who participates in the financing, planning, preparation or perpetration of terrorist acts or in supporting terrorist acts is brought to justice and ensure that, in addition to any other measures against them, such terrorist acts are established as serious criminal offences in domestic laws...."[243] The resolution also requires tightened border controls,[244] mutual assistance in criminal investigations or proceedings, including information exchange,[245] cooperation on terrorism prevention,[246] denial of a safe haven,[247] and that states become party to relevant conventions and protocols and implement them.[248] This was more than a resolution; the demands made by the Security Council in Resolution 1373 amounted to legislative action.[249]

Resolution 1373 does not include a definition for terrorism. As a result, each Member State is left to individually define terrorism. The resolution instead places its central focus on increasing the capability and capacity to fight international terrorism.[250] To that end, the Resolution established the Counter-Terrorism Committee,[251] and requires Member States to report the steps they are taking to implement the Resolution and comply with its obligations.[252] These reports cover general counter-terrorism measures in seven specific areas of domestic competence: legislation, financial asset controls, customs, immigration, extradition, law enforcement, and illegal arms trafficking.[253]

In 2003, the Security Council passed Resolution 1535[254] to express frustration with the lagging implementation of Resolution 1373. Resolution 1535 also included a series of reforms designed to enhance the Counter-Terrorism Committee's compliance-monitoring role. The most significant reform was the addition of the Counter Terrorism Executive Directorate,[255] a group of twenty experts tasked with providing technical assistance to the CTC. In 2006, the CTED began to make preliminary assessments of State implementation compliance with Resolution 1373.[256] Throughout 2008, the CTED will be making full scale assessments through field visits "tailored to the specific circumstances and the nature of the terrorist threat in the countries belonging to all regions."[257] It has taken nearly seven years for the CTC to begin the phase of helping individual Member States address the specific threat they are facing.

(B) Security Council Resolution 1540

Resolution 1540 was adopted shortly after the United States introduced a Proliferation Security Initiative.[258] The timing generated suspicion throughout the international community that the resolution was designed primarily to universalize and make mandatory, the interdiction[259] principles of the United States that had been consented to by a limited number of States at that time. It is generally agreed that the relevant international instruments on weapons of mass destruction:[260] the Chemical Weapons Convention,[261] the Non-Proliferation Treaty,[262] and the Biological Weapons Convention[263] all left a significant gap in the law. Each failed to contemplate the potential of non-State actors acquiring WMD.[264] Thus, as happened with Resolution 1373, the

Security Council filled the gap in international law to address the threat.

It would have taken years and a tremendous investment of effort to negotiate the multi-lateral treaty required to deal with this potential problem. However, the Security Council's decision to adopt this resolution under Chapter VII immediately imposed immediate and binding obligations on all Member States. Resolution 1540 aims to prevent WMD and the necessary delivery systems from falling into the hands of terrorists. It clarified the beliefs of the international community, that both the proliferation of nuclear, chemical, and biological weapons and their means of delivery constituted a threat to international peace and security. Resolution 1540 was unanimously adopted by the Security Council under Chapter VII, mandating that all States should refrain from supporting efforts by non-State actors to acquire weapons of mass destruction. Additionally, States are *required* to adopt appropriate domestic legislation and establish necessary enforcement and prevention measures. A committee modelled on the CTC was established for a two year period to oversee implementation of the resolution.[265] That mandate was later extended to April 2010.[266]

The obligations imposed by Resolution 1373 and Resolution 1540 are the type that is usually only contained in negotiated treaties.[267] Classical international law, which is built on State sovereignty and the corollary of State consent, denied all entities the power to legislate for States.[268] The Security Council's demand for action in Resolution 1373 illustrates the hegemonic nature of contemporary international law.[269]

V. LEGISLATIVE RESOLUTIONS CONSISTENT WITH SECURITY COUNCIL AUTHORITY

As previously stated, the Charter was drafted with intent for the Security Council to be the prime guarantor of peace. Article 24(1) designates the Security Council as the primary organ of the United Nations responsible for restoring or maintaining international peace and security. To enable the Council to fulfil this responsibility effectively and efficiently, the Charter endows it, under Chapter VII, with the ability to make far-reaching decisions that create binding obligations on all states.[270]

The United Nations lacks a formal process to establish the power of its organs.[271] The drafters consciously left the responsibility of interpreting the Charter provisions granting authority to the organs themselves.[272] "The power to interpret is the power to create law."[273] It should be no surprise then, that there has been criticism levelled against the Security Council for adopting Resolution 1373 and Resolution 1540. It has been argued that the Council inappropriately exercised its emergency authority under Chapter VII to establish rules with too broad an application. These critics stress either the negative authority of the Security Council's powers under the Charter,[274] or the Council's relative legitimacy when compared to the more 'democratic' General Assembly.[275] These arguments essentially espouse that the Security Council does not have the authority to create these broad obligations, and even if they do, this type of action would better be left to the General Assembly since nearly every member of the international community has a voice in the debate.[276] However, this criticism often misses the mark.

The phrase[277] 'international legislation' has been invoked by different legal scholars in a variety of contexts. It has been used broadly to explain "both the process and the product of the conscious effort to make additions to, or changes in, the law of nations."[278] It has also been used to describe the outcome of treaties,[279] the formation of customary international law, and the adoption of binding decisions by international organizations.[280] Significantly, legal scholars have already characterized previous Security Council resolutions as 'international legislation,' specifically those resolutions creating targeted sanctions, which create binding obligations on Member States.

State practice seems to indicate a preference for 'international legislation' that mirrors domestic lawmaking.[281] An observation of the hallmarks of legislation is thus warranted. The most significant characteristics of legislation are the general and abstract character of the obligations imposed.[282] These obligations may be prompted by a particular international conflict, but they are not restricted to it. Rather, the obligations are phrased in neutral terms, with the potential to apply to an indefinite number of cases, and for an unlimited time.

When Resolution 1373 states "all States shall . . . freeze without delay funds and other financial assets or economic resources of persons who commit, or attempt to commit, terrorist acts or participate in or facilitate the commission of terrorist acts,"[283] it looks like the Security Council is adopting legislation. Similarly, Resolution 1540 requires that "all States shall refrain from providing any form of support to non-State actors . . ."[284] The Security Council deliberately adopted generic resolutions[285] that create an obligation where one did not previously exist.

But by adopting the Resolutions under Chapter VII authority, the Security Council side stepped questions of legitimacy. The Security Council legitimately recognized the danger and made an Article 39 determination. It then moved forward under Chapter VII authority to close the gaps in international law. This is consistent with the purpose of the Security Council. While individual states, the General Assembly, and even the Security Council are theoretically limited by Article 2(4), the Security Council is the only constituent part of the international community that has the ability to determine that the threat or use of force is necessary based on the facts of any given situation.

The drafters anticipated solutions to prevent the same fate as the League of Nations, ensuring that the Security Council would both be better positioned and provided with authority flexible enough to respond to threats to international peace. The drafters anticipated that the Security Council would eventually fill the role of global legislator. The legal framework for the Security Council's role as global legislative exists. Now it is necessary to examine the international community's political will to accept the Security Council in that role.

VI. POLITICAL WILL OF THE INTERNATIONAL COMMUNITY

Does the international community possess the necessary political will to recognize the Security Council's legislative actions? There is much at stake as the international community grapples with the Security Council's new role. It is more than the prevention of terrorism. The Security Council's legitimacy, and, therefore, the very legitimacy of the United Nations, rests on whether the Member States do or do not recognize and enforce these new legal norms. If the Security Council fails to enforce the obligations that have been established and loses legitimacy, there is no other organ of the United Nations which possesses the 'constitutional' authority to maintain international peace and security.[286]

(A) In Theory

What the international community should do is embrace the enhanced collective security measures afforded by the Security Council in its legislative role. The Report of the High-Level Panel on Threats, Challenges and Change[287] concluded that "the central challenge for the twenty-first century is to fashion a new and broader understanding . . . of what collective security means — and of all the responsibilities, commitments, strategies and institutions that come with it if a collective security system is to be effective, efficient and equitable."[288] The panel understood its task was nothing short of reviving the 1945 consensus underlying the Charter itself: a collective security system designed to save the world from "the scourge of war."[289] When Member States recognize that the problem, in this case terrorism, is dangerous, but then cannot agree on the solution, they should be happy that the Security Council has stepped in to fill the gap.

The core theme of the high-level panel report is an appeal for a "new security consensus"[290] that underlies a "new comprehensive collective security system."[291] This new consensus rests on the common recognition by members of the international community of the actual security threats facing us in the twenty-first century. Perhaps stating the obvious, a collective security system seeks to prevent attack through collective obligations and deterrents. Scholars have used game theory to explain this process. The chain is only as strong as its weakest link.[292] In other words, the international community is safe from terrorism, only to the point of the least engaged State.

To the question: should States accept or need the help of their fellow States to ensure the security of their own citizens,[293] the panel answers with a resounding "yes." "We live in an interdependent world."[294] The report is packed with passages like: "[t]oday, more than ever before, threats are interrelated and a threat to one is a threat to all. The mutual vulnerability of weak and strong has never been clearer."[295] "No State, no matter how powerful, can by its own efforts alone make itself invulnerable to today's threats."[296]

The high-level panel's conception of this consensus rests on solidarity more than self-defence. What is required is an awareness of common threats and common responsibilities. This solidarity is both procedural and substantive. The panel actually builds on the original bargain enshrined in the Charter.[297] Nothing in the Charter allows UN Member States to infringe on the domestic jurisdiction of their fellow states except as authorized by the Security Council. The panel recognizes that consensus based on an affirmative commitment to address a wide range of threats to both human and State security will worry many States; therefore, it continues to insist on Security Council authorization prior to any action. The panel also recognizes that Member States will not put their faith in the Security Council unless it can prove to be both proactive and effective.

The high-level panel noted that "in signing the Charter of the United Nations, States not only benefit from the privileges of sovereignty but also accept its responsibilities."[298] This includes both "the obligation of a State to protect the welfare of its own peoples" and "its obligations to the wider international community."[299] These responsibilities are facts of contemporary life. The United Nations itself, through the obligations of membership, becomes the guarantor of international obligations.

Security Council resolutions passed under Chapter VII have a potentially greater sphere of influence than treaties or multilateral conventions. Both the Resolution 1373 committee and the Resolution 1540 committee are charged with assisting[300] the Member States and should be provided with the necessary resources needed to help those states comply with their obligations. It is in every individual's, and therefore every States, mutual interest.

(B) In Reality

The doctrine of incorporation describes the process by which legal norms are incorporated.[301] For some members of the international community, treaties automatically become part of the domestic legal system.[302] For others, the domestic legislature must take some action to ratify the treaty prior to incorporation.[303] This process is defined as a Monist or Dualist legal system.[304] One way to incorporate Security Council resolutions would be to treat them the same as international treaties.[305] But Security Council resolutions are not analogous to treaties.[306] Unlike a treaty or international instrument that requires broad international agreement, a Security Council resolution only requires a consensus of nine members, including all five permanent members. Trying to equate treaties with Security Council resolutions might also stretch the doctrine of incorporation, since the document to be incorporated was nonexistent at the time of the treaty.

Enhancing Member State compliance with these obligations is often a simple but expensive matter of capacity building.[307] It is impossible to measure the political will of the international community through legal norms. In fact, this discussion nearly abandons the law and turns to politics. However, there is a relevant tool to assist with measuring the will of the international community to accept the Security Council's legislative role; member state compliance with the reporting obligations created by both resolutions. It illuminates both what the State has done and demonstrates the individual states' willingness to comply.

Resolution 1373 established a 90 day deadline for submission of the first reports.[308] The deadline, December 27, 2001, passed without total compliance of the initial reporting requirement. Only 119 out of 192 nation-states had submitted reports to the CTC.[309] The international community was either pushing back against the Security Council, or it was generally incapable of complying with the obligations. Ambassador Greenstock encouraged non-compliant States to submit the required reports as soon as possible, and thanked those that had complied.[310] The Security Council, frustrated by non-compliance, passed Resolution 1456[311] in January 2003. It encouraged all States to follow the obligations, including the reporting obligation established by Resolution 1373.[312] It wasn't until July 15, 2003, nearly a year and a half after the deadline, before the CTC could inform the Security Council that it had received the required first reports from all Member States.[313]

Reporting compliance to the 1540 Committee is far worse. Resolution 1540 established a six month deadline for submission of the first reports.[314] A third of the Security Council missed the reporting deadline of October 24, 2004.[315] Even today, almost four year later, only 137 States have submitted their first report to the committee.[316]

Compliance with the resolutions provides clues as to the mindset of the international community towards the Security Council creating international obligations that have a direct impact on domestic affairs. The record of compliance is not good. This could be caused by either a desire to retain nationalistic power (not ceding authority to the Security Council to alter domestic legal norms), concern that the Security Council was overstepping its bounds of authority, or just a plain inability to do what the international community is asking. It is clear that accepting the Security Council in this role will require a reconfiguration of the notion of Sovereignty.[317] This "new sovereignty" represents the right to and the capacity to participate in the international institutions which allow their members, working together, to accomplish the ends that individual governments could once accomplish alone. The nation state is no longer king.

VII. NEXT STEPS FOR THE SECURITY COUNCIL

Where does the Security Council go now? The reporting requirements enable the subsidiary organs, the CTC and the 1540 committee, to monitor compliance with the respective resolutions and also to engage Member States in a dialogue about compliance.[318] The CTC has managed this noncompliance through persuasion and acculturation rather than requesting the Security Council to impose sanctions on any UN member.

The first thing that the Security Council should do is take initiative and provide clear guidance to the international community by supplying an operative definition of terrorism.[319] This will help the Member States as they pass domestic legislation to comply with the new rules while allaying fears about human rights violations.[320] It will also help Member States grasp the true extent of the problem of international terrorism. Many definitions have been proposed, but none of them is uncontroversial. They are either too wide or too narrow. Yet, without an operative definition of terrorism, one can neither identify an act of violence as terrorist nor condemn (or justify) that act. If the international community does not know the true extent of the problem, there is little it can realistically do in order to solve it.

The next step is to assist the Member States with developing an increased capacity to fight the clearly defined problem. That may mean providing both technical and financial support from within the United Nations or, more specifically, from the permanent members of the Security Council. It only takes one state not living up to its obligations for terrorism to retain a place in the modern era and put everyone at risk.

Finally, the Security Council must ensure that the obligations under Resolution 1373 and Resolution 1540 are fully implemented.

This may mean establishing either a reward system for those in compliance, or a system of punishment for those who are not.[321] This system could include expanded opportunities for involvement with Security Council initiatives and activities. Perhaps it is those who have managed to become compliant who are in the best position to provide technical assistance to those who are still non-compliant. The structure of the Security Council probably makes it easier and more productive if a system of punishment strong enough to prod compliance is established.[322] If all else fails, the Security Council should pursue direct enforcement as provided for in Article 41 against Member States in non compliance.[323]

VIII. CONCLUSION

It took 56 years, but the Security Council has finally matured into the role envisioned by the drafters of the Charter. The Security Council has the competence to act as a global legislator. It is simply a matter of acceptance by the Member States. The doctrine of sources provides a roadmap to find the sources of international legal norms and methods for using those norms. The Doctrine informs international lawyers and the Courts that a treaty, while one-dimensional, is a clear representation of the law between States that is based on consent. Further that customary law is the still the most robust source of international legal norms but it is very difficult to pinpoint their existence. Finally, that the secondary sources of judicial opinions and academic writing can point in general to the existence of international legal norms but cannot be trusted as authorities establishing those norms.

Once the lawyers know where to look and how to apply the law, they may be surprised to learn that the Charter has moved beyond the Cold War and developed a 'constitutional' character. The Security Council has taken advantage of its new found productivity to assess its power and make a legitimate determination that it has authority to do much more. As a result, the Security Council felt no reluctance to move quickly to fill the voids in international law that have allowed terrorism to flourish for the past four decades. But the character of the Security Council, with the power located in the hands of the permanent members, has caused some hesitation.

While the international community has been reluctant to accept the Security Council role, there are some distinct advantages. The Security Council is flexible and can act faster to address situations of international concern than either the process of custom formation or treaty negotiation. This was clearly shown with establishment of the effective international legal regimes found in Resolutions 1373 and Resolutions 1540.

The jury is still out as to whether the international community possesses the political will and commitment to principle to accept the Security Council as a global legislator. The concern is that one State, particularly the United States, could dominate the Security Council and use it to enact global legislation.

Notes

1. U. N. Development Programme [UNDP], Human Development Report, 88 (1994).
2. Press Release, Secretary-General, Secretary-General Annan Addressing Assembly on Terrorism, Calls for 'Immediate, Far-Reaching Changes' in UN Response to Terror, U.N. Doc. SG/SM/7977/GA/9920 (Oct. 1, 2001).
3. Ramsey Kleff, Terrorism: The Trinity Perspective, in Terrorism and Political Violence: The Limits and Possibilities of Legal Control 15 (1993) (noting evidence of terrorism by the Israelites in the Old Testament).
4. Press Release, General Assembly, Agreement on Comprehensive Terrorism Convention Remains Elusive, Assembly's Legal Committee is Told, U.N. Doc. GA/L/3296 (Oct. 11, 2006). The Representative of Saint Vincent and the Grenadines recalled the 1973 terrorists hijacking and explosion of a Cuban Airways plane off the coast of Barbados in which all 73 people aboard were killed. *Cf.* Jerry Markon, *Interrogator Testifies About Hamdan's Work With Bin Laden*, Wash. Post., July 24, 2008, at A16 (recounting that during his interrogation, Salim Ahmed Hamdan, bin Laden's driver said "he had heard bin Laden saying he didn't expect the operation...would be that successful"). 2,819 people were killed in the terrorist attacks on September 11th terrorist attacks. *9/11 by the Numbers: Death, Destruction, Charity, Salvation, War, Money, Real Estate, Spouses, Babies, and other September 11 statistics*, N.Y. Mag., (Sept. 5, 2002), available at *http://nymag.com/news/articles/wtc/1year/numbers.htm* (last visited Aug. 20, 2008).
5. Paul Wilkinson, Terrorism Versus Democracy: The Liberal States Response 13 (2001).
6. For a list of terrorist organizations *see* Office of Counterterrorism, United States Department of State, Fact Sheet (Oct. 11, 2005), at *http://www.state.gov/s/ct/rls/fs/37191.htm. See also* The Security Council Committee established pursuant to resolution 1267 (1999) concerning Al-Qaida and the Taliban and Associated Individuals and Entities, The United Nations Security

Council, The Consolidated List established and maintained by the 1267 Committee with respect to Al-Qaida, Usama bin Laden, and the Taliban and other individuals, groups, undertakings and entities associated with them (Aug. 12, 2008), available at *http://www.un.org/sc/committees/1267/consolidatedlist.htm* (last visited Aug. 20, 2008).

7. Brian Jenkins, International Terrorism: A New Mode of Conflict, in 48 California Seminar on Arms Control and Foreign Policy 1 (1975); *see also* Tel-Oren v. Libyan Arab Republic, 726 F.2d 774, 795 (D.C.Cir.1984) (Edwards, J., concurring) (noting "the nations of the world are so divisively split on the legitimacy [of terrorism] as to make it impossible to pinpoint an area of harmony or consensus"), cert. denied, 470 U.S. 1003 (1985).

8. Louis Rene Beres, *The Legal Meaning of Terrorism for the Military Commander*, 11 Conn. J. Int'l Law 1 (1995) (noting that the term [terrorism] has become so comprehensive and vague to render legitimate acts of aggression terrorism).

9. *See* Abraham D. Sofaer, *Terrorism and the Law*, 64 Foreign Aff. 901, 903-06 (1986).

10. *See* Eric Hobsbawm, The Age of Extremes: A History of the World, 1914-1991 560 (1994).

11. Press Release, Secretary-General, 'Our Place is Beside Those in Distress', Secretary-General Tells Staff at Special Meeting for Terror Victims, U.N. Doc., SG/SM/7956 (Sept. 14, 2001).

12. S.C. Res. 1368, UN SCOR, 56th Sess., 4382nd mtg., UN Doc. S/RES/1368 (September 12, 2001).

13. *Id.*

14. *See* Section IV *infra* for a detailed discussion of the legislative and administrative obligations.

15. *See* Paul C. Szasz, *The Security Council Starts Legislating*, 96 Am. J. Int'l. L. 901, 901 (2002).

16. U.N. Charter art. 38.

17. U.N. Charter art. 39.

18. *See generally* Jianmeng Shen, *The Relativity and Historical Perspective of the Golden Age of International Law*, 6 Int'l Legal Theory 15 (2000). Notable positivists include: Alberico Gentilis (1552-1608); Richard Zouche (1590-1660); Cornelis van Bynkershoek (1673-1743); Georg Wilhelm Friedrich Hegel (1770-1831); Heinrich Triepel (1868-1946); F.L. Oppenheim (1858-1919); Georg Jellinek (1851-1911); Hans Kelsen (1881-1973).

19. *See Id.* Notable naturalists include: Saint Thomas Aquinas (1225-1274); Francisco de Vitoria (1486-1546); Francisco Suarez (1548-1617); Sammuel Pufendorf (1632-1694); Thomas Hobbes (1588-1679); John Locke (1632-1704).

20. *See* Malcolm N. Shaw, International Law 40-44 (1997).
21. Arthur Nussbaum, A Concise History of the Law of Nations 148 (1954) (noting that German legal scholar Sammuel Pufendorf (1632-1694) "sets out to prove that every rule actually observed among nations is nothing but the law of nature" that was established by God.)
22. The heavens are home to "the super-sensual world of the mind and the eternal abode of ideas." G. Robert Blakey & Brian J. Murray, *Threats, Free Speech, and the Jurisprudence of the Federal Criminal Law*, 2002 B.Y.U.L. Rev. 829, 1093 (2002). *See also* Dennis Lloyd, The Idea of Law 70-71 (1976) (providing, as a characteristic of natural law, that humankind and all matters of the universe are guided by gods and the spirits of the supernatural).
23. *See* Nussbaum, *supra* note 21 at 147-164.
24. *See* Hans Kelsen, Principles of International Law 243 (1966).
25. *See* J. G. Starke, An Introduction to International Law 23-24 (1989).
26. Cornelis von Bynkershoek, Quaestiones juris publici (Questions of Public Law) (Tenney Frank trans., London, H. Milford 1930) (1737) (asserting that the law of nations is that which is observed in accordance with the light of reason, between nations. "[W]e may safely follow this definition, which establishes two distinct bases of this law: namely, reason and custom. But whatever manner we may define the law of nations, and however we may argue upon it, we must come at last to this conclusion, that what reason dictates to nations, and what nations observe between each other... is the only law of those who are not governed by any other").
27. *See generally* Christopher A. Ford, *Judicial Discretion in International Jurisprudence: Article 38(1) (c) and "General Principles of Law,"* 5 Duke J. Comp. & Int'l L. 35 (1994).
28. Statute of the International Court of Justice art. 38, June 26, 1945, 59 Stat. 1055, 1060, available at *http://www.icj-cij.org/icjwww/ibasicdocuments/ibasictext/ibasicstatute.htm.* (last visited Aug. 20, 2008).
29. See Michael Byers, War Law 4 (2005). "Treaties may be referred to by any number of different names, including 'charter', 'convention', 'covenant', 'exchange of notes', or 'protocol'."
30. *See* P. Corbett, *The Consent of States and the Sources of the Law of Nations*, 6 Brit. Y. B. Int'l L. 22, 25 (1925). "Treaties considered as agreements are acts of consent; considered as documents they are records of evidence of consent."
31. Martti Koskenniemi, From Apology to Utopia 398 (2006) (explaining that a treaty is more responsive to changing wills and interests than custom).
32. *See* I.M. Lobo Souza, *The Role of Consent in the Customary Process*, 44 Int'l & Comp. L.Q. 521 (1995).

33. *See* United Nations Treaty Collection, available at *http://untreaty.un.org*. (Last visited Aug. 20, 2008).

34. The 1945 United Nations Conference on International Organization [UNCIO], June 26, 1945. The Charter was finally ratified on October 24, 1945.

35. U. N. Charter pmbl., para. 3.

36. 1 L. Oppenheim, International Law: A Treatise 546-47 (1955) (noting that the power and importance of treaties arise from the underlying custom of considering treaties binding on the signatories).

37. *See* Daniel Mazzini, *Stable International Contracts in Emerging Markets: An Endangered Species?*, 15 B.U. INT'L L.J. 343, 355 (1997) (discussing *pacta sunt servanda* in the context of international project finance arbitration).

38. Mark W. Janis, An Introduction to International law 14-15 (1998) (defining "law of treaties" as the "accepted rules respecting the making, and the amendment, invalidity, and termination of agreements among states").

39. Vienna Convention on the Law of Treaties, May 23, 1969, U.N. Doc A/ Conf. 39/27 at 289 (1969), 1155 U.N.T.S. 331.

40. *Id.*

41. Discovering the shared intent of the parties is the stated goal of the International Court of Justice. *See* South West Africa Cases (Eth. v. S.Afr.; Liber. v. S.Afr.), 1962 I.C.J. 319, 341 (Dec 21) (Van Wyk, J., dissenting).

42. *Supra* note 39 at art. 24, para. 2. "[F]ailing any [provision of the treaty respecting entry into force], a treaty enters into force as soon as consent to be bound by the treaty has been established for *all* the negotiating States." (Emphasis added). *See also* Byers, *supra* note 29 (noting that a third party can become bound by the treaty through the process of 'accession').

43. *See* John Currie, Public International Law 226 (2001).

44. *See supra* note 39. The Vienna Convention does not specifically govern treaty termination. One may therefore infer that termination is governed by the parties and absent some limiting factor that the default term is infinite.

45. North Sea Continental Shelf (F.R.G. v. Den. & Neth.), 1969 I.C.J. 3, 38 (Feb. 20) (discussing customary international law as having "equal force for all members of the international community" and not being subject to any "right of unilateral exclusion"). *See also* Jonathon I. Charney, *Universal International Law*, 87 Am. J. Int'l. L. 529, 531 (1993). "[T]reaties ... require the consent of individual states to be binding on them ..."

46. *See* United Nations Treaty Collection: Conventions on Terrorism, available at *http://untreaty.un.org/English/Terrorism.asp* (last visited Aug. 20, 2008).

47. See W. Michael Reisman, *International Legal Responses to Terrorism*, 22 Hous. J. Int'l. L. 3, 28 (1999).
48. *See* discussion *infra* regarding treaty formation.
49. Paul Reuter, Introduction au droit des traites 38 (1972). "Custom is even more central than the treaty."
50. Prosper Weil, *Towards Relative Normativity in International Law?*, 77 AJIL 413, 433-434 (1983) (noting that the classic theory of customary law is based on a delicate equilibrium between allowing customary norms to change without consent from every individual state and allowing individual states to escape being bound by legal norms they do not recognize).
51. *See supra* note 38 at 44.
52. Customary law is distinct from custom. Harold J. Berman, Law and Revolution 8 (1983). "Custom, for example, in the sense of habitual patterns of behaviour, is distinguished from customary law, in the sense of customary norms of behaviour that are considered to be legally binding."
53. Restatement (Third) of the Foreign Relations Law of the United States §102(2) (1987). "Customary international law results from a general and consistent practice of states followed by them from a sense of legal obligation." *See also* ICJ Statute 38 *supra* note 28. The International Court of Justice (ICJ) defines custom as "evidence of a general practice accepted as law."
54. Anthony A. D'Amato, The Concept of Custom in International Law 270 (1971) (asserting that custom "is rooted in the desire of the international community for order and security-aims").
55. *See* Charney *supra* note 45 at 532. (discussing various theories of state obligation to abide by international law).
56. *Id.* at 531.
57. S. S. "Lotus" (Fr. v. Turk.), 1927 P. C. I. J., ser. A, No. 9, at 1, 28 (merits). This case involved a question of Turkish compliance with international law regarding the institution of criminal proceedings pursuant to Turkish law. The proceedings were against a French officer aboard the Lotus, which collided with the Boz-Kourt. The Court held that a "negative" state practice, consisting of abstention from criminal proceedings, cannot, in itself, be seen as sufficient evidence of *opinio juris*.
58. Jordan J. Paust, International Law of the United States 1 (1996) "(C)ustomary international law actually has two primary components which must generally be conjoined: (1) patterns of practice or behaviour, and (2) patterns of legal expectation, 'acceptance' as law, or opinio juris." *See also* Michael Byers, Custom, Power and the Power of Rules: International Relations and Customary International Law 130 (1999).
59. *See* D'Amato *supra* note 44 at 58. (noting that there is no consensus as to how much time a practice must be maintained to evidence existence of

a custom). *See also* G. I. Tunkin, *Remarks On the Juridical Nature of Customary Norms of International Law*, 49 Cal. L. Rev. 419, 420 (1961) (arguing that the element of time is not dispositive as to whether a customary law exists).

60. *See* Tunkin *Id.* at 419.

61. Ian Brownlie, Principles of Public International Law 6-7 (2d ed. 1973) (noting that uniformity and consistency of the practice, not generality of the practice evidence custom).

62. For a history of international law, *see* Nussbaum, supra note 21.

63. *See* H.W.A. Thirlway, International Customary Law and Codification: An Examination of the Continuing Role of Custom in the Present Period of Codification of International Law 17 (1972).

64. *Id.* at 47 (referring to opinio juris as "the psychological element in the formation of custom.").

65. *See* Maurice H. Mendelson, *Formation of Customary International Law*, 272 Recueil des Cours 155, 183 (1998).

66. Int'l L. Ass'n, Comm. on Formation of Customary (Gen.) Int'l L., Statement of Principles Applicable to the Formation of General Customary International Law 29-30 (2000), available at http://www.ila-hq.org/pdf/customarylaw.pdf (quoting Thirlway, *supra* note 63). "The question of the subjective element in customary law is highly controversial.... 'The precise definition of ... the psychological element in the formation of custom, the philosopher's stone which transmutes the inert mass of accumulated usage into the gold of binding legal rules, has probably caused more academic controversy than all the actual contested claims made by States on the basis of alleged custom.'"

67. *See* Byers, *supra* note 58 at 130-131.

68. *See* Andrew T. Guzman, *A Compliance-Based Theory of International Law*, 90 Cal. L. Rev. 1823, 1833-1834 (2002).

69. Continental Shelf (Libya v. Malta), 1985 I.C.J. 13, 29 (June 3). "The material of customary international law is to be looked for primarily in the actual practice and opinio juris of States ...." *See also* Continental Shelf *supra* note 64 at 44. "The States concerned must therefore feel that they are conforming to what amounts to a legal obligation."

70. *See* Lotus *supra* note 57 at 18. "The rules of law binding upon States therefore emanate from their own free will..." *See also* Louis Henkin, *International Law: Politics, Values and Functions*, 216 Recueil Des Cours D'Academies de Droit Int'l 9, 27 (1989). "[A] state is not subject to any external authority unless it has voluntarily consented to such authority."

71. *Id.*

72. One criticism of this theory is that internalization of any particular legal norm does not necessarily mean that the state has accepted that norm

because it is the right thing to do. Koh argues that through a process of interaction, interpretation, and internalization a state may simply accept that the underlying norm is helpful and therefore valuable in the long term. Other states may express no opinion about the value of the rule and follow it as a matter of routine. Still other states may only internalize the fact that the norm is widely accepted by others. In other words, a state may follow the rule because it has an internalized fear of reputational harm or other negative consequences that could result from noncompliance. *See* Harold Hongju Koh, *The 1998 Frankel Lecture, Bringing International Law Home*, 35 Hous. L. Rev. 623, 642 (1998) (noting repeated participation in the transnational legal process is a constructivist activity that helps to reconstruct the national interests of the participating nations).

73. *Id.* at 632. "In Professor Henkin's famous phrase, 'almost all nations observe almost all principles of international law and almost all of their obligations almost all of the time.' But if this is so, why do they obey?"

74. *Id.* at 647. *See* also David Dyzenhaus, Emerging From Self-Incurred Immaturity, 6 (Institute for International Law and Justice, Global Administrative Law Series Working Paper No. 2005/1, 2005), available at *http://www.iilj.org/publications/2005-1Dyzenhaus.asp.* (noting that the process of interpretation confers legislative authority on bodies and validity on constitutional statues on legal documents or simply on values that are considered fundamental to legal order).

75. *Id.*

76. *See* Harold Hongju Koh, *Why Do Nations Obey International Law?*, 106 Yale L.J. 2599, 2646 (1997).

77. *Supra* note 76 at 655.

78. Andrew T. Guzman, *Saving Customary International Law*, 27 Mich. J. Int'l L. 115, 124-127 (2005) (explaining that customary international law can result from a belief that non-compliance with a rule will be met by sanctions, including harm to a state's reputation).

79. *Supra* note 76 at 655-663.

80. *Frederic* L. Kirgis, Jr., *Custom on a Sliding Scale*, 81 AJIL 146 (1987) (arguing that the greater the moral value, the less actual state action necessary to establish custom.

81. *Id.* at 149.

82. *See* Koskenniemi, *supra* note at 2 (arguing that finding traditional custom solely on the strength of state practice alone allows it to become an apology for state power).

83. *See* JANIS, *supra* note 38 at 46. "Without *opinio juris*, there may exist only a history lesson more or less devoid of legal significance."

84. *See* G. J. H. Van Hoof, Rethinking the Sources of International Law 86 (1983).

85. Bin Cheng, *Custom: The Future of General State Practice In a Divided World*, *in* the Structure and Process of International Law: Essays in Legal Philosophy Doctrine and Theory 513, 532 (1983).

86. *Id.* at 549.

87. *Id.* Based on this theory, there is strong evidence that the Bush Doctrine, first proclaimed by the U.S. in response to the terrorist attacks of September 11, 2001, that States harbouring terrorist are as guilty as the terrorist, became an instant custom during the days and weeks following the attacks.

88. *See supra* note 45.

89. Hereinafter "ICJ"

90. *See* discussion *supra* on customary legal norms. *See also* Katherine N. Guernsey, *The North Continental Shelf Cases*, 27 Ohio N.U. L. Rev. 141, 153 (2000).

91. *Id.* Some scholars have argued that treaties and international conventions can create instant customary law. *See* Craig L Carr & Gary L. Scott, *Multilateral Treaties and the Environment: A Case Study in the Formation of Customary International Law*, 27 Denv. J. Int'l L. & Pol'y 313 (1999).

92. *Supra* note 69 at para. 74. "Although the passage of only a short period of time is not necessarily . . . a bar to the formation of a new rule of customary international law on the basis of what was originally a purely conventional rule, an indispensable requirement would be that within the period in question, short though it might be, State practice, including that of States whose interests are specially affected, should have been both extensive and virtually uniform in the sense of the provision invoked;—and should moreover have occurred in such a way as to show a general recognition that a rule of law or legal obligation is involved."

93. See Van Hoof, supra note 84 at 86. *Cf.* Peter Malanczuk, Akehurst's Modern Introduction to International Law 45-46 (7th ed. 1997) (discussing the possibility of "instant customary international law" which relies solely on *opinio juris* without regard to state practice and relevance of time).

94. Van Hoof *Id.*

95. *Id.*

96. *See supra* note 38 at 55.

97. *See* discussion *supra* notes 49-71.

98. Joyner, *U.N. General Assembly Resolutions and International Law: Rethinking the Contemporary Dynamics of Norm-Creation*, 11 Cal. W. Int'l L.J. 445, 459-60 (1981) (arguing "general principles" are actually just norms consolidated out of customary practice).

99. *See* Statute of the ICJ *supra* note 28. The "general principles" category is typically read narrowly. *See* Virally, *The Sources of International Law* in

Manual of Public International Law 143-48 (M. Sorensen ed. 1968) (explaining the various interpretations of this peculiar category.)

100. *See* Effect of Awards of Compensation Made by the U.N. Administrative Tribunal, 1954 I.C.J. 47, 53 (July 13).

101. The Corfu Channel Case, (U.K. & N.Ir. v. Alb.), 1949 I.C.J. 4, 18 (Apr. 19) (merits) (holding that "[t]his indirect evidence is admitted in all systems of law, and its use is recognised by international decisions").

102. *Id*. Application for Review of Judgment No. 158, 1973 I.C.J. 166, at 177; Application for Review of Judgment No. 273, 1982 I.C.J. 325, at 338-40 & 356. *See also* Brownlie, *supra* note 61, at 18; Rudolf Schlesinger, *Research on General Principles of Law Recognized by Civilized Nations*, 51 Am. J. Int'l L. 734, 736-77 (1957).

103. *See* Diane Penneys Edelman, *It Began at Brooklyn: Expanding Boundaries for First-Year Law Students by Internationalizing the Legal Writing Curriculum*, 27 Brooklyn J. Int'l L. 415, 417 (2002) (citing J. G. Starke, Starke's International Law 44 (11th ed. 1994).

104. *See* Rosalyn Higgins, Problems & Process: International Law and How We Use it 22-28 (1994).

105. *See* Edward M. Morgan, *Act of Blindness, State of Insight*, 13 B.U. Int'l L.J. 1, FN 62 (1995).

106. *See* Roger P. Alford, *The Proliferation of International Courts and Tribunals: International Adjudication in Ascendance*, 94 Am. Soc'y Int'l L. Proc. 160, 160 (2000).

107. *See* Louis B. Sohn, *Sources of International Law*, 25 Ga. J. Int'l & Comp. L. 399, 401 (1996).

108. *United States v. Yousef*, 327 F.3d 56, 101 (2d Cir. 2003) (quoting Id.). "I submit that states really never make international law .... It is made by the people that care; the professors, the writers of textbooks and casebooks, and the authors of articles in the leading international law journals.... This is the way international law is made, not by states, but by "silly" professors writing books [.]"

109. Martti Koskenniemi, Sources of International Law 28 (2000) (citing Robert Y. Jennings. *What is International Law and How Do We Tell It When We See It?*, Schweitzerisches Jahrbuch, Inter-nationales Recht 37, 60 (1981)). "I doubt whether anybody is going to dissent from the proposition that there has never been a time when there has been so much confusion and doubt about the tests of the validity - or sources - of international law, than the present."

110. In *The Paquete Habana*, 175 U.S. 677 (1900), the U.S. Supreme Court demonstrated the classical method for ascertaining international legal principles by analyzing interactions between individual nations for several centuries.

111. For a great chronology of the League of Nations *see* Gary B. Ostrower, The League of Nations From 1919 to 1929 119-159 (1996).

112. Bruno Simma *et al.*, The Charter of the United Nations, A Commentary 2 (2004).

113. August 21, 1944 to October 7, 1944.

114. The United Nations is the result of two extraordinary conferences – Dumbarton Oaks from late August to early October 1944 and San Francisco from late April to late June 1945. *See generally* Stanley Meisler, United Nations: The First 50 Years 2 (1995).

115. *Id.*

116. *Supra* note 112.

117. *See* Charles Malik, Man in the Struggle for Peace 124 (1963).

118. John Linarelli, *Peace-Building*, 24 Denv. J. Int'l L & Pol'y 253, 276 (1996). "Freezing the Charter in time would seriously distort the purposes of the Charter and hamper efforts to allow the collective security system envisioned by the framers to respond to change in the international legal and political order".

119. U.N. Charter art. 103. "In the event of a conflict between the obligations of the Members of the United Nations under the present Charter and their obligations under any other international agreement, their obligations under the present Charter shall prevail."

120. *See* Mattias Kumm, *Section VI: Constitutional and Administrative Law: Beyond Golf Clubs and the Judicialization of Politics: Why Europe has a Constitution Properly So Called*, 54 Am. J. Comp. L. 505, 508 (2006).

121. *Id.*

122. *Id.*

123. Eduard Shevardnadze, the former Foreign Minister of the former Soviet Union between 1985-1990 captured this on the eve of the first Iraq War when he stated "we are becoming the United Nations and we're returning to our own global constitution; the United Nations Charter." Antonio F. Perez, *On the Way to the Forum: The Reconstruction of Article 2(7) and Rise of Federalism Under the United Nations Charter*, 31 Tex. Int'l. L.J. 353, 373 (1996)

124. *See* W. Michael Reisman, *The Constitutional Crisis in the United Nations*, 87 A.J.I.L. 83 (1993).

125. *See* Steven Ratner, *The Security Council and International Law*, in The UN Security Council: From the Cold War to the 21st Century 591, 591-606 (2004).

126. U.N. Charter art. 7(1)

127. *See* U.N. Charter arts. 40 & 41 (providing the Security Council with the authority to use non-military and military measures to maintain

international peace and security. The Security Council is the only organ of the United Nations to have this authority.)

128. U.N. Charter art. 24.
129. Please imagine the difficulty of getting all 192 Member States to agree on a resolution that required immediate attention.
130. U.N. Charter art. 25.
131. U.N. Charter art. 29.
132. U.N. Charter art. 33(1). These are negotiation, enquiry, mediation, conciliation, arbitration, judicial settlement, resort to regional agencies or arrangements, or *other peaceful means* of their own choice. (emphasis added).
133. U.N. Charter art. 36(1).
134. *See* U.N. Charter art. 34.
135. U.N. Charter art. 37 (2).
136. *Supra* note 16.
137. U.N. Charter art. 1. "To maintain international peace and security, and to that end: to take effective collective measures for the prevention and removal of threats to the peace, and for the suppression of acts of aggression or other breaches of the peace, and to bring about by peaceful means, and in conformity with the principles of justice and international law, adjustment or settlement of international disputes or situations which might lead to a breach of the peace.
138. U.N. Charter art. 33.
139. *See* J. M. Sanderson, *Dabbling in War: The Dilemma of the Use of Force in United Nations Intervention,* in Peacemaking and Peacekeeper for the New Century 145, 148 (1998).
140. *See* Mats R. Berdal, *The Security Council, Peacekeeping and Internal Conflict after the Cold War,* 7 Duke J. Comp. & Int'l L. 71, 74 (1996).
141. Brian Urquhart, *The United Nations, Collective Security, and International Peacekeeping,* in Negotiating World Order: the Artisanship and Architecture of Global Diplomacy 59, 62 (1986). "[T]he technique of peace-keeping is a distinctive innovation by the United Nations. The Charter does not mention it. It was discovered, like penicillin. We came across it, while looking for something else, during an investigation of the guerrilla fighting in northern Greece in 1947."
142. The United Nations Truce Supervision Organization (UNTSO) went to the Middle East to monitor the truce in the 1948 Arab-Israeli War. *See* Boutros Boutros-Ghali, The Blue Helmets: A Review of United Nations Peacekeeping 17 (3d ed. 1996).
143. Certain Expenses of the United Nations, 1962 I.C.J. Rep. 151, 166. "The operations known as UNEF and ONUC were not enforcement actions within the compass of Chapter VII...."

144. *Id.* at 167.
145. *See* discussion *supra* notes 49-67 regarding custom formation.
146. *See* Thomas G. Weiss, *New Challenges for UN Military Operations: Implementing an Agenda for Peace*, Wash. Q. 51, 52 (Winter 1993).
147. *See* L.C. Green, The Contemporary Law of Armed Conflict 324 (1993).
148. *See generally* Major Joseph P. "Dutch" Bialke, *United Nations Peace Operations: Applicable Norms and the Application of the Law of Armed Conflict*, 50 A.F. L. Rev. 1, (2001).
149. *See* Michael Stopford, *Peace-Keeping or Peace-Enforcement: Stark Choices for Grey Areas*, 73 U. Det. Mercy L. Rev. 499, 502 (1996).
150. *See* Press Conference by Security Council President (Apr. 2, 2004), available at *http://www.un.org/News/briefings/docs/2004/pleugerpc.DOC.htm* (noting that on April 2, 2004, there were 15 peacekeeping operations under way, including complex mission, with 5 more to be built in the coming weeks and months. That meant 49,000 soldiers were in the field and peacekeeping operations might double the number of soldiers in the field within the following year.)
151. *See* United Nations, *UN Peacekeeping: Some Questions and Answers*, How has peacekeeping evolved?, available at *http://www.un.org/Depts/dpko/dpko/faq/q4.htm.* "The end of the Cold War precipitated a dramatic shift in UN peacekeeping. Freed from bipolarization, the Security Council established larger and more complex UN peacekeeping missions, often to help implement comprehensive peace agreements between protagonists in intra-State conflicts."
152. U. N. Charter art. 24, para. 1 (authorizing the Security Council to allocate power to subsidiary organs "in order to ensure prompt and effective action by the United Nations").
153. U. N. Charter art. 42.
154. *Supra* note 17.
155. U. N. Charter art. 40.
156. Caroline Case 29 BFSP 1137, 1138 (1837).
157. *Supra* note 6 at 621. "With the adoption of Resolution 598 (1987), the view of the permanent and other members of the Security Council has become quite clear that orders on the basis of Article 40 are formally binding."
158. U. N. Charter art. 41.
159. U. N. Charter art. 40. These sanctions may include complete or partial interruption of economic relations and of rail, sea, air, postal, telegraphic, radio, and other means of communication, and the severance of diplomatic relations.
160. *See* Gary C. Hufbauer and Barbara Oegg, *Targeted Sanctions: A Policy Alternative*? 32 Law & Pol'y Int'l Bus. 11 (2000).

161. *See generally* Gary C. Hufbauer et al., Economic Sanctions Reconsidered (2000). Sanctions were used by the United Nations Security Council against the following States: Iraq (1990), Somalia (1992), Haiti (1993), Rwanda (1994), and Sierra Leone (1998).
162. *See* Pamela Constable, *Flights of Frustration*, Wash. Post, December 6, 1999, at A17.
163. *See, e.g.*, Amy Borrus, *Hitting Sudan in the Pocketbook: Pension Funds Are Taking Notice of a Growing Push to Cut Ties to the Rogue State*, Bus. Week, May 2, 2005, at 25 (describing the increasing political pressure for state pension funds to divest from companies that have substantial ties with Sudan).
164. U. N. Charter art. 42.
165. *See* League of Nations Covenant art. 16. The League of Nations only had authority to recommend application of armed force against an aggressor.
166. The historical truth is that the world organization would have never been established if the privileges of being permanent members of the Security Council had not been granted to the victorious powers of the Second World War. See statement of US Secretary of State, Cordell Hull (made shortly after the establishment of the United Nations): "... our government would not remain there a day without retaining the veto power", The Memoirs of Cordell Hull, Vol.2 1664 (1948).
167. UN Charter art. 2(4): 'All members shall refrain in their international relations from the use or threat of force against the territorial integrity or political independence of any state or in any other manner inconsistent with the purposes of the United Nations.'
168. U. N. Charter art. 2(6).
169. U. N. Charter art. 2(7).
170. U. N. Charter art. 15(1).
171. U. N. Charter art. 24(3).
172. U. N. Charter art. 10.
173. U. N. Charter art. 12.
174. U. N. Charter art. 12(1).
175. U. N. Charter art. 24(2)
176. U. N. Charter art. 1.
177. U. N. Charter art. 2.
178. U. N. Charter art, 1(1).
179. Legal Consequences for States of the Continued Presence of South Africa in Namibia (South West Africa) Notwithstanding Security Council Resolution 276, Advisory Opinion, 1971 ICJ REP. 16, 52 (June 21). This position was sanctioned by the ICJ in approvingly citing the opinion of

the UN Secretary-General that "Members of the United Nations have conferred upon the Security Council powers commensurate with its responsibility for the maintenance of peace and security. The only limitations are the fundamental principles and purposes found in Chapter 1 of the Charter."

180. *Supra* note 35.

181. Another proposal to amend Article 1(1) so as to read "to maintain international peace and security in conformity with the principles of justice and international law" was not accepted at the San Francisco Conference. Rudiger Wolfrum, *Article 1, in* the Charter of the United Nations: A Commentary 52 (Bruno Simma ed., 1994).

182. U. N. Charter art. 1(1), art. 25 and arts. 39-42.

183. *See* Hans Kelsen, the Law of the United Nations 294-5 (2000).

184. *See* Hans Köchler, *The United Nations Organization and Global Power Politics: The Antagonism Between Power and Law and the Future of World Order*, 5 Chinesejil 323 (2006).

185. U. N. Charter art. 27 (3) requiring that "decisions on substantive matters considered by the Security Council must be made by an affirmative vote of the majority including the concurring vote of the permanent Members."

186. U. N. Charter art. 27(2).

187. Sydney D. Bailey, The Procedure of the Security Council 214-23 (2d ed. 1988) (noting that double vetoes were cast on the Spanish question in 1946, the Greek frontier question in 1947, and the Czechoslovak question in 1948).

188. *See* Richard Hiscocks, The Security Council: A Study in Adolescence 109 (1973).

189. U. N. Charter art. 52.

190. U. N. Charter art. 52.

191. U. N. Charter art. 24(1).

192. *See* Feld, Jordan, and Hurwitz, International Organizations: A Comparative Approach 204-211 (1994).

193. U. N. Charter art. 52(1).

194. U. N. Charter art. 52(2).

195. U. N. Charter art. 53(1).

196. U. N. Charter art. 53(2). There is an exception to this rule. Actions against 'enemy states' defined as "used in paragraph 1 of this Article ... as any state which during the Second World War has been an enemy of any signatory of the present Charter."

197. U. N. Charter art. 54.

198. U. N. Charter art. 96.

199. U. N. Charter art. 7(1).

200. Francisco Vicuna & Christopher Pinto, *Peaceful Settlement of Disputes, Prospects for the 21st Century*, in the Centenial of the first International Peace Conference, Reports & Conclusions 111 (2000) (noting that the ICJ does not obtain authority to review Security Council decisions from either the U.N. Charter or the Court's authorizing statute).

201. Vera Gowlland-Debbas, *The Relationship Between the International Court of Justice and the Security Council in Light of the Lockerbie Case*, 88 Am. J. Int'l L. 643, 664 (arguing that the Charter did not altogether rule out judicial review of the Security Council by the ICJ).

202. *Id.* at 664 (noting that the Conference specifically rejected the Belgian proposal to allow for judicial review of Security Council decisions). *Cf.* W. Michael Reisman, *The Constitutional Crisis in the United Nations*, 87 Am. J. Int'l L. 83, 84 (1993) (noting that while the Belgian proposal failed in 1945, many States continue to seek judicial review of Security Council actions).

203. *See generally* Marcella David, *Passport to Justice: Internationalizing the Political Question Doctrine for Application in the World Court*, 40 Harv. Int'l. L. J. 81, 144 (1999) (addressing the possibility of having an international court review the legality of Security Council resolutions).

204. Michael William Dowdle, *Of Parliaments, Pragmatism, and the Dynamics of Constitutional Development: The Curious Case of China*, 35 N.Y.U.J. Int'l L. & Pol. 1, 18 (2002) (noting that China has not embraced the concept of judicial review).

205. *See* Certain Expenses supra note 143 at 155.

206. *See* Southwest Africa *supra* note 179 at 45.

207. *See* Provisional Measures Order of April 14, Case Concerning Questions of Interpretation and Application of the 1971 Montreal Convention Arising from the Aerial Incident at Lockerbie (Libya v. U.S.), 1992 I.C.J. 114, 140; see also, id. at 156 (concurring opinion of Shahabudden, J.); *id.* at 174-75 (dissenting opinion of Bedjaoui, J.); *id.* at 192-93 and 196 (dissenting opinions of Weeramantry, J.).

208. LaGrand Case (F.R.G. v. U.S.) 2001 I.C.J. 104 (June 27), in print at 40 I.L.M. 1069, 1078-79 (June 27, 2001).

209. *See* ICJ Statute, art. 59. *See also* Press Release, International Court of Justice, LaGrand (Germany *v.* United States of America) (June 27, 2001), available at: *www.icj-cij.org/presscom/index.php?pr=355&pt=1&p1=6&p2=1*) (noting that the ICJ could exercise jurisdiction in order to fulfil the functions provided it in Article 59).

210. Deborah D'Angelo, *The "Check" on International Peace and Security Maintenance: The International Court of Justice and Judicial Review of Security Council Resolutions*, 23 Suffolk Transnat'l L.Rev. 561, 586-7 (2000)

(discussing invalidation of Security Council Resolution 748 by the ICJ based solely on a technicality). *See also* South West Africa *supra* note 41 (holding that Security Council Resolution 284 is valid). *See generally* Application of Convention on Prevention and Punishment of Crime of Genocide (Bosn. & Herz. v. Yugo.), 1993 I.C.J. 325, 439-40 (Sept 13) (separate opinion of Judge Lauterpacht) (refusing to invalidate Security Council Resolution 713 regardless of the possibility that the resolution violated the doctrine of *jus cogens*).

211. U. N. Charter art. 12, para 1.

212. U. N. Charter art. 94(2)

213. *See supra* note 28.

214. With the mutual agreement to withdraw the Libyan cases against the United States and The United Kingdom, the ICJ lost the perfect opportunity to answer the question of whether it had the authority to invalidate Security Council resolutions. *See* Scott S. Evans, *The Lockerbie Incident Cases: Libyan-Sponsored Terrorism, Judicial Review and the Political Question Doctrine*, 18 MD. J. Int'l L. & Trade 21, 75 (1994) (noting that the Lockerbie cases highlighted the judicial review conflict between branches of the United Nations).

215. *See* Inocencio Arias, *Humanitarian Intervention: Could the Security Council Kill the United Nations?*, 23 Fordham Int'l L.J. 1005, 1013-14 (2000) (contemplating that the United Nations' loss of credibility is due to the excessive power of the permanent members on the Security Council).

216. This concept was pioneered in American constitutional law. During the early years of the American Republic, Chief Justice John Marshall struck down a Congressional statute enlarging the U.S. Supreme Courts appellate jurisdiction. The very idea of written constitutionalism, wrote Marshall, requires that the Constitution be considered a law superior to the ordinary enactments of legislatures constituted there under. *See Marbury v. Madison*, 5 U.S. 137 (1803). "If ... [in the event of a conflict between a constitutional rule and an ordinary law] the courts are to regard the constitution; and the constitution is superior to any ordinary act of the legislature; the constitution, and not such ordinary act, must govern the case to which they both apply." *Id.* at 177.

217. The Court's primary emphasis is rightly on the peaceful settlement of international disputes. Cases that come before the Court have parties that have agreed that they should do so. A general willingness to abide by the Court's decisions can therefore be imputed to the parties in advance. However, this does not create an actual mechanism to impose the Court's decisions on obstinate parties. That only happens once the Security Council makes an independent decision to do so, and only then in response to a threat to the peace. *See* M.N.S. Sellers, *The Authority of the International Court of Justice*, 8 Int'l Legal Theory 41, 46 (2002) (noting that The ICJ is ill-equipped to determine the content of international law for precisely the same reasons that it is capable of settling

international disputes, which is to say, because the Court is subject to the political control and oversight of interested States).

218. *See* generally Michael J. Matheson, *Judicial Review in International Organizations: ICJ Review of Security Council Decisions*, 36 Geo. Wash. Int'l L. Rev. 615 (2004).

219. *See supra* notes 184-188 and the surrounding discussion.

220. *Open the Club*, ECONOMIST, Aug. 29, 1992, at 10. "America, Britain and France dominate decision-making; Russia is out of things and China intent on its own affairs."

221. *See* U.N. Charter art. 23(1). Consideration to be elected to fill a non-permanent seat on the Security Council should be "in the first instance to the contribution of Members of the United Nations to the maintenance of international peace and security and to the other purposes of the Organization, and also to equitable geographical distribution."

222. David D. Caron, *The Legitimacy of the Collective Authority of the Security Council*, 87 A.J.I.L. 552 (1993) (assessing the legitimacy of Security Council action).

223. Ian Johnstone, *Legislation and Adjudication in the UN Security Council: Bringing down the Deliberative Deficit*, 102 A.J.I.L. 275 (2008) (discussing a shift in the paradigm of legitimacy from membership and voting rules to the quality of deliberations).

224. *See* Ian Hurd, After Anarchy: Legitimacy and Power at the United Nations 30-40 (2007).

225. *See* Dyzenhaus *supra* note 74 at 32.

226. *Id.* (noting that if legal power is exercised according to common law values, it will be legitimate, which is to say the power will have authority or the character of legality).

227. S.C. Res. 1373, U.N. SCOR, 56th Sess., 4385th mtg., U.N. Doc. S/1373 (2001).

228. *See* Dyzenhaus *supra* note 74 at 6. *See also* S.C. Res. 1214, U.N. SCOR, 52d Sess., 3952d mtg. at 1, U.N. Doc. S/PV.1214 (1998) (condemning certain acts of the Taliban in Afghanistan); S.C. Res. 1189, U.N. SCOR, 52d Sess., 3915th mtg. at 1, U.N. Doc. S/PV.1189 (1998) (condemning the terrorist bombings in Kenya and Tanzania); S.C. Res. 731, U.N. SCOR, 47th Sess., 3033d mtg. at 51, U.N. Doc. S/731 (1992) (condemning the destruction of Pan Am flight 103 and UTA flight 772 "and the resultant loss of lives").

229. *See supra* note 227.

230. S.C. Res. 1540, U.N. SCOR, 59th Sess., 4956th mtg., U.N. Doc. S/1540 (2004).

231. See *supra* note 227; see also supra note 230.

232. *Id.* The Committees established by Resolution 1373 and Resolution 1540 provide oversight and theoretical compliance enforcement. For example,

the committees would be well within their rights to analyze country reports, provide encouragement to governments taking resolute and effective steps to implement the respective Resolutions, and draw attention to states that do not take these legal obligations seriously.

233. Id.

234. *See* Mark Kantor, *The War on Terrorism and the End of Banking Neutrality*, 118 Banking L.J. 891, 896-97 (2001) (stating that Security Council Resolution 1373 supports the USA PATRIOT Act's expanded power to confiscate foreign assets); Serge Schmemann, *United Nations to Get a U.S. Antiterror Guide*, N.Y. Times, Dec. 19, 2001, at B4 (reporting statements made by U.S. officials that the Counter-Terrorism Committee would enable the United States to export its antiterrorism legislation around the world).

235. *See* United Nations General Assembly, 25th Plenary Meeting, UN Doc. A/56/PV.25, at 3 (Oct. 15, 2001). The representative of Costa Rica, referring to Resolution 1373, said, "In short, for the first time in history, the Security Council enacted legislation for the rest of the international community."

236. *See* Szasz *supra* note 15 at 901.

237. *See* Jose E. Alvarez, *Hegemonic International Law Revisited* 97 Am. J. Int'l L. 873, 874 (2003)

238. *See, e.g.*, General Assembly's Elimination Declaration of 1994 G.A. Res. 49/60, U.N. Doc. A/RES/49/60 (Dec. 9, 1994). *See also* International Convention for the Suppression of the Financing of Terrorism, U.N. GAOR 6th Comm., 54th Sess., U.N. Doc. A/RES/54/109 (1999).

239. *See supra* note 227 at 1 (b).

240. *Id.* at 1 (c).

241. *Id.* at 1(d).

242. *Id.* at 2(a).

243. *Id.* at 2(e).

244. *Id.* at 2(g).

245. *Id.* at 2(f). Id. at 3(b).

246. *Id.* at 3(c).

247. *Id.* at 2(c).

248. *Id.* at 3(d).

249. *See* Press Conference, *supra* note 150. The Security Council President, referring to the planned adoption of Resolution 1540, said, "Starting with the creation of the Counter-Terrorism Committee and now weapons of mass destruction, that Council would be needed more and more to do that kind of legislative work."

250. *See* Jeremy Greenstock, Ambassador from the United Kingdom, Chair of the Counter-Terrorism Committee, Presentation at the "Combating International Terrorism: The Contribution of the United Nations" Symposium in Vienna, Austria (June 3-4, 2002) available at http://www.un.org/Docs?sc?committees/1373/ViennaNotes.htm.

251. *Supra* note 219 at 12 (noting that the committee's authority looks "aJministrative"). [Hereafter "CTC"].

252. *Supra* note 78, at 6.

253. *See supra* note 227.

254. S.C. Res. 1535, U.N. SCOR, 59th Sess., 4936th mtg., U.N. Docs. S/Res/1535 (2003).

255. Hereinafter "CTED."

256. Organizational Plan for the Counter Terrorism Executive Directorate, UN Dco. S/2008/80, enclosure, at 4, para. 5 (b) (Feb. 8, 2008).

257. *See* Briefing by Hus Excellency, Mr. Neven Jurica, Chairman of the Security Council Committee established pursuant to resolution 1373 (2001) concerning Counter-Terrorism to the Security Council, (May 6, 2008), available at *http://www.un.org/sc/ctc/pdf/briefing1_NJ_06may.pdf* (last visited Aug. 20, 2008).

258. *See* The Proliferation Security Initiative, United States Department of State, available at *http://usinfo.state.gov/products/pubs/proliferation*. The PSI is a global initiative aimed at stopping shipments of weapons of mass destruction (WMD), their delivery systems, and related materials worldwide. (last visited Aug. 20, 2008).

259. *Id.* "This set of principles identifies specific steps for effectively interdicting [Weapons of Mass Destruction] shipments and preventing proliferation facilitators from engaging in this deadly trade."

260. Hereinafter "WMD"

261. *See* Convention on the Prohibition of the Development, Production, Stockpiling and Use of Chemical Weapons and on Their Destruction, G.A. Res. 47/39, U.N. GAOR, 47th Sess., 74th mtg., U.N. Doc. A/RES/47/39 (1993).

262. *See* Treaty on the Non-Proliferation of Nuclear Weapons, July 1, 1968, 21 U.S.T. 483, 729 U.N.T.S. 161 (entered into force Mar. 5, 1970).

263. *See* Convention on the Prohibition of the Development, Production, and Stockpiling of Bacteriological (Biological) and Toxin Weapons and on their Destruction, 26 U.S.T. 571, 1015 U.N.T.S. 163 (1972)

264. *See* U.N. SCOR, 59th Sess., 4950th mtg. at 2, U.N. Doc. S/PV.4950 (2004) (providing statements by Representatives of nearly all 15 Members of the Security Council and some 20 non-Council Members at a public Security Council meeting to discuss a draft of what became Security Council Resolution 1540).

265. Resolution 1540 Committee. More information available at: www.un/org/sc/1540.

266. S. C. Res. 1810, U.N. SCOR, 64th Sess., 5877th mtg., U.N. Docs. S/Res/1810 (2008).

267. *See* Nicholas Rostow, *Before and After: The Changed U.N. Response to Terrorism Since September 11th*, 35 Cornell Int'l L.J. 475, 482 (2002).

268. *See* Szasz *supra* note 15 at 901.

269. *See generally* Rosemary Foot, *et al.*, The United States and Multilateral Institutions (2003).

270. U. N. Charter art. 25. *See also* U. N. Charter, art. 2(6). "The Organization shall ensure that states which are not Members of the United Nations act in accordance with these Principles so far as may be necessary for the maintenance of international peace and security."

271. J. A. Frowein & N. Kirsch, Introduction, in The Charter of the United Nations: A Commentary 701, 710 (2d ed. 2002) (arguing that every organ of the U. N. must determine its own jurisdiction, and further that "such a determination is binding only if supported by the Member States in general").

272. Statement of Committee IV/2 of the San Francisco Conference, Report of Committee IV/2 of the United Nations Conference on International Organizations, San Francisco, p. 7, UNCIO Doc. 933, IV/2/42(2) (June 12, 1945); 13 UNCIO Documents, 703, at 709-10.

273. Oscar Schachter, *United Nations Law*, 88 Am. J. Int'l. L. 1, 6 (1994) (discussing the development of law and new rules through the process of applying and interpreting the Charter).

274. *See generally* Jared Schoot, *Chapter VII as Exception: Security Council Action and the Regulative Ideal of Emergency*, 6 Nw. U. J. Int'l Hum. Rts. 24 (2007)."

275. *See* Stefan A. Talmon, *The Security Council as World Legislature*, 99 Am. J. Int'l L. 175 (2005).

276. *See supra* note 219 at 15. "[P]arliament's monopoly on legislative power is rooted in the claim that only the people's representatives have authority to make law, although the justification for the formal doctrine of the separation of powers need not be democratic. It can, for example, reside in a Hobbesian argument about the need to concentrate legislative power in one body."

277. 278.

279. *See* 1 International Legislation: A Collection of Texts of Multipartite International Instruments of General Interest, at xiii (1931).

280. *See* discussion *supra* note 25.

281. *See* Oppenheim *supra* note 36 at n. 9.

282. *See* Krzysztof Skubiszewski, *International Legislation*, *in* 2 Encyclopaedia of Public International Law 1255 (1995).

283. *Kaahumanu v. County of Maui*, 315 F.3d 1215, 1220 (9th Cir. 2003) (holding in part that in the United States, courts determine whether an action is legislative by considering four factors: (1) whether the act involves ad hoc decision making, or formulation of policy; (2) whether the act applies to a few individuals, or to the public at large; (3) whether the act is formally legislative in character; and (4) whether it bears all the hallmarks of traditional legislation. (citing Bechard v. Rappold, 287 F.3d 827, 829 (9th Cir.2002)).

284. *Supra* note 227 at para. 1(c).

285. Supra note 230

286. *See* Agenda, June 12, 2003, The United Nations Security Council, 4772nd mtg., UN Doc. S/PV.4772, at 5 (2003), available at *http://www.iccnow.org/documents/UNSCpv1422debate12June03.pdf.* The representative of New Zealand defined a "generic resolution" as one "not in response to a particular fact situation."

287. Masahiko Asada, *WMD Terrorism and Security Council Resolution 1540: Conditions for Legitimacy in International Legislation*, IILJ Working Paper 2007/9, note 88 (2007) (noting that with few exceptions, such as the question of admission for membership or expelling a member of the United Nations, the General Assembly does not have the authority to adopt a resolution with a legally binding effect).

288. *See* A More Secure World: Our Shared Responsibility, Report of the High-Level Panel on Threats, Challenges and Change, UN Doc. A/59/565, at 8 (2004), available at *http://www.un.org/secureworld/report.pdf* (last visited Aug. 20, 2002).

289. *Id*. Synopsis at 11.

290. *Supra* note 35.

291. *See supra* note 287. The title of part I of the High-Level Panel Report is "Towards a New Security Consensus."

292. *Id*. at para. 28.

293. Game theory is a discipline of mathematics that seeks to model human decision making. Avinash K. Dixit & Barry J. Nalebuff, Thinking Strategically: The Competitive Edge in Business, Politics, and Everyday Life (1991) (offering a nontechnical explanation of game theory). *See also* R. Duncan Luce & Howard Raiffa, Games and Decisions: Introduction and Critical Survey (1957) (providing a technical explanation of game theory).

294. The high-level panel addresses this point somewhat indirectly, noting that when a state fails in its responsibilities to its own people or to the international community, "some portion of those responsibilities should be taken up by the international community, acting in accordance with the Charter of the United Nations . . . to help build the necessary capacity or supply the necessary protection, as the case may be." *Supra* note 287 at para. 29.

295. *Id.*

296. *Id.* at 19.

297. *Id.* at 21.

298. U. N. Charter art. 2(7) reads: "Nothing contained in the present Charter shall authorize the United Nations to intervene in matters which are essentially within the domestic jurisdiction of any state or shall require the Members to submit such matters to settlement under the present Charter; but this principle shall not prejudice the application of enforcement measures under Chapter VII."

299. *See* High-Level Panel Report, *supra* note 287 at 21.

300. *Id.* at 22.

301. *Supra* note 227. See also *supra* note 230.

302. *See generally* Laurence H. Tribe, American Constitutional Law 772-80 (2nd ed. 1988) for an example of incorporation from the United States.

303. *See* Restatement of Foreign Relations Law of the United States § 131 introductory note, at 41 (Tent. Draft No. 1, 1980). "International law and international agreements of the United States are law of the United States and supreme over the law of the several states." *Cf.* Curtis A. Bradley, The Charming Betsy Canon and Separation of Powers: Rethinking the Interpretive Role of International Law, 86 Geo. L. J. 479 (1998) (noting that in the United States legal system, only self-executing treaties have direct effect under domestic law).

304. *Supra* note 219 at 7 (noting the Canada has a dualist system which requires the domestic legislature to take some action before international legal norms have domestic effect).

305. This is essentially a Monist v. Dualist distinction. In a dualist legal system, international law exists on a parallel system to domestic law. In a monist legal system, international law is a subset of domestic law and is used in resolving disputes in domestic courts. *See* George E. Edwards, *International Human Rights Law Violations Before, During, and After Hurricane Katrina: An International Law Framework For Analysis*, 31 T. Marshall L. Rev. 356, 359-60 (2006).

306. See Gregory J. Kerwin, *The Role of United Nations General Assembly Resolutions in Determining Principles of International Law In United States Courts*, 1983 Duke I.J. 876 (1983).

307. Professor Mary Ellen O'Connell objects that Security Council resolutions are not analogous to treaties because Security Council resolutions are binding even without the consent of states subject to them. *See* Mary Ellen O'Connell, *UN Resolution 1441: Compelling Saddam, Restraining Bush*, Jurist, available at *http://jurist.law.pitt.edu/forum/forumnew73.php* (last visited Aug. 20, 2008)

308. The Counter-Terrorism Committee facilitates the provision of technical assistance by disseminating best practices; identifying existing technical,

financial, regulatory and legislative assistance programmes; promoting synergies between the assistance programmes of international, regional and sub-regional organizations; and, through CTED, serving as an intermediary for contacts between potential donors and recipients and maintaining an on-line directory of assistance providers, all within the framework of resolution 1373 (2001). *See* Security Council, Counter-Terrorism Committee, *Technical Assistance*, available at *http://www.un.org/sc/ctc/page2.html*. (last visited Aug. 20, 2008).

309. The Resolution passed on September 28 and reports were due by December 28, 2004.

310. *See* Letter dated 15 January 2002 from the Chairman of the Security Council Committee established pursuant to resolution 1373 (2001) concerning counter-terrorism addressed to the President of the Security Council, U.N. Doc. S/2002/67 (January 15, 2002).

311. *Supra* note 233.

312. S. C. Res. 1456, U.N. SCOR, 58th Sess., 4388th mtg., U.N. Doc. S/RES/1456 (2003).

313. *Id*. at 1. The Security Council also buried a stern warning in the text of Resolution 1456. "States must ensure that any measure taken to combat terrorism comply with all their obligations under international law, and should adopt such measures in accordance with international law, in particular international human rights, refugee, and humanitarian law." *Id*. at 6. The Security Council presumably added this after successive UN High Commissioners for Human Rights had testified that more attention to human rights was urgent and necessary. *See* United Nations, Office for the High Commission on Human Rights, Terrorism and Human Rights, available at *http://www.unhchr.ch/terrorism*. However, note that Resolution 1456 was not adopted under Chapter VII authority and therefore does not create binding obligations on states.

314. *See* Letter dated 15 July 2003 from the Chairman of the Security Council Committee established pursuant to resolution 1373 (2001) concerning counter-terrorism addressed to the President of the Security Council, U.N. Doc S/2003/710 (July 15, 2003).

315. The Resolution passed on April 28 and reports were due by October 28, 2004.

316. Burkina Faso: Jan. 4, 2005; Croatia: Nov. 29, 2004; Libya: Apr. 12, 2005; Panama: July 12, 2005; South Africa Jan. 31, 2005.

317. *See* United Nations Security Council, 1540 Committee, List of National Reports by Submitting Member States, available at *www.un.org/sc/1540/nationalreports.shtml*. (Last checked Aug. 20, 2008).

318. *See* Abram Chayes & Antonia Handler Chayes, The New Sovereignty: Compliance with International Regulatory Agreements 4 (1995).

319. Ryan Goodman & Derek Jinks, *How to Influence States: Socialization and International Human Rights*, 54 Duke L.J. 621, 635 (2004) (defining "persuasion" as "the active, often strategic, inculcation of norms ... [in which] actors are consciously convinced of the truth, validity, or appropriateness of a norm, belief, or practice").

320. Greenville Byford, *The Wrong War*, 81 Foreign Aff. July-August 2002, at 34 (discussing the current subjective nature of defining terrorism).

321. Richard Goldstone, *A Decade in Human Rights Law: International Human Rights and Criminal Justice in the First Decade of the 21st Century*, 11 Hum. Rts. Br. 3, 6 (2004) (noting the Security Council has been lax in efforts to ensure that civil liberties and human rights will be respected).

322. *See supra* note 317 at 22-28 (1995) (advocating a "management" approach to treaty compliance that emphasizes non-coercive mechanisms to monitor behaviour, build capacity, and persuade states to comply with their treaty commitments).

323. *See* Edward Weisband, *Discursive Multilateralism: Global Benchmarks, Shame, and Learning in the ILO Labor Standards Monitoring Regime*, 44 Int'l Stud. Q. 643 (2000) (assessing naming and shaming strategies used to promote compliance with labour conventions). *See also supra* note 219 at 31. "[I]n a properly functioning legal order the penalties of disobedience will outweigh the rewards and so the sanctions attached to primary rules provide sufficient reason to legal subjects for obedience."

324. *Cf.* J. Craig Barker, *The Politics of International Law-Making: Constructing Security in Response to Global Terrorism*, 3 J. Int'l L. & Int'l Rel. 5, 16 (2007) (claiming that "it is unlikely that the United Nations Security Council would use sanctions against non-cooperating states in the context of Resolution 1373").

IP ENFORCEMENT MECHANISMS TO COMBAT PIRACY: THE CONTEXT OF SOFTWARE PIRACY

Mohammad Monirul Azam and*
*Abdul Hamid Chowdhury***

Software piracy, the unauthorized duplication and distribution of software, is a worldwide problem that is growing at an epidemic pace. In this paper we attempt to define software piracy and its global scenario. In the second section, we outlined the causes of piracy, the debate between the free software and software protection. It also includes the socio-economic impact of software piracy, impacts on the users and its alleged involvement with the organized crime. In the third section, we discussed the legal mechanisms to curb software piracy at the international, regional and national levels. The next section deals with the alternative measures to tackle the software piracy. Section five analyzed the effectiveness of the international and national legal measures to combat software piracy. We attempt to examine the national measures in the light of the TRIPS agreement because it is the most comprehensive IP agreement adopted at the international level, which imposed upon all the member countries of the WTO to ensure effective enforcement mechanisms. Finally we concluded with a few recommendations to deter software piracy and thereby to exploit the benefits of IP.

1. INTRODUCTION

Software piracy, the unauthorized duplication and distribution of software, is a worldwide problem that is growing at an epidemic pace. The cost and impact of software piracy is enormous. Whenever a piece of pirated software is used, a company is deprived of its earnings. Piracy undermines the software market, making it less lucrative for software companies to continue to offer innovative and high quality software. It also hurts the consumer. Frequently, pirated software does not include documentation or

* Assistant Professor at the Department University of Chittagong, Chittagong-4331, Bangladesh.

** Assistant Professor at the Department of Business Administration, Islamic University, Chittagong (IIUC), Bangladesh.

provide access to customer support, and, or, future software upgrades. Most importantly, pirated software is illegal and a crime in most countries. International, regional and national legal measures are increasingly empowering software creators to protect their assets. An increase in penalties for pirating software and a larger push for wider enforcement are attempts to curb the rising piracy rates worldwide. Furthermore, new anti-piracy technologies are being incorporated to prevent and deter the software piracy.

In this paper we first attempt to define software piracy and its global scenario. In the second section, we outlined the causes of piracy, the debate between the free software and software protection. It also includes the socio-economic impact of software piracy, impacts on the users and its alleged involvement with the organized crime. In the third section, we discussed the legal mechanisms to curb software piracy at the international, regional and national levels. The next section deals with the alternative measures to tackle the software piracy. Section five analyzed the effectiveness of the international and national legal measures to combat software piracy. We attempt to examine the national measures in the light of the TRIPS agreement because it is the most comprehensive IP agreement adopted at the international level, which imposed upon all the member countries of the WTO to ensure effective enforcement mechanisms. This agreement not only pressed for the national enforcement measures but also provides dispute settlement mechanisms for IP related issues between the member states. Finally we concluded with a few recommendations to deter software piracy and thereby to exploit the benefits of IP.

1.1 What is Software Piracy?

"Software" is the set of instructions, which tell a computer what to do[1]. Without software, a computer is just a useless lump of silicon, metal and plastic. As the cost of computer hardware has declined, the importance of software has increased; software is where the action and the money are these days.

"Software piracy" to a large extent has become a generic term for the illicit duplication of copyrighted computer software. However some organization working to prevent infringement of software copyright prefer to use the term software theft rather than software piracy because sometimes the term piracy create a shadow that it is not illegal rather simply prohibited practices and thereby relegating the seriousness of the theft.

Software piracy, or theft, occurs when users illegally duplicate software for profit, produce counterfeit copies of a software package and sell it as a legitimate product, or make multiple copies of software and distribute it to others. Parties that participate in software piracy include commercial users, software resellers, consumers and computer hackers. Even it is now possible to find literally hundreds of websites devoted to software piracy. While all types of software piracy are illegal, software piracy can be categorized based on scale, severity, monetary motivation, and the ability for enforcement. Considering the nature and scope of the piracy, it can be divided into (1) commercial piracy[2]; (2) corporate piracy[3]; and (3) softlifting[4].

The law of most of the countries does not expressly address contributory infringement for software piracy[5]. In fact, specific or particularized knowledge of infringing activity is not essential to liable anyone for contributory infringement. Therefore, the term software piracy is expanding day by day. Keeping in mind this broad perspective, it can be considered that a person who has a role in copying, or who provides facilities, directions, knowledge or encouragement, will be liable for software piracy.

1.2 Software Piracy-The Global Scenario

Although there is no universally well-recognized report on software piracy, it is undisputable fact that software piracy is a global problem increasing day by day. For every two-dollar's worth of PC software purchased legitimately, one dollar's worth was obtained illegally. In the Third Annual Business Software Alliance's (BSA) and IDC Global Software Piracy Study[6], May, 2006 on 97 countries, the median piracy rate was 64 per cent—meaning half of the countries studied in the report have a piracy rate of 64 per cent or higher[7]. Therefore, whether developed or developing countries, software piracy is a problem around the world. Even the seizures of pirated Microsoft products alone exceeded $1.7 billion[8].

In a comparative analysis of the software piracy of last two years, BSA study of 2006 reported that the worldwide personal computer (PC) software piracy rate stayed the same at 35 per cent while losses increased by over $1.6 billion and the PC software piracy rate increased in four of the regions, including Western Europe, Asia Pacific, Latin America and the European Union. However, in Middle East/Africa and Central/ Eastern Europe the rate is decreased slightly and in North America stayed the same.

2. CAUSES OF PIRACY

2.1 Quantitative and Qualitative Approach of the Phenomenon

Software is an integral part of the global economy. The large growth in software application makes developing software a big business with potentially large profits. Software enables users and business to do more with their systems, and the need for software is growing. But software is not free, and depending on the type of software, it can cost large amounts of money. Wherever there is potential for large profits and there exists a high demand, illegal methods for satisfying the demand at a lower cost also exist. But money is not the only motivation. Power, satisfaction, and lack of education are also factors for fueling the software piracy industry.

The BSA Study of May 2006 identified the following factors[9] that contribute to differences in piracy rate across the regions or country to country—the strength of intellectual property protection, the availability of pirated software and Cultural differences.

It is worth noting to mention the study of *Donald Merron and David G Steel*[10], where they identified the following factors for the causes and increase of software piracy :

(a) Income level and development of the country concerned,

(b) Cultural notion of rights (Private Vs Collective),

(c) Social and Economic Institutions and

(d) Well-educated population and state expenditure for research and development (R&D).

On the other hand, some scholars would like to say that the ultimate reason of the causes of software piracy is two folds[11]-

(i) Failure of the public authorities and commercial organizations to communicate to the consuming public of the dangers from the use of unauthorized products and of the harmful social welfare effects from this trade and

(ii) The inadequacy of deterrent penalties by the judicial authorities.

Furthermore, Internet facilitating the easy reproduction and distribution of pirated software.However, enormous scale of software piracy is successful owing to the unique nature of computer programs[12].

2.2 Free Software and Protection

Free software development, also known as 'open source[13],' is a phenomenon in which volunteer programmers collaboratively develop software on the Internet, and then make it available, along with its source code. Interestingly, free software has recently become a competitive alternative to unauthorized copying. Many free software solutions have finally sufficient functionality to replace proprietary systems and they are available 'Free as in speech, not as in beer.'

Free software makers or developers although not gaining direct economic benefits for disclosing the whole source code, it offers a possibility to market their skills globally and thus might help in finding jobs from rich countries or-more realistically-from a local subsidiary of a multinational software company.

However at the international legal regime as developed by WIPO and WTO has not given that much concern for free software because most of the member countries especially developed countries has feared that opening the door for a discussion about the limits of intellectual property rights under the free software agenda could have unwanted long-term implications to their national interests. This is why, Lois Boland, director of international relations for the U.S. Patent and Trademark Office said that *"...open source software runs counter to the mission of WIPO, which is to promote intellectual property rights[14]"*

Interestingly countries like India, Chile and Brazil, which have been pushing otherwise aggressively for more flexible intellectual property rights regime, have not yet forced the issue on the table. Even in the WIPO Development Agenda, which is mostly sponsored by the developing countries, refers to free software ("open source") only once.

Although there is fundamental political debate between the free software and strict IP law to protect software, it is possible to find some common ground for the proponents of strong intellectual property and the free software movement. In the developed countries strict IP law could protect software. But in the developing and least developed countries situation may be different. In the developing countries the promotion of free software could be used as a non-controversial way to teach about the fundamental concepts of copyright. Consequently, if free software could help creating a social norm "one should obey copyright", which would be beneficial in the long run for every copyright industry equally and obviously software industry as well[15]. Thus, instead of fighting against free software, it could be used as a tool because to create a field for future protection is better than not getting any benefit forever.

2.3 Impact of Software Piracy

(a) Economic and Social Impact

Software piracy has many depressing economic consequences: local software industries crippled by competition with pirated software from abroad and Government do not get tax revenues and non creation of new jobs from lack of a legitimate market. In December 2005, IDC and the BSA released their second study on the economic benefits of lowering piracy[16]. In a software market that is projected to grow to over $70 billion from $40 billion within the next five years, the industry is poised for tremendous losses due to piracy. According to the Organization for Economic Co-Operation and Development, counterfeit and pirated items including software piracy that are traded internationally are thought to account for about 176 billion US dollars even by conservative estimates[17].

In the study, IDC concluded that decreasing piracy by 10 percentage points over four years would add more than 2.4 million new jobs and almost $70 billion in tax revenues to local governments worldwide. Most of that new employment and most of an additional $400 billion in GDP would be added to local economies.

The European Union, United States and Canada experienced significant dollar losses, yet had relatively low piracy rates. This is because their markets are so large, and in such enormous markets even small piracy rates can add up to large losses. Only in 2005, the United States lost $6.9 billion as a result of software piracy[18]. The software piracy rate in EU is 37%. The cost of software publisher in the region is over 8 million Euros[19].

As counterfeiting activities have become rampant, counterfeiters create distribution channels and establish an economic and even political presence in society. Some economies are supported by these activities, which create local job opportunities[20].

Such attitude of the government may have long-term harmful effects on the foreign direct investment (FDI) in the software and ICT sector in a country and local software industries. The lack of IP protection will discourages manufacturers of legitimate goods from establishing their facilities in those countries. Such decisions result in a loss of FDI, as well as the concomitant technology transfer and foreign know-how, which normally accompany FDI. Loss of FDI also manifests itself in a loss of foreign income, which ultimately affects a country's balance of payments[21]. Local creators, inventors, and SMEs, in the field of ICT and software industry may also be discouraged that their products will be illegally copied and sold, thus precluding a return on investment and future growth.

In social terms, the damage suffered by businesses because of counterfeiting and piracy is reflected ultimately in its impact upon employment. Initially, employment may improve in those countries where pirate and counterfeit goods are produced. However, where local industries are developed which are dependent upon intellectual property rights, the local capacity to produce infringing products may have an ultimately harmful effect upon employment. Only considering EU, with a 10 point drop in software piracy rates, Western Europe's IT sector could grow to over 330 million euros by 2006, adding over 200, 000 new jobs[22].

(b) Effects on Consumers/Users

To the extent that consumers participate in a contraband market, this undermines respect among ordinary citizens for the law. Studies have shown that the initial act of law breaking can influence subsequent behavior. Once people develop a taste for cheating, they keep on cheating. Thus, a key societal consequence of participating in a contraband market is that it serves to sanction tax evasion and other forms of law breaking[23].

Again, using pirated software is also risky for users. Apart from the possible legal threat of using pirated software, those who use pirated software may also face the following problems:

- Increase the chances that the software will not function correctly or will fail completely;
- Forfeit access to customer support, upgrades, technical documentation, training, and bug fixes;
- Have no warranty to protect themselves;
- Increase their risk of exposure to a debilitating virus that can destroy valuable data;
- May find that the software is actually an outdated version, a beta (test) version, or a nonfunctioning copy;
- Are subject to significant fines for copyright infringement; and
- Risk potential negative publicity and public and private embarrassment and in the case of an organization, negative publicity that could cause irreparable harm to the business etc[24].

(c) Piracy and Organized Crime

Organized criminal elements are deeply involved in counterfeiting and piracy of software due to opportunities of easy reproduction technologies, need less investment of time, physical space and money, high-profit potential and relatively low risk. There are a number of reasons for the dramatic increase in IP crime in recent years.

-First, many forms of IP can be produced with minimal start up costs making IP crimes accessible to larger numbers of people;

-Second, international enforcement of IP laws is virtually nonexistent; and

-finally, domestic enforcement of IP laws has been inadequate and consequently the level of deterrence has been inadequate.

Profits from counterfeiting and piracy of software and other goods are often used to fund other criminal activities; and unfortunately, the criminal enforcement infrastructure as well as the public, does not always view counterfeiting and piracy of software as the serious crimes that they are. The active involvement of organized crime in counterfeiting and piracy is a proven, irrefutable fact[25]. Counterfeiting and piracy is becoming more attractive than drug trafficking, since high potential profits can be obtained without the risk of major legal penalties. Organized criminals often combine counterfeiting and piracy with terrorism and smuggling[26].

The World Economic Forum in Davos in January 2003 was informed by the World Customs Organization (WCO) that the trade in counterfeit and pirate products was as high as US$450 billion per annum and was controlled by organized crime and was being used to fund terrorist activity[27].

At the Third Global Congress on Combating Counterfeiting and Piracy held in Geneva from 30 to 31 January 2007, government officials, business leaders, and international law enforcement bodies like Intellectual Property Crime Unit of Interpol and WCO officials also hinted towards the link between the organized crime, terrorism and piracy and that is why called for an even greater marshalling of efforts and resources to counter the escalation in counterfeiting and piracy[28].

3. HOW TO TACKLE SOFTWARE PIRACY?

3.1 Cooperation and Coordination at the International, Regional National Level

Software piracy has serious repercussions on the entire ICT industry and on the broader knowledge economy. As mentioned earlier, software piracy not only carry mere infringement of intellectual property rights but also constrain growth within the software industry and weaken economies in the form of lost jobs and tax revenues. Against this backdrop intellectual property right is meaningless unless they can be enforced into practice. Therefore, cooperation and coordination at the international, regional and national levels is a must for technical, financial and legal initiatives to deter piracy.

3.2 Enhancing the Legal Framework

3.2.1 International Legal Measures

At first it is the Berne and Paris Convention incorporated certain provisions relating to enforcement against counterfeit and pirated goods[29]. These conventions provided that disputes between countries could be brought before the International Court of Justice. But no Member State has ever resorted to this remedy[30]. Perhaps due to voluntary or non-binding nature of these enforcement provisions discouraged the member countries to take recourse to this mechanism.

However, compulsory or mandatory enforcement mechanism was first taken up in the Uruguay Round and resulted in the TRIPS Agreement. Part III of the TRIPS Agreement specifies certain minimum standards for the enforcement of IPRs. All Members are under obligation to implement these standards, which include General Obligations, Civil and Administrative Procedures and Remedies, Provisional Measures, Special Measures Related to Border Measures, and Criminal Procedures.

These provisions obliges signatories to provide a enforcement mechanism so that IPR holders can effectively assert their rights, seize infringing goods, seek remedies against criminal enterprises and infringing goods, and seek the assistance of those agencies of government which have responsibilities in these matters, such as the courts, police, customs, and other administrative agencies.

On another level, when Members of WTO have disputes with other Members concerning, *inter alia*, the effective enforcement of IPRs, they are able to proceed in certain stages to bring their complaints through the Dispute Settlement Mechanism. These procedures are based upon mandatory jurisdiction in the WTO where there are sufficiently weighty remedies to ensure compliance, and in the event of proven noncompliance, to effect remedial compensation to the aggrieved Member. This is a noteworthy experiment to ensure the enforcement of intellectual property under the multilateral trading system.

Furthermore, in 1996 to address the growing trends of online piracy, the World Intellectual Property Organization (WIPO) adopted new copyright treaties to enable better and more effective enforcement against digital and online piracy. In order to ensure protection of copyrighted works in the digital age, countries need to update national copyright laws to implement the obligations of the WIPO copyright treaties.

These treaties address provisions on new tools to fight software piracy by technological protection measures and Internet piracy. Some countries have already implemented them in their national legislation, new legal actions are being taken and a new body of case law is growing up, which can successfully take the enforcement fight into cyberspace as well[31].

3.2.2 Regional Legal Measures

In below we outlined only regional legal measures in Europe:

(i) Regulation on the border enforcement of intellectual property rights (4 May 2000) On July 1, 2004 a revised Council Regulation setting forth custom measures in relation to goods suspected of infringing IPRs entered into force.

(ii) Directive on measures and procedures to ensure the enforcement of intellectual property rights (29 April 2004): It is the centerpiece of the EU's anti-piracy mechanism. The directive includes rules on searches and seizures, provides for injunctive relief, and harmonizes criteria for calculating damages.

(iii) Proposed Directive on criminal measures aimed at ensuring the enforcement of intellectual property rights (12 July 2005): This Directive lays down the criminal measures necessary to ensure the enforcement of intellectual property rights. These measures shall apply to IPRs provided for in Community legislation and/or national legislation in the Member States[32]. Member States shall ensure that all intentional infringements of an intellectual property right on a commercial scale, and attempting, aiding or abetting and inciting such infringements, are treated as criminal offences[33].

(iv) Copyright Directive: This directive provides for the technological protection measures to protect the rights of copyright owner.

(v) Software directive: E. C. Software Directive (the Software Directive) makes it mandatory on the Member States to protect computer programs, by copyright, as literary works within the meaning of the Berne Convention for the Protection of Literary and Artistic Works[34]. The Directive expressly provided exclusive rights for the software or computer programs. Member States have been directed to provide in accordance with their national legislation, appropriate remedies against a person committing any of the following acts[35]:

(a) any act of putting into circulation a copy of a computer program knowing, or having reason to believe, that it is an infringing copy;

(b) the possession, for commercial purposes, of a copy of a computer program knowing, or having reason to believe, that it is an infringing copy,

(c) any act of putting into circulation, or the possession for commercial purposes of any means the sole intended purpose of which is to facilitate the unauthorized removal or circumvention of any technical device which may have been applied to protect a computer program.

As in the following section of this paper I will analyze the effectiveness of the international and national legal measures in the context of the TRIPS enforcement obligations, it would not be out of place to mention here something regarding the effectiveness of the EU legal measures to combat piracy in general and software piracy in particular.

The EU copyright, software and enforcement directives respectively were critically examined by the IP scholars. The copyright directive was criticized for seriously flawed for its failure to achieve harmonization, too narrow room for free uses, leaves no flexibility for copyright law to adapt itself to future technological developments and inappropriately discriminates against digital technology and overly broad legal protection for technological measures and thereby threatens to replace copyright law with technological monopolies[36]. The same is almost true for the software directive as well. On the other hand enforcement directive also lacks the effective mechanisms to fight against piracy because it proposes an across the board instrument intended to deal horizontally with all kinds of IP infringement without making a difference between the pirates and legitimate competitors[37]. This distinction is very crucial because piracy poses specific enforcement questions, which have to be tackled by, specialized investigative and enforcement tools[38]. Again the directive appear to be toothless because no where in its long winded test is to be found a provision which compel the pirates to declare assets and pirated property under the *de facto* control of him through his associates[39]. This kind of provision would be very useful to destroy the long chain of software piracy. But it is ignored in the directive rather it included only order to communicate under article 6 (2) of the directive.

3.2.3 *National Legal Measures*

Although with the launching of the TRIPS agreement now there is effective international framework to deal with software piracy, without effective national legal measures in line with TRIPS agreement software piracy will continue to increase. Ultimately it is the national authority or court that has to deter software piracy within their national borders. To impose a fear of consequences, there must be some form of liability for the act of software piracy and this liability must be able to be proven in a court of law. The liability may rest with the pirate and the provider of the distribution. In this paper we will deal with national law of three countries to deter software piracy. Starting from the relevant law of USA, a country having biggest software market, it will deal with the laws of the Singapore, a country having very deterrent law to curb software piracy and has considerable success to reduce piracy when it is increasing globally. Finally it will deal with the laws of Bangladesh to combat software piracy, which is a least developed country (LDC) and yet to implement the TRIPS agreement (enjoying the transitional period until July 11, 2013), but trying to fight huge amount of software piracy in the local market.

4. ALTERNATIVE MEASURES

4.1 Technological Measures, Ethical Measures, Social Measures

Apart from the absolute legal protection measures, there are some alternative methods like technological (protective) measure and ethical and social (preventive) measures to prevent software piracy. Technological devices with adequate legal support would be a most effective measure for curbing software piracy by the offline users and online pirates as well.

A large number of ways to prevent software piracy at the technical level have been researched and implemented. A distinction can be drawn between those controls that act to prevent the duplication of software, and those that increase the likelihood of offenders being caught and prosecuted.

Technical measures that increase the difficulty of duplicating software can be categorized as obfuscation, encryption and simple checks. Code obfuscation is the deliberate altering of program code, whether at the source, object or machine code level[40].

Encryption can also be used to encipher program input and output streams, whether they are streamed to disk files or to other devices. A key is then required to be able to make use of the encrypted matter.

Another simple check is registration systems, which involve the user of the software acquiring a special unique string of characters and digits that the program demands are entered before it is first run, or at the time of installation[41].

"Guards" are hardware or software modules that monitor the running program and ensure that it has not been tampered with in any way[42].

The WIPO Internet Treaties, the WCT and WPPT, bind the Contracting Parties to provide legal protection and effective remedies against the circumvention of effective technological measures that are used by the right holders.

Article 11 of the WCT, entitled "Obligations Concerning Technological Measures," provides:

> "Contracting Parties shall provide adequate legal protection and effective legal remedies against the circumvention of effective technological measures that are used by authors in connection with the exercise of their rights under this Treaty or the Berne Convention and that restrict acts, in respect of their works, which are not authorized by the authors concerned or permitted by law."[43]
>
> The social and ethical issues of software piracy are another way to counter piracy. In fact it considers that the "right to fair compensation" is a basic principle of "universal" ethics. If we consider that purchasing software is the only fair compensation for the authors and distributors of that software, then software piracy is in breach of this set of ethics and social norms.

4.2 Greater Awareness among the Stakeholders

4.2.1 Role of the Educational Institutions

The Educational institutions can play a prime role for the promotion and protection of the intellectual property rights and at the same time it will aware the people about IP rights and will encourage the students to come up with their new innovation and to seek protection for their IP rights as well. Ultimately when consumers will not be interested to buy pirated software due to educational campaign, piracy will diminish automatically. As the saying goes, when the buying stops the selling stops[44]. The Ministry of Education in the developing and least developed countries may take steps to heighten public awareness for IPR protection by including a standard IP education part in the textbooks at the school and college levels. In Bangladesh under the street law program students of schools and colleges are provided basic education on IP, Environment and Democracy[45].

4.2.2 Role of the Software Users and Corporate Bodies

Software user especially corporate bodies have a great role to play to fight against the software piracy. Every corporate body should use genuine software and should encourage their employee to do the same. Ultimately, the fight against counterfeiting and piracy has to involve the public, since it is its purchasing power, which causes these practices to flourish. National anti-counterfeiting and anti-piracy campaigns could be used to indicate the link between intellectual property, crime and job losses, the debilitating effects of organized crime, and the dangers to health and safety of infringing goods.

4.2.3 Role of the Software Developers

As intellectual property rights are ultimately private rights, right holders have the largest immediate financial stake in ensuring the protection of those rights. For this reason, rights holders have been particularly willing to assist in enforcement efforts by providing information to assist in the identification of infringing products and in co-operating in awareness and training programmes.

The border control provisions of the TRIPS Agreement envisages that in the first place it will be the rights holders who will apply to the Customs authorities to intercept shipments of counterfeit and pirated products. Inevitability the rights holders will be in the best position to identify infringing products[46]. Therefore, software developers should also act as united force against the software piracy[47].

4.2.4 Pro-active Role of the Intellectual Property Offices

The role of the IP offices is crucial for the development of IP culture in a particular country. Intellectual Porperty offices may take initiatives to aware the peoples about IPR's and at the same time it should conduct frequent raid/visit as the case may be, in the hot-spots(places where software piracy is rampant),super markets and bringing criminal cases against the pirates . Furthermore, IP offices should also review its action and effectiveness of the relevant laws and regulations time to time and will submit reports to the Government to reshape the IP laws and enforcement mechanisms in the country. In some countries special units within the government apparatus have been set up to deal with IP matters[48]. Their functions includes from receiving complaints to investigate, bring matters before the jurisdiction of competent courts and cooperation with other relevant bodies and rights holders.

5. EFFECTIVENESS OF THE LEGAL ENFORCEMENT MEASURES: A SURVEY OF ISSUES

5.1 Effectiveness of the International legal Measures (WIPO Treaties and TRIPS Agreement)

As mentioned earlier, although Berne and Paris convention provides for the enforcement of IP rights at the international level, theses provisions are not effective. The main reason of the no-effectiveness of these provisions is mainly due to the inherent jurisdictional problems of the International Court of Justice (ICJ), which is primarily responsible for the judicial enforcement of IP rights under the Berne and Paris Convention. International court of justice as opposed to the national courts follows the voluntary nature of jurisdiction. Therefore it has no mandatory enforcement mechanisms like the national courts. The jurisdiction of the ICJ is still depends on the consent of the states to initiate any proceedings before it[49]. Therefore unless or until both the states consented to any measures or voluntarily refer any case before ICJ, it lacks jurisdiction to entertain the same, which is the major drawback to enforce the IP rights through ICJ[50].

Whereas the obligation under the TRIPS agreement although has incorporated mandatory and effective enforcement mechanism, it is yet to be implemented by all the WTO member states. The agreement will be implemented by different member stated under the different time frame on the basis of the stage of development of that particular country. Suppose in this study, the author is concentrating on the enforcement efforts of USA, Singapore and Bangladesh, which has three separate time frames for TRIPS-compliance system[51]. Therefore, despite mandatory provisions, the enforcement mechanism is yet to be fully effective across the member states.

As mentioned earlier, major feature of TRIPS is its requirement in Part III that WTO members include a specific minimum set of effective enforcement procedures for all categories of IP, including copyright (but not including moral rights)[52]. Even developed states which have long been accustomed to enforcing IP rights may need to change their laws and practices to comply with TRIPS obligations; so it is not surprising that developing states also may have to make changes.

The general obligations that TRIPS imposes include, in broad detail, the following:

> -Remedies to prevent and cure infringement must be expeditious and must be effective to deter further infringement (art. 41.1).
>
> -Abuses of procedure and barriers to legitimate trade should be avoided (art.41.1).
>
> -Due process must be guaranteed (arts. 41.2-41.4, & 42). In particular, there must be:
>
> -Fair procedures that are "not unnecessarily complicated or costly" and that do not impose "unreasonable time-limits or unwarranted delays[53]".

Thus TRIPS provided a framework of minimum obligation for enforcement to the extent that it is possible under the infrastructure and socio-economic circumstances prevailing in the concerned member countries. But it failed to adopt an approach of complete harmonization in the field of enforcement of intellectual property rights. During the negotiation process, the approach of universal recognition and execution of trans-boundary court judgments (Judgments of one country in another country) was also rejected from the outset because this would probably work only in a relatively 'homogenous environment'. In fact, the formulation of 'minimum basic stock of procedural regulations guided by the intention to achieve the 'best possible effectiveness' and tie this stock of regulations to result oriented criteria instead of setting out all the details reflects a certain Anglo-American pragmatism which need not necessarily always conform with Continental-European concepts of formal procedural fairness. This result oriented approach triggered in the adoption of vague phrases such as 'effective', 'expeditious', 'reasonable, 'undue', 'unwarranted', 'fair and equitable', and 'not unnecessarily complicated', or costly etc[54].

But what kind of remedies will be effective and what not and when it would be expeditious and adequate yet to be explored. There have been no WTO panel reports or Appellate Body decisions to date regarding inadequate enforcement of IPRs. There has been only one complaint filed in the WTO against inadequate IPR enforcement—a complaint filed by the United States in June 1998 against Greece and the European Union because of the Greek Government's failure to enforce its intellectual property laws effectively against television stations that broadcasted U.S. copyrighted works without authorization. On March 22, 2001, after extensive consultations, Greece, the European Union and the United States formally resolved this WTO dispute without a decision by a dispute settlement panel.

Again, given the financial requirements and legal and factual sophistication in identifying inconsistencies and effectiveness in intellectual property laws and trade practices and thereafter in bringing complaints to the WTO-Dispute Settlement Body(DSB), the developed countries like the USA, EU countries, Canada or Japan are structurally best positioned. On the other hand, the developing and least developed countries have to face formidable challenges while taking of the benefits under the DSB due to lack of specialized human resources and financial resources. The size and amount of trade or economic power of a particular developing or least developed country is so marginal, which made it unlikely that such retaliation would harm the opposite developed country[55]. At the same time, the voluntary nature of determine compensation is also a major drawback of the dispute settlement system. The right of filling official cases and obtaining ruling from the Panel has to expand to include additional actors beyond the sovereign member states. Individuals and certain groups that bear the effect of the WTO rulings have to be able to hold their governments. The initiative of including reports of civil society in the panel hearings is already a step in the right direction, but is not sufficient. Leveling the playing fields for all participants of the process by providing more assistance to developing and least developed countries is necessary to preserve the integrity of the system.

5.2 Effectiveness of the National Legal Measures (Compliance with TRIPS)

5.2.1 USA

In implementing its obligations under the TRIPS Agreement, the **United States** made a number of amendments to its substantive intellectual property laws, including, for example, expanding the acts that constitute patent infringement to include importing or offering for sale of an article claimed in a patent or produced by a process claimed in a patent, and providing new Federal remedies against bootlegged audio and video recordings. As laid down in the report of US Government on the Review of US Legislation on Enforcement at the TRIPS Council, no further amendments were required to implement the obligations of Part III of the TRIPS Agreement because the US enforcement system already provided protection consistent with those obligations[56].

A number of procedures as required by the TRIPS agreement are available in USA to deter software piracy such as civil procedure like injunctions, Criminal procedures (imprisonment and fines etc), Administrative and Special border measures (by Customs) etc.

State courts in the United States have jurisdiction over claims of infringement of state registered or common-law trademarks, misappropriation of trade secrets, or unfair competition. On the administrative level, the United States International Trade Commission has jurisdiction over cases brought under section 337 of the Tariff Act of 1930, which applies to claims of violations of all forms of intellectual property rights involving imported products. The US Customs Service is authorized to seize counterfeit trademarked goods and pirated copyrighted works presented for entry into the United States[57].

Federal copyright law automatically protects software from the moment of its creation[58]. The rights granted to the owner of a copyright are clearly stated in the Copyright Act, Title 17 of the US Code. The Act gives a copyright owner "the exclusive rights" to "reproduce the copyrighted work" and "to distribute copies ... of the copyrighted work" (Section 106). It also states that "anyone who violates any of the exclusive rights of the copyright owner ... is an infringer of the copyright" (Section 501), and sets forth several penalties for such conduct.

However, those who purchase a license for a copy of software do not have the right to make additional copies without the permission of the copyright owner, except when it is necessary to: (i) copy the software onto a single computer in order to use the software, (ii) make a backup copy "for archival purposes only", which are specifically provided in the Copyright Act and (iii) copy the software during activation of the computer in order to repair the computer (Section 117).

A plaintiff can establish copyright infringement by showing "(1) ownership of a valid copyright, and (2) copying of constituent elements of the work that are original[59]."

A copy of an infringing computer program has been made when an "electronic copy of the signals that tell a computer what to do [are] . . . stored [by an infringer] on a device like a floppy disk or a hard drive[60]."

In *Microsoft Corporation vs. Suncreast Enterprise et al*[61] the Court held that the sale of counterfeit software was sufficient to establish liability for copyright infringement, trademark infringement, false designation of origin and unfair competition.

In *Ellison Vs. Robertson*[62], the Court defines the three possible theories of liability, which would be applicable for software piracy: direct infringement[63], contributory infringement[64] and vicarious liability[65].

Those who copy are liable for the resulting copyright infringement whether or not they knew their conduct violated federal law. Penalties include liability for damages suffered by the copyright owner plus any profits of the infringer that are attributable to the copying, or statutory damages of up to $150,000 for each work infringed. The unauthorized duplication of software is also a Federal crime if done "willfully and for purposes of commercial advantage or private financial gain (Title 18 Section 2319(b))." Criminal penalties include fines of as much as $250,000 and jail terms of up to 5 years[66]. Furthermore, USA implemented WCT and WPPT through the Digital Millennium Copyright Act (DMCA) that provides the technological protection measures to protect software.

In USA the role of the law enforcing agency and its cooperation with the law enforcing agency of other countries to deter piracy in general and software piracy in particular is very remarkable. In the Case of *United States of America Vs. Robin Rothberg, et al*[67] FBI seized the equipment of a computer software piracy group called "Pirates with Attitudes (PWA)," an organization "dedicated to the illegal reproduction and distribution of copyrighted software over the Internet, for the use and benefit of members of PWA, and of those persons to whom PWA members further distributed that software (over 54,000 software programs and worth in excess of

$ 10 million) with the cooperation and assistance of Canadian law enforcement personnel.

Although USA provides a very effective enforcement mechanism to prevent software piracy, it is some way over protective creating obstacles for fair use and the procedure is very costly for the small software developers. Again a broad array of protection for software like copyright, patent, trade mark, trade secret etc sometimes make it uncertain and too much cumbersome.

5.2.2 *Singapore*

Singapore recognizes the importance of intellectual property as a national resource and in attracting foreign investment in its development as a knowledge-based economy. To develop intellectual property as a strategic and competitive resource and to make the country as the hub of IP, Singapore has already adopted an essentially pro-active IPR policy for the development of high value added and creative-content industries. Intellectual Property of Singapore (IPOS) is very active in policy making and in the drafting of legislation relating to enforcement of intellectual property rights.

In Singapore generally the rights holders themselves via civil actions can enforce IP rights whereas the Intellectual Property Rights Branch of the Criminal Investigations Department of the Singapore Police Force responsible for the criminal enforcement activities (e.g. raids on software pirates). Border enforcement measures are carried out by Singapore Customs.

The Intellectual Property Rights Warrant Enforcement Unit (IPRWEU) was set up on 15 Feb 95 as a dedicated law enforcement unit for the execution of Intellectual Property Rights (IPR) related search warrants. In the year 2000, the unit expanded into the present Intellectual Property Rights Branch (IPRB). The formation of the Branch demonstrated the Singapore Government's strong stance against intellectual property rights offences.

In Singapore, enforcement procedures and remedies (including border measures) are available under the various intellectual property legislations or under the common law to enable effective action against acts of infringement[68]. Both civil and criminal remedies may be resorted to. In a civil action injunction, damages or account of profits maybe ordered. The court may also order the delivery up and/or destruction or other disposal of infringing goods and materials and implements for their production. In criminal prosecutions imprisonment, monetary fines, seizure, forfeiture and destruction of infringing goods and materials and implements for their production may be ordered.

In relation to software piracy on a commercial scale, if a person who, at a time when copyright subsists in a work, makes for sale or hire, sells or lets for hire, or by way of trade offers or exposes for sale or hire or by way of trade exhibits in public or imports for the purposes of trade or distributes either for the purpose of trade or for other purpose but to such an extent as to affect prejudicially the copyright owner any article which he knows, or ought reasonably to know, to be an infringing copy of the work shall be guilty of an offence carrying a fine of $10,000 per infringing article up to a maximum of $100,000 and/or an imprisonment sentence of up to 5 years[69].

In addition, it is also an offence carrying a fine up to a maximum of $20,000 and an imprisonment term of 2 years to make or to have in one's possession an article specifically designed or adapted for making infringing copies when the person knows or ought reasonably to know that the article is to be used for making infringing copies. Singapore law provides that where a person is found to have more than 5 copies of any one's work, it is presumed that the infringing copies were not for personal use[70].

Under Section 139 of the Copyright Act, any person who, by any means, publishes, or causes to be published, in Singapore an advertisement for the supply in Singapore (whether from within or outside Singapore) of a copy of a computer program which is an infringing copy shall, unless he proves that he acted in good faith and had no reasonable grounds for supposing that copyright would or might thereby be infringed, be guilty of an offence and shall be liable on conviction to a fine of up to $20,000 or to imprisonment for a term not exceeding 2 years or to both.

Since the enactment of the Manufacture of Optical Discs Act (MODA)[71] in 2004, Singapore police regularly visit various plants to prevent the manufacturing of unauthorized optical discs, which are mostly used for software piracy. Again under the Regulation 3 of Imports and Exports Regulations, any party who wishes to import replication and mastering equipment for manufacture of optical discs must obtain permit from the Director General of Customs to do so.Any party who imports without permit shall be guilty of an offence[72]. The initiatives of Singapore Police and Custom to destroy the counterfeiting rings and to tackle piracy were very significant over the years.

Statistics on Number of Raids and Total Value Seized by Singapore Authorities:

Year	*Copyright Raids*	*Trademark Raids*	*Total Raids*	*Total Value Seized*
2000	308	146	454	S$16,310,436.28
2001	308	183	491	S$15,553,324.95
2002	284	207	491	S$9,415,266.00
2003	266	160	426	S$33,185,092.00
2004	126	190	316	S$12,665,969.00
2005	61	168	229	S$19,774,083.00

Source: Singapore Police Force, Films and Publications Department and Customs and Excise Department

It is worth noting that the Judiciary of Singapore considers the cases of piracy and counterfeiting very seriously. In this regard, the observation of Yong Pung How CJ in the case of *Ong Ah Tiong v Public Prosecutor [2004] SGHC 11*[73]*, is remarkable:*

> "Singapore is a prominent business hub with a reputation for upholding intellectual property rights. It is manifestly in the public interest to deter potential criminals who are inclined to use Singapore as a distribution centre or a base for transshipment of counterfeit products to neighboring countries. I therefore agreed with the sentiments of the trial judge that the appellant's intention of re-exporting the counterfeit items rather than of selling them in Singapore was not of any mitigating value whatsoever"

The CJ further held that the trial judge rightly recognized the government's strong efforts to promote Singapore as a regional intellectual property centre and the concomitant need to clamp down on piracy of intellectual property.

In is also fascinating to know that in the original suit the trial judge, while determining a sentence for piracy and counterfeiting considered *"all the circumstances in which the offences were committed, including the nature and extent of the infringements, and the manner in which the infringements were carried out*[74]*". (Emphasis added)*

It is also worth noting that Singapore adopts the 3 'Es' (Education, Engineer and Enforcement) approach in combating piracy[75].

Education: IPRB consider that education is the one of the most effective ways to fight piracy. As the saying goes, when the buying stops the selling stops. In Singapore, the Intellectual Property Office of Singapore (IPOS) is responsible for educating the public to heighten its awareness on piracy issues. The IPOS conducts regular anti-piracy campaigns like mobilising artists for walkabouts, concerts and school talks to propagate the message to members of public that the intellectual property of artists and rights owners should be respected. IPOS also works with the IPRB to spread the message across to the schools.

Engineer: Singapore Government promotes an environment where public can gain easy access to genuine products with reasonable pricing. In this, the intellectual property owners are strongly encouraged to price their products reasonably. In government agencies and schools, only genuine products are used. The Singapore government is actively promoting innovation and creativity among Singaporeans to be inventors and creators ourselves. With more and more genuine ideas generated, people will respect the intellectual property of others.

Enforcement: When the two above 'Es' do not produce the desired results, the 3rd 'E'-Enforcement is the last resort. The IPRB adopts a 2-prong approach – police initiated and collaborative, towards enforcement. The police initiated approach is targeted at syndicates, icons and hot spots and the collaborative approach is targeted at retail piracy.

Under the collaborative approach, the IPRB act in the interest of justice by executing the Search Warrant, ensuring law and order during the raids and to take custody of the seized exhibits. No arrest is made in this instance. The benefit of this approach is that the IPR owners determine the pace and scope of the enforcement action. In addition, the punishment meted out can be similar to that of the criminal proceeding, depending on the merits of the case.

On the basis of analysis of law, relevant case law, working procedure and communication with relevant bodies, it is reflected that the reasons behind the success of the Singapore in reducing software piracy are as follows:

1. Education and Campaign programs by IPOS along with relevant national bodies and non-governmental organization having expertise in the relevant field[76].

2. Effective Cooperation and coordination among the Singapore Custom, Police and other relevant bodies to ensure different remedies where appropriate.
3. Tough law to prevent software piracy (as amended in 2005, which has very positive impact to reduce piracy).
4. Very active role of the Singapore Police and its special unit to raid hot spots, markets and to initiate tough proceedings against the pirates.
5. Active role of Singapore Custom to prevent software piracy and manufacture and export and import of related equipments under Manufacture of Optical Discs Act and Export and Import Regulation.
6. prevent internet piracy by prohibiting any kinds of technological means for software piracy.
7. Cooperation between the law enforcing agency and the rights holders.
8. Last but not the least, the successful application of the 3 'Es' (Education, Engineer and Enforcement) approach in combating piracy.

5.2.2. Bangladesh

Piracy of intellectual property rights including software piracy is a common phenomenon in Bangladesh[77]. Although Bangladeshi nationals feel piracy keenly, the harm from piracy in Bangladesh is significant for the U.S. and other foreign right holders. Piracy is so rampant, Bangladeshi record/music producers compelled to take it so seriously to enforce their own rights, calling it "a matter of life and death" for their local Bangladeshi companies[78]. But responses of the government of Bangladesh is not adequate, both in terms of the results from enforcement actions taken, as well as from the standpoint of publicizing results of actions in order to create necessary deterrence[79].

However, as least developed country, Bangladesh required to implement the TRIPS agreement by July 11, 2013. Bangladesh has already started the process and recently promulgated new legislations in the field of intellectual property rights and is in the process of strengthening its IPR regime. The Copyright law as enacted in 2000 is almost TRIPS compliance and the law commission of Bangladesh drafted new patent and design law and trademarks law in compliance with the TRIPS agreement, which will replace the existing laws in the concerned fields. With the help of WIPO and EU, intellectual property offices of Bangladesh especially the Trade Marks Registry and the Patents Office are being in the process of modernization both in terms of facilities and working procedures. Enforcement mechanisms to deter software piracy in Bangladesh is depends not only on intellectual property related laws but also some other general laws like the civil enforcement mechanism is regulated by Copyright Act along with Code of Civil Procedure, 1908 and criminal enforcement mechanism is regulated by the Copyright Act and Code of Criminal Procedure, 1898.

Under the Code of Civil Procedure, 1908 (Order 39, rule 2) a court has powers to order temporary injunctions. A temporary injunction may be passed to restrain an infringement of an intellectual property right[80]. Under the Code of Civil Procedure (Order 39, rule 7), the court has the authority to pass an order for the preservation, detention or inspection of any subject matter of the suit[81]. The law authorizes judges to order the payment to the right holder of adequate damages to compensate the injury he suffered. Section 76 of the Copyright Act, 2000, empower the court to order the infringer to pay adequate damages to the right holder to compensate for the injury that he has suffered because of the infringement. Section 93 of the same Act authorizes the police to raid and seize the pirated software. But unfortunately this provision is hardly applied due to lack of knowledge among the law-enforcing agency regarding the software piracy and gravity of it.

Customs has a more visible and important role with respect to enforcing IPRs at the borders, as the TRIPS Agreement provides detailed provisions on customs procedures. But due to the low policy priority given to IPR enforcement, customs offices in Bangladesh have scarce resources to combat piracy at the border. Custom authority has the power to order that infringing goods are to be placed outside channels of commerce or destroyed[82].

Although section 15 of the Customs Act, 1969 empowered the custom authority of Bangladesh to take border measures against the pirated goods[83], similar provisions yet to be included in copyright law (which is mainly applied in Bangladesh for software protection) and that is why, Custom authority is either reluctant to take action or ignorant about the pirated software.

Criminal Offences in Bangladesh can either be cognizable or non cognizable[84]. All offences under the Copyright Act are cognizable. Under the Copyright law[85] and Penal Code[86] of Bangladesh, criminal penalties are available against copyright piracy and trademark counterfeiting. The Court before which any offence under the Copyright Act is tried may, whether the alleged offender is convicted or not, order that all copies of the work or plates or recording equipment in the possession of the alleged offender, which appear to it to be infringing copies, or plates, or recording equipment used or intended to be used for the purpose of making infringing copies, be destroyed or delivered to the owner of the copyright or otherwise dealt with as the Court may think fit[87].

It is quite interesting to note that although copyright law in Bangladesh protects software, law-enforcing agency in most of the occasions and even software developers proceed to take action against the software piracy under the penal code. Till date as per study of this author on the law reports of Bangladesh as decided by the Supreme Court of Bangladesh, there is no case law on the software piracy. However, District Judges Court in Dhaka[88] for the first time decided a case on Software piracy in 2002. In that case more popularly known as the *Bijoy Keyboard Case,* the Court applied the Copyright Act and showed very tough view against the software piracy and illegal use of trademark of Plaintiff's software (*Bijoy*) by the defendant. Again in another case, the Supreme Court of Bangladesh showed a very liberal approach towards the application of international IP related conventions/ treaties/agreements, as case may be within the domestic jurisdiction of Bangladesh[89]. This is a very remarkable development in Bangladesh for the effective enforcement of intellectual property laws in line with international standard like the TRIPS agreement and WCT[90] etc.

On the basis of field reports, interview with experts and officials, relevant laws and case laws, it is reflected that the enforcement mechanisms of Bangladesh to prevent software piracy is not satisfactory due to following reasons:

1. Lack of effective and deterrent criminal enforcement system
2. Most of the procedural laws in Bangladesh like Code of Civil Procedure and Code of Criminal Procedure is yet

to be updated, which are mostly enacted during the British colonial time and not suitable to address the modern phenomenon of software piracy and other computer crime (hacking, cracking, virus distribution etc.)[91].

3. Lack of competent police and custom officials having expertise on intellectual property laws.
4. Lack of awareness among the general user regarding the gravity of software piracy.
5. Poor infrastructure and resources for the intellectual property teaching in general and awareness program on piracy in particular[92].
6. Delay in civil and criminal adjudications and cost of litigations[93].
7. Despite the enactment of information technology law in 2006 to provide protection for technological protection measures to prevent software piracy, due to lack of technological knowledge among the police and custom officials to monitor internet piracy, it is not effective till date.
8. Extremely poor border procedure to deter software piracy from the outside of borders[94].
9. Low priority and ignorance about the gravity of software piracy.
10. Lack of coordination and cooperation among the official of different bodies.
11. Last but not the least, the debate or dilemma in Bangladesh among the scholars despite its WTO membership that TRIPS may not be beneficial for Bangladesh let alone it's enforcement mechanisms. For the proper implementation of the TRIPS agreement (being a member of the WTO) and for introducing the effective enforcement mechanisms Government should settle this dilemma immediately on the basis of proper study[95].

6. RECOMMENDATIONS AND IN LIEU OF CONCLUSION

Being a Member of the WTO, all member countries are under obligation to comply with the enforcement provisions of the TRIPS Agreement. There are in addition good policy reasons why a country should enforce intellectual property rights. In developed countries, there is good evidence that intellectual property is, and has been, important for the promotion of invention in some industrial sectors, particularly the pharmaceutical, chemical and petroleum industries as well as biotechnology and software and ICT industries. For developing countries, the nurturing of indigenous technological capacity through the intellectual property system has also proved to be a key determinant of economic growth and poverty reduction. The enforcement of intellectual property rights thus protects local commercial and industrial innovation, as well as encouraging technology transfer and foreign investment. Enforcement is therefore is to be considered as a developing country's economic development strategy as well.

Thus, for true economic, social, and cultural development to occur, intellectual property must play a crucial role and to ensure that crucial role of IP, they must be enforced throughout society. However, enforcement is a multi-layered concept. It cannot be achieved only through the police, customs, and courts. Without political will, the appropriate legislative framework, and a sustainable IP practices, there can be no enforcement, and ultimately, the country and its economy will suffer.

To fight against piracy in general and software piracy in particular (as that is the most used IP rights in this digital age) and to declare a country as the 'Home of IP' (IP protector country) to attract foreign direct investments in the ICT sector and to harness the 'Beauty of IP' (benefits of IP) to ensure economic growth and sustainable progress of the software industries and IP intensive enterprises, a country at least should take following steps:

Implement the TRIPS and WIPO Copyright Treaty

A country should make its laws in compliance with the TRIPS agreement and at the same time it should adopt the provisions of the WCT to prevent online software piracy[96]. Among other things, these measures make sure that software cannot be pirated by ensuring that protected works are not made available online without the author's permission, and that copy protection tools are not hacked or circumvented.

Not Mere Paper Tiger and Awareness is the Key

Strong copyright laws are essential, but meaningless and would be mere paper tiger without effective mechanisms to enforce them.

Governments must fulfill their obligations by adopting and enforcing IP laws consistent with the TRIPS agreement. However mere tough law without awareness among the peoples may not be effective. Reducing software piracy requires a fundamental shift in the public's attitude. In this regard, the successful application of the 3 'Es' (Education, Engineer and Enforcement) approach in combating piracy in Singapore may be a effective model to be replicated in other countries.

Trained and Knowledgeable Enforcement Staffs

Too often, software piracy is treated harmless or not considered as a serious offence and the punishment is too insignificant to be an effective deterrent. In this regard, Countries should elevate their enforcement of intellectual property by:

(a) creating specialized intellectual property enforcement units at the national and local levels, and providing dedicated resources to investigate and prosecute intellectual property theft,

(b) increasing cross-border mutual cooperation among police, custom and other enforcement agencies to improve coordination among law enforcement in various countries[97], and

(c) supporting training of law enforcement and judiciary officials and providing better technical assistance to ensure that the people on the front lines of piracy enforcement are equipped with the tools they need to deal with the changing nature of intellectual property theft.

Set Example

One of the most effective mechanisms for public persuasion may stem from governments themselves by sending a strong and clear signal that the government will not tolerate software piracy, and is vigorously managing its own software assets[98].

Let us contribute in our respective countries for the effective enforcement of IP rights and thereby making our respective country *'Home of IP'* to exploit the *'Beauty of IP'*. IP protection to deter software piracy cannot be viewed in isolation. It is a global effort, which requires all stakeholders to work closely with one another. Again, solving software piracy requires a combination of education, technology, legislature, and enforcement. Anti-piracy methods must be effective in deterring piracy and not hinder the legal use of the software by the user. A successive and viable solution for piracy prevention is a solution that incorporates both hardware and software protection in conjunction with education about intellectual property rights. It is also important to provide choices for quality software at fair prices[99].

Notes

1. In the United States of America, under the copyright Act of 1976, A Computer Program is defined as "a set of statements or instructions to be used directly or indirectly in a computer in order to bring about a certain result." 17 U.S.C. § 101. Computer programs fall within the definition of literary works. *Lexmark Int'l, Inc. v. Static Control Components, Inc.*, 387 F.3d 522, 533 (6th Cir. 2004).The EU Directive 91/250 does not define the term computer program as such, however it has made several provisions regarding the protection of computer programs. Article 10.1 of the TRIPS agreement requires member states to recognize computer programs as literary works. But there is no definition of the software or computer program in the TRIPS agreement. As it is not defined in the TRIPS agreement, members may keep the definitions they adopted under their domestic laws prior to entry into force of TRIPS. See for details, Resource Book on TRIPS and Development, UNCTAD-ICTSD in IPRs and Sustainable Development, Cambridge Univ. Press, USA, p. 152.
2. Commercial piracy refers to the illegal duplication of software for the purpose of distribution and sale. *In Microsoft v. CMOS Technologies, Inc., et al., 872 F. Supp. 1329 (D. N.J., 1994)* USA, the defendants purchased and sold nearly 30,000 units of stand alone counterfeit software after receiving notice of its counterfeit status. Microsoft filed suit and obtained seizure and temporary restraining orders. The Court found that defendants engaged in the unauthorized distribution of counterfeit software. In *Microsoft v. Grey Computer, et al., 910 F. Supp. 1077 (D. Md. 1995), co*-defendants purchased and copied Microsoft software without the accompanying personal computers and sold the software to others. Here, the defendants asserted their alleged lack of knowledge as a defense. The Court found that the defendants had in fact received notice of the counterfeit products and were computer software professionals and therefore held liable for copyright infringement.
3. Corporate piracy entails copying of software for direct financial gain. Corporate pirates often find that the size and scope of their company's software usage makes tracking and enforcement of software copyrights exceedingly difficult. Corporate piracy encompasses the activities of not only corporations and businesses, but also educational institutions, government entities, etc.

4. Softlifting is the software equivalent of shoplifting. Softlifting occurs when a person purchases a single licensed copy of a software program and loads it on several machines, in violation of the terms of the license agreement. When one copies a friend's software package, or brings a backup copy home from work for personal use, or borrows a program from the library and makes a copy of it, each of these acts amounts to softlifting. Softlifting is that piracy which goes on in our homes and behind closed doors, where no one can see it happening. It is not intended for direct financial gain, and is believed by many to be perfectly legal.For details see, D.HORNIK, *Recent Development Combatting Software Piracy: The Softlifting Problem*, 7 J.L. & Tech 377, 378 (1994).

5. Nevertheless, US federal courts have held that a person who knowingly causes, induces, or materially contributes to the infringing conduct of another may be held liable as a contributory infringer. See for details, *Playboy Enterprises, Inc. v. Russ Hardenburgh, Inc.*, 982 F. Supp. 503, 508 (1997).

6. Despite the report of BSA is higly controversial, the author used the data due to lack of any other source on global software piracy from any universally recognised authority. The main criticism against the BSA is that it is simply serving the interest of a corporate lobby, self appointed global police and legislature and even examining the situation of other countries without considering the knowledge of the law of that particular country, ignoring the sovereign right of law making of a country BSA simply consider US law and sometimes campaign using disgraceful notice to even genuine customers. It is quite interesting to note that in a Belgian case, the Court declared the campaign of BSA to some extent illegal and to be removed immediately and it has also forbidden BSA to operate as a Non-Profit Organisation as the Court consider the activities of BSA entirely commercial. See for deials, J.DOUGLAS, *BSA (A) Belligerence Stepping on Sovereignty*, available at www.zdnet.com/au/mews/business/soa/BSA_A_*belligerencesteppingonsovereignty/0,139023166,120265924,00.htm and IT Week December 1, 1997, available at www.itweek.co.uk/vnunet/mews/2095430/bsa-campaign-illegal-rules-belgian-judge/*

7. The Third Annual Business Software Alliance's (BSA) and IDC Global Software Piracy Study, May, 2006, p. 1.

8. Statement of R.LAMAGNA (Microsoft Corporation) before the House Subcommittee on Courts, the Internet, and Intellectual Property, *Oversight Hearing on International Copyright Piracy: Links to Organized Crime and Terrorism,*(March 13, 2003).

9. *Kamil Idris, Intellectual Property: Engine of Economic Growth, WIPO, Switzerland*, p. 5.

10. D. Merron and D. Steel, *Which Countries Protect Intellectual Property? The Case of Software Piracy*, Eco.Inquiry, April 2000, pp. 159-174.

11. M. Blakeney, *Overview of IPR Enforcement Developments,* EC-ASEAN Intellectual Property Rights Co-operation Programme (ECAP II), May, 2003, Bangkok.

12. This unique nature of software, which is facilitating piracy may be illustrated as follows:In most countries those who seek to ride on the backs of others must first take time to understand and recreate the work of their competitors. Thus the original work enjoys 'lead time' over the imitations it has inspired, in which time it can begin to eatablish a footing on the market. However, in the computing insdutry, the digitisation of information allows programs to be copied, manipulated and disected at such a great speeds and at such a little expense that 'lead time' is virtually non-existent. Consequetly consumers cannot distingush between the original and the second generation work. The only obvious difference is likely to be their relative price. See for details, D. J. M. Attridge, *'Copyright protection for computer programs'* in EIPR Issue 12 2000 p. 563.

13. The term 'free software' is often misunderstood. The father of free software Stallman clarifies its meaning by explaining that it refers to software that is 'Free as in speech, not as in beer.' Thus, the term describes software that one is able to use freely, without limiting restrictions. There are many software programs that are available at no cost, such as freeware or shareware, yet they do not provide the same freedoms that 'free software' provides. Stallman states that a piece of software can be called 'free software' if a user has the freedom to use it for any purpose, to modify it, and to redistribute either copies of modified versions, either without cost or for a fee. For details see, R. Stallman, "The GNU Operating System and the Free Software Movement," available at *http://www.opensource.org/advocacy/faq.php*, accessed on November 12, 2006.

14. The biggest beneficiaries of free software are currently big information technology service firms such as IBM and HP–most of them based in the U.S. Also, the most important Linux-distribution companies RedHat and SuSE (i.e. Novell) are from the U.S. This makes the U.S position quite complex.

15. One of the possible mechanism to use free software for IP enforcement is to encourage the software companies to distribute software freely or with a minimum price to the educational institutions in the developing and least developed countries with a precondition that there must be a mandatory course curriculum on the IP and negative impacts on the piracy. It may be somehow a bit different from the idea of free software as prevalent now. Whereas as the cocept of Stallman when he states that a piece of software can be called 'free software' if a user has the freedom to use it for any purpose, to modify it, and to redistribute either copies of modified versions, either without cost or for a fee may be used for the Government Campaign to promote the respect of IP law from the view point that people will have the option to use this kind of software and to exploit the benefits of it and in other kinds of software user have to pay and can be used under some restrictions. Therefore, in this way

customer would be educated not to use pirated software or to use with restrictions or without restrictions , as the case may be.

16. Available at *www.bsa.org / idcstudy*, accessed on October 30, 2006.
17. To view the preliminary findings of the OECD study 'Counting the Cost: The Economic Impacts of Counterfeiting and Piracy' presented at the WIPO conference, availavle at *http://www.oecd.org/dataoecd/12/7/38015608.pdf*, accessed on February 15, 2007.
18. Software Piracy in the United States–Fact Sheet, available at www.bsa.org, accessed on September 25, 2006.
19. BSA and IDC global software piracy study, 2004.
20. *Supra note 9, p. 309.*
21. *Ibid, pp. 312-13.*
22. BSA and IDC study on the benefit of reducing software piracy, 2003.
23. M. Blakeney, *Guidebook On Enforcement of Intellectual Property Right,* Queen Mary Intellectual Property Research Institute Queen Mary, University of London, UK, 2003, p. 10.
24. for details see; *http://www.siia.net/piracy/faq.asp;* accessed on September 25, 2006.
25. *Supra note* 9, p. 309.
26. Supra note19 p. 13; According to media reports, the FBI had compiled strong evidence that the terrorists who bombed the World Trade Center in 1993 financed their activities with counterfeit textile sales from a store located on Broadway in New York City.
27. *Supra note* 9, p. 11.
28. See for details proceedings of the Third Global Congress on Combating Counterfeiting and Piracy held in Geneva from 30 to 31 January 2007, details available at *http://www.wipo.int/edocs/prdocs/en/2007/wipo_pr_2007_475.html*
29. Article 28 of the Paris Convention, 1883 and Article 33 of the Berne Convention, 1886 respectively.
30. Supra note 9, p. 313.
31. *Supra note 9*, p. 309.
32. Article 1 of the draft Criminal measures directive.
33. Article 3 of the draft Criminal measures directive.
34. See Article 1, E. C. Software Directive.
35. See Article 7, E.C. Software Directive.
36. T. Vinje, *Should We begin Digging Copyright's Grave,* 2000, EIPR, Issue 12, pp. 551-562.

37. M. Ricolfi, *The Proposed IP Enforcement Directive: Tough on Legitimate Competitors, Weak against Pirates*, IIP, Anno II Fasc.1-2004, pp. 3-12.
38. *Ibid*, p. 4.
39. *Ibid*, p. 8.
40. The idea is to hide the very purpose of the code, thereby making it more difficult to understand and alter. This is a protection against reverse engineering, which may allow a pirate to duplicate more easily by analysing the code for protections against duplication and circumvent these. Obfuscation may be carried out statically, or it may be introduced as part of the executing code.
41. This occurs in most popular business and development software, for example Microsoft Office (Office 2002) and Macromedia Dream weaver (Dream weaver 2002).
42. It works as a system to guard against illegitimate modification of code by implementing a network of mutually reinforcing software agents within an executable program. The guards use checksums on key areas of code and on each other to ensure no modifications have taken place and take some action such as crashing the program if a modification is detected.
43. WIPO Copyright Treaty, Article 11 (Adopted December 20 1996).
44. For details See,Intellectual Property Crime Prevention initiatives in Singapore (on file with author, collected by email communication with Singapore Custom, Police and IPOS).
45. In fact the University law students under the supervision of Faculty members conduct all these street law classes. The author of this paper has the experience to conduct street law programs both as a student and faculty member as well. For details see, M.Azam, *Sharing the Experiences of Transformation of Legal Education in Bangladesh*, Seminar Paper, Global Alliance for Justice Education Conference, May 3-4, 2006, Fordham Law School, New York, USA.
46. An example of rights holder co-operation with the enforcement authorities is the establishment in the People's Republic of China of the Quality Brands Protection Committee (QBPC), which was founded in 2000. The QBPC consists of 76 foreign companies, such as Compaq, Siemens and Kodak, with investments in China totalling some $US 14 billion. The QBPC cooperates in the fight against counterfeiting with local administrations.
47. In Bangladesh, a number of copyright owners (especially software and audio-video) formed an organisation named after 'Movement Against Piracy(MAP)' which campaign against piracy around the country and with the aid of law enforcing agency visit different hot spots and super markest time to time to seize pirated software and CD-VCD; See for details, A report on the activities of MAP published in Daily Shamokal, January 15, 2007, Dhaka, Bangladesh.

48. See for details, A.Hirst, *The role of the Government authorities in the enforcement of Intellectual Property rights* , WIPO Workshop for Judges, Beirut, December 7, 1999.

49. Article 36(2) of the Statute of the International Court of Justice.

50. For details on the jurisdictional problems of the ICJ see, R.Anand, *ICJ and Contemporary conflicts*, New Delhi, 1974, N. Singh, *The role and Record of the ICJ*, Nijhoff Publishers, The Netherlands, 1989, R.Hoque, *Jurisdictional Problems of the ICJ: Towards an Alternative Framework of the ICJ*, BJL, Vol. 3, No.1, 1999.

51. For USA, January 1, 1995, For Singapore, January 1,2000 and for Bangladesh July 11, 2013 (for Pharmamceutical patents untill January 1, 2016).

52. Articles 41.1 and 9.1 of the TRIPs Agreement.

53. The establishment of a special IP court is not mandatory or not required by the TRIPS (art. 41.5).

54. See for details, F.K.Beier-G.Schricker (Eds.), *From GATT TO TRIPS-The Agreement on Trade Related Aspects of Intellectual P[roperty Rights, IIC Studies*, Max Planck Institute, Munich, Germany, 1996.

55. For example, in Bannana III case before the WTO-DSB, Ecuador received WTO authorisation to cross retaliate the EC(now EU) by targetting European Intellectual property rights and trade in services as well as product based tariffs. But the size and power of the Ecuadorian economy is not so strong to harm the EU countries. See for details, Dispute Settlement System under the WTO: An Appraisal, CU Journal of Law, Vol. VII, 2002, pp.107-120.

56. Review of US Legislation on Enforcement at the TRIPS Council, IP/ Q4/USA/1, December 18, 1998, p. 1.

57. In USA Customs officials are responsible for making their decisions in good faith in accordance with the authority granted to them by statute. Decisions of the Customs Service are review able in court under Chapter 7 of title 5 of the United States Code. A reviewing court can decide all relevant questions of law, interpret constitutional and statutory provisions, and determine the meaning or applicability of the terms of an agency action. Section 706(1) authorizes the court to compel action that it determines has been unlawfully withheld.

58. It is worth noting that US Congress's authority to legislate concerning copyright issues derives directly from the U.S. Constitution. Article 1, Section 8, Clause 8 of the Constitution grants to Congress the power to "promote the Progress of Science and the Useful Arts, by securing for limited times to authors and inventors the Right to their respective Writings and Discoveries." Congress codified modern copyright law with the U.S. Copyright Act of 1976; apart from the copyright protection, since Diamond Vs Diehr (450 US. 584, 1978) the US Patent and Trademark

office has taken a liberal view towards protection of software under the patent law. Software is also protected under the trade secret law.

59. *Ellis v. Diffie*, 177 F.3d 503, 506 (6th Cir. 1999).

60. *Wilcom Pty. Ltd. v. Endless Visions*, 128 F. Supp. 2d 1027, 1031 (E.D. Mich. 1998) and *Apple Computer, Inc. v. Franklin Computer Corp.*, 714 F.2d 1240, 1248-49 (3d Cir. 1983).

61. 2006 US Dist. LEXIS 32824, Case No-C035424JFCHRL.

62. 357 F.3d 1072, 1076 (9th Cir, 2004).

63. To prove a claim of direct copying infringement, a plaintiff must show that he owns the copyright and the defendant himself violated one or more of the plaintiff's exclusive rights under the copyright Act.

64. To prove a claim of contributory infrigement, a plaintiff must show that the defendant with knowledge of the infriging activity, 'induces, causes or materially contributes to the infringing conduct or another'.

65. A corporate officer may be held vicariously liable under the Copyright Act when: (1) the officer personally participated in the actual infringement; or (2) the officer derived financial benefit from the infringing activities as either a major shareholder in the corporation, or through some other means such as receiving a percentage of the revenues from the activity giving rise to the infringement; or (3) the officer used the corporation as an instrument to carry out a deliberate infringement of copyright; or (4) the officer was the dominant influence in the corporation, and determined the policies which resulted in the infringement; or (5) on the basis of some combination of the above criteria.

66. The US Department of Justice enforces the criminal provisions of US intellectual property laws. It deals with all enforcement of federal criminal laws, not just those dealing with intellectual property, but it does have specialists within the Department who deal with violations involving intellectual property.

    Section 509 of the Copyright Act, 17 U.S.C. § 509, provides for the seizure and forfeiture of infringing copies and articles of infringement used in criminal copyright infringement. Agents, officials or persons authorized by the US Attorney General, perform the seizures. These procedures can be instituted upon the government's showing of probable cause; a criminal indictment or criminal conviction is not required.

67. Case No. 00 Cr 85, United States District Court for the Northern District of Illinois, Eastern Division, 2001 U. S. Dist. Lexis 21119.

68. Review of Singapore Legislation on Enforcement at the TRIPS Council, IP/Q/SGP/1, September 20, 2000, p. 1.

69. Section 136 of the Copyright Act of Singapore.

70. From Official Communication with Singapore Police (on file with author)

71. Under section 4 of the Manufacture of Optical Discs Act, no party shall engage in the manufacture for sale or other commercial purpose of any CDs,VCDs, CD-ROMs, DVD-ROMs in any place except under the authority, and in accordance with the terms and conditions of a licence.
72. This regulation is very important to control piracy from the source/ root or point of origin. The penalties for a first conviction are a fine not exceeding S$ 100,000/-or upto 3 times value of goods, whichever is greater and /or imprisonment for up to 2 years. For a second conviction the fine payable shall not exceed S$200,000/-or upto 4 times value of goods, whichever is greater and/or imprisonment for upto 3 years.
73. In this case, the appellant appealed that the sentence inflicted on him was excessive. He was the managing director of a company selling electronic goods, was the sole partner actively involved in running the business. He was convicted on three charges of having in his possession for the purposes of trade articles with falsely applied trade marks under s 49(c) of the Trade Marks Act (the "TMA"). Three charges were taken into consideration for sentencing purposes. The appellant was sentenced to a total of 32 months' imprisonment.
74. The trial judge referred *OhCheng Hai v Ong Yong Yew* [1993] 3 SLR 930 at 937 case to consider what kind of punishment may be awarded.
75. The author collected information about this approach using email communication with IPOS, Singapore Custom and Police Authority.
76. The necessity of education programs side by side the role of police is reiterated by the A.Jong, Head of Singapore police forces IP Rights Branch: 'Our actions against pirates addressing the supply side of the piracy problem whereas education is also important to discourage the public and consumers from looking for and using pirated software'. (Communication with Singapore Police and collection of an interview of A. Jong, Head of Singapore police forces IP Rights Branch-on file with author).
77. As reported in International Intellectual Property Alliance 2007 Special 301 Report on Bangladesh: The local music companies are regularly complaining about growing piracy problems, especially the fact that music albums of the leading Bangladeshi music labels are being pirated in the outskirts of key urban areas. The music industry of Bangladesh is at the same time undergoing steady growth in terms of new music production companies in the sector. These companies aspire to create quality music and have no intention to engage in piracy, so protecting their interests should be paramount to the Bangladeshi government. As to broadcast piracy, the local television industry has also expanded with four new channels coming into operation, Channel One, Bangla Vision, Baisakhi, and STV.
78. *See Bangladesh Music Producers Take Law Into Own Hands To Fight Piracy*, August 17, 2006, at *http://www.channelnewsasia.com/stories/entertainment/ view/225343/1/html* (describing a record producer-launched "Movement

Against Piracy" campaign, raiding shops in the capital Dhaka and the southeastern port city of Chittagong to catch traders selling pirated CDs and cassettes, and quoting senior campaign member, and CEO of G-Series, Nazmul Haq, as saying, "we had no choice but to take the law into our own hands as piracy has almost sent our business to the graveyard. It's (a) matter of life and death for us"). Raids run by local industry revealed 99% piracy. Haq was further quoted as saying, "in the last four years alone, as many as 10 big and respected companies have had to close because of piracy."

79. In Bangladesh's Trade Policy Review at the World Trade Organization in September 2006 (minutes released in November 2006), the government of Bangladesh essentially indicated that it does not keep regular copyright enforcement statistics, but that "efforts are being made for collecting such data," that the records/data in relation to seizure or confiscation are maintained by Bangladeshi Customs manually in a register, but that there are other enforcement agencies like BDR (Bangladesh Rifles), Coast Guard and Police who are also responsible for enforcement of copyright regulations within their respective jurisdictions, and can supply such information "when available and [when] a request is received." In addition, the government noted that "since several agencies are involved in enforcement of copyright, no consolidated information [on raids, prosecutions, convictions, etc.] is available right now." With respect to optical disc plants and piracy, the government indicated that it took note of the concerns expressed in the report regarding optical disc manufacture in Bangladesh and would place the matter "under investigation." *See* World Trade Organization, Trade Policy Review Body, 13 and 15 September 2006, WT/TPR/M/168/Add.1 (published November 10, 2006).

80. In granting a temporary injunction, there has to be firstly, a prima facie case, secondly, the accrual of irreparable loss or injury and lastly, the balance of inconvenience in the favour of the petitioner.

81. Such an order may be passed on application by any party to the suit. An application by the plaintiff for such an order may be made after notice to the defendant at any time after the institution of the suit.

82. Section 16 of the Customs Act, 1969 provides that the Govt. by notification in the official Gazzette may prohibit or restrict importation of goods of specified description by air, land or sea. Section 17 of the same Act empowered the authority for the confiscation of the prohibited and pirated goods.

83. Goods specified under section 15 shall not be brought, whether by air or land or sea, into Bangladesh.

84. In respect of cognizable offences the police are authorized to initiate criminal proceedings on its own on information of the offence being committed. In the case of non cognizable offences, the police initiate criminal proceedings at the order of a magistrate to whom a complaint

has been made under Section 190 of the Code of Criminal Procedure, 1898.

85. Section 84 of the Copyright Act, 2000 as amended by section 38 of the Copyright (Amendment) Act, 2005 provides that person liable for software piracy shall be punishable with imprisonment which may extend to three years, or with fine which may extend to TK. three lac, or with both

86. Section 482-488 of the Penal Code, 1860.Section 486 provides that ... Whoever sells, or exposes, or has in possession for sale or any purpose of trade or manufacture, any goods or thing with a counterfeit trade mark or property mark be punished with imprisonment of either description for a term which may extend to one year, or with fine or with both.

87. Section 84-89 of the Copyright Act, 2000.

88. which is the court of first instance to deter piracy and software piracy as well. But judgment of this court is not reported in any law reports.

89. *Sunil Kumar Das Vs. Canon Kabushiki Kaisha*, 57 DLR, 2005 pp. 93-100, in this case the court held that new dimension has been added to traditional concept of local market. The world has become a small one for all practical purposes and one should not strictly adhere to the traditional concept of national/local market. There are free movement of the commodities and capitals. Keeping in mind all these factors, the law must be given a new interpretation to suit the needs of the day. Finally the court applied the well-known provision of the Paris Convention not to allow a national company from using a popular mark and thereby preventing imitation of marks.

90. WCT is yet to be ratified by Bangladesh.

91. Code of Civil Procedure and Code of Criminal Procedure enacted in 1908 and 1898 respectively.

92. Although Chittagong, Dhaka and Rajshahi University respectively offering intellectual property program and some awareness programs, all these are not adequate.

93. On and average to settle a dispute under the regular procedure of the court, it takes around 10 years due to huge backlog of cases and workload of the judges. Judges who supposed to decide IP infringement cases are already burdened with huge cases, therefore IP cases are given mostly low priority.

94. Bangladesh having a very long land and coastal border with India and Myanmar, it is very difficult by the Bangladesh Custom to prevent software piracy from the outside of borders without the active support of Custom of Indian and Myanmar. One of the Custom officials from Bangladesh (unwilling to disclose his identity) said in fact at least 50% of software piracy in Bangladesh can be eliminated with the active

support of Indian Custom to prevent entry of cheap blank optical discs and pirated software. (Field Visit on January 20-25, 2007). Unfortunately till date there is no cooperation regarding this and even it is not in the agenda of two countries while discussion among the Custom and border forces of two countries.

95. However in a recent case for piracy (by the successful invocation of the TRIPS agreement and WPPT) against the one Indian film director for piracy of the song of one Bangladeshi music group, Indian Court ruled in favour of Bangladeshi music group. This case gained a momentum to show that to some extent TRIPS would be beneficial for the Bangladesh to protect the creative works like software, songs, books of Bangladeshi authors in abroad; The Hon. Justice S. K. Mukherjee of Calcutta High Court took *prima facie* cognizance of the matter and passed an interim order on 19 May 2004. In his learned judgment, the justice ordered the respondents to remove the pirated song from the soundtrack of the movie *Murder*. The court order further barred the respondents from manufacturing, selling, distributing or marketing any music cassette or disc containing the song and the order as to award for damages was pending for final adjudication. See for details, (WTO Case Study 3 available in www.wto.org), A.K.Azad, Managing *The Challenges of WTO Participation: Rock 'N Roll In Bangladesh: Protecting Intellectual Property Rights In Music.*

96. However, Microsoft urges to include the provisions of the WCT in the TRIPS agreement to give them more weight for enforcement.

97. Cooperation with Interpol and WCO for IP crime should be strengthened.

98. This can be achieved by implementing software management policies to set an example that the private sector should follow. For a government to demonstrate its commitment to enforcing intellectual property protections in the private sector, it must demonstrate that it is willing to do so in the public sector as well.

99. For details on the importance of fair and reduced price of software as an alternative method to curb software piracy and ensure greater software protection, see, the study of A. Story, *Intellectual Property and Computer Software- A Battle of Competing Use and Access Visions for Countries of the South,* UNCTAD-ICTSD Project on Intellectual Property Rights and Sustainable Development, May 2004, Geneva, Switzerland.

ESTABLISHING A LINK BETWEEN TRADE AND THE PROTECTION OF HUMAN RIGHTS*

*Mohammad Naqib Ishan Jan***

1. INTRODUCTION

Trade may successfully be conducted in an environment that is free from human rights violations. Gross violation of human rights resulting from *inter alia* unfair trade policies of certain industrialized countries were the main cause of the First and the Second World Wars in 1930s and early 1940s respectively. No one wish to experience a Third World War for this war would be far more dangerous, more destructive than its predecessors and if it occurs all peaceful activities, including free trade may be halted. A secure and peaceful world in which free trade can prosper necessitates protection of all human rights whether these rights fall within the category of 'first', 'second' or 'third' 'generations of rights'[1]. These are legal rights and most of the States members of the World Trade Organizations (WTO) agreed while signing or ratifying 'international human rights instruments' to protect them. The protection of these rights ensures respect to the dignity and sanctity of human life and enables the States to prevent situations that threaten international peace and security. World's security, which is already under a threat by unjust and often illegal unilateral behaviour of certain powerful States against the weaker ones, may be worsened if States fail to adopt fair trading

---

* This paper was presented at the Regional Conference on Trade, WTO and Sustainable Development: A Cause for Concern?", 23-24 April 2007, Kuala Lumpur, Malaysia.

** Associate Professor, Ahmad Ibrahim, Faculty of Laws, International Islamic University Malaysia, LLB (IIUM), MCL (IIUM) & PH.D (IIUM), *naqib@iiu.edu.my*

policies or to avoid adopting among themselves trade agreements that are contrary to their international human rights obligations.

The question here is whether States parties to the WTO have taken international human rights obligations into account in formulating and implementing their international trade agreements, and if they have done so, which in some areas not, then the question is why today more than one billion people, mostly in the developing and least developed countries, are condemned in want of food, potable water, health care, education and other basic necessities of life. Condemning a great number of human beings in want of these basic necessities of life is surely amount to a total violation of human rights including all social, economic, cultural, civil and political rights. In spite of the fact that international human rights law and international trade law do enjoy certain shared features, yet it has been alleged that much of such a total violation of human rights is due to certain unfair aspects of the later law adopted by the WTO member States.

This paper, after briefly examining the shared features of both laws, discusses the areas where the two laws conflict with each other and thereafter explores the question as to which law shall prevail in case of conflict. The paper also examines the legality and the effectiveness of 'unilateral' or 'collective' trade related measures that are occasionally taken to 'improve human rights situations' in target states. In examining these questions the paper refers to both international human rights law (as contain in the United Nations Charter, International Bill of Rights[2] and international custom), and international trade law adopted by the WTO Member States. After analyzing the relevant rules of both laws, the paper concludes that there is link between free trade and the protection of human rights, including economic, social and cultural rights and that since 'the promotion and protection of human rights is a matter of priority for the international community', the WTO Member States must make sure that whatever trade policy they agreed upon or going to agree in future must not in any way compromise their capacity to respect their international human rights obligations and that the trade rules that they have adopted or going to adopt must be just and must not, in any way, undermine the protection of human rights.

2. COMMON CHARACTERISTICS OF INTERNATIONAL TRADE AND HUMAN RIGHTS LAWS

The linkage between international trade law and international human rights law is evident from their shared temporal and objective features. Both international human rights law and international trade law are post-World War II phenomena, as the international human rights law which codifies legal provisions governing 'human rights' in various 'international human rights instruments' was adopted immediately after the adoption of the WTO's predecessor, the General Agreement on Tariffs and Trade (GATT[3]). GATT was established by western nations on a provisional basis in 1947[4] and it remained the only multilateral instrument governing international trade until the establishment of the WTO in 1995[5]. GATT did pave the way for the liberalization of trade among its members helping them to reduce or eliminate a range of trade barriers that were in existence and it also made a freer trade to become an engine of economic, social and political growth in Europe and Japan. The formation of the GATT in 1947 was followed by the adoption of the Universal Declaration of Human Rights (UDHR) in 1948[6]. The UDHR, which is considered as the "spiritual parent" of human rights law [7], has inspired the adoption of the International Covenant on Civil and Political Rights (ICCPR)[8] and the International Covenant on Economic, Social and Cultural Rights (ICESCR)[9]. Of the WTO's 150 members 116 have ratified the ICESCR and 119 have ratified the ICCPR and therefore all these member States are legally bound to observe, respect and fulfill their human rights obligations under these treaties[10] in good faith[11].

The primary purposes of both international human rights law and international trade law were the prevention of the recurrence of the events of the Second World War which destroyed world's peace and security and caused massive human suffering and devastation[12]. States while adopting the United Nations Charter in 1945 expressed their determination in Preamble to the Charter:

> [T]o save succeeding generations from the scourge of war, which twice in our lifetime has brought untold sorrow to mankind, and to reaffirm faith in fundamental human rights, in the dignity and worth of the human person, in the equal rights of men and women and of nations large and small, and to establish conditions under which justice and respect for the obligations arising from treaties and other

sources of international law can be maintained, and to promote social progress and better standards of life in larger freedom.

One of the main purposes of the United Nations (UN), as spelt out in Article I (3) of its Charter, is the promotion of, and respect for human rights. The Charter in its Article 55 (c) obliges the UN to promote "universal respect and observance of human rights and fundamental freedoms for all". This is why all the UN members under Article 56 of the Charter "pledge themselves to take joint and separate action in cooperation with [UN] Organization for the achievement of the purposes set forth in Article 55". The use of the term 'pledge' implies a legal obligation[13] on the parts of Member States to work toward fulfillment of their obligation in respecting human rights[14].

The UDHR, which constitutes an authoritative interpretation of the UN Charter in relation to human rights[15], was adopted within months of the WTO's predecessor, the GATT. It too "sought to protect individuals from the abuses of the kinds millions in Europe and Asia had been subjected to in the 1940s, before and during the War"[16]. The main purpose behind establishing the GATT was also to protect individuals and nations from the reoccurrences of the beggar-my-neighbour policies as pursued by some countries in the past. The beggar-my-neighbour policies involved competitive devaluations, discriminatory trade barriers which led to a deep and persistent economic slump, the implosion of trade, the collapse of the international monetary system, and the termination of international lending as well as worsening domestic economic problems, including unemployment and inflation[17]. GATT was established with a hope of keeping the effects of the economic depression out of their countries that was threatening peace and security of these countries. Thus, both international human rights law and international trade law were aimed at removing the causes of insecurity, which were perceived to be the violation of human rights and the practice of unfair trading policies[18], including the policy of 'beggar-thy-neighbour' economic policy[19].

The international human right law and the international trade law, which were negotiated and adopted by sovereign States having binding effect on the member countries, require States to take active steps to create the conditions in which "free" trade can take place or respect for human rights can be guaranteed[20].

Both laws are based on non-discrimination; the rule of law; access to courts and adjudication of disputes; promotion of social welfare through peaceful cooperation among free citizens;[21] and the two sets of laws assume that if respected they will naturally lead to the increased general well-being of people all over the world[22].

3. AREAS OF CONFLICTS BETWEEN INTERNATIONAL HUMAN RIGHTS LAW AND TRADE LAW

Lately, however, some aspects of the WTO agreements have developed in isolation from human rights law failing to ensure the general well-being of all people for they adversely affect people's basic human rights. These agreements, which are the result of the 1986–94 Uruguay Round negotiations, signed at the Marrakesh ministerial meeting in April 1994, include the GATT 1994[23], the General Agreement on Trade in Services (GATS)[24] and the Agreement on Trade-Related Aspects of Intellectual Property Rights (TRIPs)[25]. These are the three pillars of the WTO that contain provisions which may adversely affects social, economic and cultural rights, particularly the right to food, right to health, right to education and right to development and if these rights are affected people's right to enjoy civil and political rights can also be frustrated[26]. For instance, WTO Agreements on Agriculture (AoA) contains provisions in it that badly affects the right to food to millions of people in the developing and least developed countries while Agreement on Trade-Related Aspects of Intellectual Property Rights (TRIPS) adversely affects the right to health. These are some of the areas of conflict between international trade law and human rights law that this paper seeks to explore.

3.1 WTO Agreement on Agriculture and its Effect on Human Rights

The Agreement on Agriculture (AoA), which was adopted during the Uruguay Round negotiations by the WTO member States in 1994 and came into force, like the other WTO agreements, in 1995[27], is based on three pillars, namely market access[28], domestic support[29] and export subsidies[30]. In its preamble, the AoA says the aims of WTO are to raise living standards, ensure full employment and increase incomes and that AoA, as part of the WTO Agreement, is meant to further these aims. The question here is whether the AoA has accomplished these lofty aims? Well, the proponents of the AoA are of the view that "liberalization in agriculture trade have beneficial effects for aggregate world income, as inefficiencies in production and trade will gradually be removed"[31]. The critics, however, disagree and say that from a human rights perspective the AoA has certain key failures:

> First of all the AoA is an export oriented agreement that puts emphasis on expanding production and exports, favouring transnational commodity traders and processors over small-scale agricultural sectors in the developing countries. In other words, it is not in any way improving the livelihoods of millions of people in the developing and least developed countries who are involved in agricultural production as it is very difficult for these people to export their products[32], but it rather benefits the privileged minorities that have access to resources, infrastructure, credit and foreign markets to export their agricultural goods.

Secondly, the AoA has increased the market power of transnational commodity traders and processors, while taking power away from the producers[33]. Giant Companies, like, for example, Cargill, which runs a huge financial services unit, a seed and fertilizer business and is one of the top three beef producers in the United States (US) running a worldwide transportation business, gain most of the share in the agricultural market by consolidating and acquiring productive resources and by extending their activities beyond simply producing. Giant companies that run 'vertically integrated businesses' are more interested in high sales volumes and to achieve this they sell sale their agricultural goods at low price on world market leaving farmers out of business and thereby deprive them to earn their basic necessities of life[34].

Finally, the AoA, despite its aim to avert dumping[35], has failed to prevent dumping. The Institute for Agriculture and Trade Policy (IATP), which has documented export dumping from United States based multinational corporations onto world agricultural markets for the last 15 years, says that the US is one of the world's largest sources of dumped agricultural commodities, such as wheat, corn (maize), soybean, rice and cotton[36]. These commodities are grown in the US and are dumped consistently since the WTO's inception in 1995 on the world market well below the cost of production[37]. Dumping, which is one of the most damaging of all current distortions in world trade, has created a situation where the agricultural products produced by small farmers in developing counties are put in competition with cheaper subsidized agricultural production from developed countries and thereby crippling the developing countries agricultural sector–a sector that is vital for food security, rural livelihoods, poverty reduction and the generation of foreign exchange. In a study on the impact of AoA in 14 countries, the UN Food and Agricultural Organization (FAO) concluded that:

> "For many developing countries, key agricultural sectors that were vital for the economy in terms of food security, employment, economic growth and poverty reduction, were being seriously eroded owing to the inability to compete with cheap imports [from the rich countries]"[38].

The AoA is, thus, unfair as it allows rich countries to protect their subsidies to agriculture, and at the same time dump the surpluses all over the developing and least developed countries depriving them of the right to control imports of food and other agricultural products, and also forces the governments of those countries to reduce and eventually end their subsidies to farmers[39]. Many developing countries, especially least developed countries, have liberalized well beyond WTO commitments while industrialized countries still heavily protect their agriculture through subsidies and tariff structures. Liberalization, if unilateral, results in 'food insecurity'[40], deprives people of the right to food and creates situations of poverty. Food security is best assured when food is locally produced, processed, stored and distributed, and is available on a continuous basis regardless of climatic and other variations.

The agricultural trade policy formulated under the AoA is therefore in conflict with international human rights law as the former has affected many internationally-recognized human rights, including the right to life, to food, to health, to work and to be free from discrimination. These rights, which are set out in the ICCPR, ICESCR, and the Convention on the Rights of the Child (CRC), are legally binding as most of the States in the world have ratified at least one of these treaties. Furthermore, States, while adopting the Millennium Development Goals, emphasized their commitment to combat poverty, hunger and disease[41]. A similar commitment was made in 2004 by 188 States members of the Food and Agriculture Organization (FAO)[42].

Since international human rights law requires States to respect, protect and fulfill human rights, including the right to food, they must abide by it and one way to do this is to formulate their agricultural trade policies in line with their obligation under international human rights law. States will be able to 'respect' human rights if they avoid taking actions that deprive people of their existing access to adequate standard of living. They will be able to 'protect' human rights if they formulate and enforce laws that prevent third parties, including powerful people and corporations, from depriving individuals of their access to adequate standard of living including food. States are not only obliged to respect and protect but they are also required observe human rights. Observance of human rights requires States to identify vulnerable sector of the society groups, particularly the poor, and implement policies to ensure that public service providers can meet their human rights obligations to provide everyone, whether poor or rich, with essential services, including food, potable water, health care and education. However, the ability of the public sector to provide these essential services to the public, as explained below, is adversely affected by the General Agreement on Trade in Services (GATS).

3.2 GATS and Human Rights

Prior to the adoption of GATS there was no services agreement in the GATT. GATS, which came into force with the founding of the WTO in 1995, is the first legally enforceable trade agreement that covers trade in services and investment. Its scope is wide, covering over 160 sectors of national life, from tourist attractions, to retail sales, to mail delivery, to insurance, including such critical sectors as telecommunications, water supply, energy, health and education. It allows foreign and domestic service providers to compete to provide services in all these areas. It basically considers all service activities as commodities that can be bought and sold for profit. This not only raises questions as to whether, e.g., water is a human right to be ensured or a commodity to be sold, but it also raises questions as to what is the role and responsibilities of governments in providing essential services to their populations. Historically, both governments of developed and developing countries felt it is their social contracts responsibilities to provide their populations with essential human services including health, education, water, electricity and social safety nets. Most of these public services are also human rights, which under the Universal

Declaration of Human Rights, governments are required to ensure for all persons living within their jurisdiction.

The concept of public service is slowly but surely being eroded in favour of private service provider by the general practice of liberalization of trade in services[43] and also by the legal requirements of the GATS. The 'national treatment obligation' provided by the GATS[44] requires a member country to subsidies public service including foreign private provider of the same service. The priorities of public and private providers of services are different and so are their services to the communities. The private sector is profit oriented having no obligation to provide services to rural areas or people in poverty while the public sector has the obligation of serving all citizens and therefore must often subsidize the service to ensure that it is available to everyone whether poor or rich. The poor would suffer if a WTO member country implement its GATS national treatment obligation by either subsidizing both public and private suppliers or by cutting out subsidies to public suppliers altogether. Consequently, those who can afford to buy the services will enjoy them and those who cannot afford to buy services will either experience diminished access or no service at all in that sector. For instance, in Bolivia, the city of Cochabamba privatized its water system by contracting it out to a foreign company. The result was an increase in the cost of water of close to 200%, making it a commodity available only to those who could afford it and disenfranchising the people who could not. The people rebelled and the city took back the water system.

Although Article 1 of GATS excludes "service supplied in the exercise of governmental authority" from the process of trade liberalization, the definition of government services under Article 1 (3) (c) of the GATS is very narrow as it include only those services which are supplied neither on a commercial basis, nor in competition with one or more service suppliers". Article 1 of the GATS appears to be vague as most public services, such as health and education, often have a fee and are provided by both public and private suppliers, and the ambiguity of language in this Article virtually leaves all public services open to liberalization and privatization. Liberalization of essential services, like water, health and education may surely benefit the transnational corporate service providers but it is not so helpful for realization of human rights as it adversely affects the poor.

GATS also targets domestic regulations limiting them to only "ensure the quality of the services."[45] Domestic regulations, which cover, for example, access to water, public safety, development, education and health, etc, must protect people's rights and to ensure certain social and cultural values and objectives. Domestic regulations must not be limited only to ensure the quality of the service but they must ensure that all people, whether rich or poor, have access to the necessary services. Therefore, there is a need for a strong governmental regulation in service sector to ensure these services to everyone not only to 'have' but also to 'have not'. These services, including potable water, education and health care, should not be categorized as commodities but they rather be kept as human rights.

3.3 WTO Agreement on TRIPS and its Effect on Human Rights

Health care-a component part of the right to health-is however adversely affected by the Agreement on Trade-Related Aspects of Intellectual Property Rights (TRIPS Agreement) as it contains rules that makes it difficult for the poor people, particularly in developing and least developed countries, to have access to affordable medicines. The TRIPS Agreement, which was adopted by WTO Members in 1994 and came into force on 1 January 1995, has a number of rules[46] and the relevant one here is its rule on patent that is the concern of human rights advocates because it grants exclusive rights over the manufacture, use or sale of an invention[47]. The rule on patent rights is controversial[48] in the sense that it can keep prices of drugs artificially high and thereby hindering the realization of the right to health and its underlying determinants including a wide range of socio-economic rights, such as access to nutritious food, potable water and healthy environment[49]. It has incapacitated the developing and least developed countries to have access to or provide medicines for their population, particularly the poor ones[50] and it has made them unable to meet their obligation under international human rights law to provide their people with appropriate health care which is a component part of their right to health.

The right to health, which is enshrined in Article 12 of the International Covenant on Economic, Social and Cultural Rights (ICESCR), Article 24 of the Convention on the Rights of the Child (CRC) and is further protected by other international and regional legal instruments, including the World Health Organization Constitution, the Convention on the Elimination of All Forms of Discrimination Against Women, the African Charter on Human and Peoples' Rights, as well as by several national constitutions[51], is meant to all people, whether they are rich or poor, whether they live in developed countries or in developing or least developed countries. In other words, it must be enjoyed by people everywhere. In practice, however, it is the rich people, mostly in the developed world, who fully enjoy this right while the poor people in other countries are mostly denied the full enjoyment of this fundament right and the denial of this right basically means the denial of all civil and political rights as well as social, cultural and economic rights. This is because when people suffer from ill-health and consequently, duc to un-accessibility of medicines, die, they neither enjoy their right to health nor they enjoy any other rights under international human rights law. It is sad to note, as pointed out by the World Health Organization (WHO), that an estimated one third of the world's population, mostly in the developing and least developed countries, lacks access to essential medicines, and that over 50 percent of people in poor countries in Africa and Asia do not have access to even the most basic essential drugs.

Access to essential medicines, which depends on sustainable financing, reliable supply systems and affordable prices, is already a serious challenge for the developing and least developed countries as these countries are poor and technologically least advanced. They are already unable to comply with their obligations under international human rights law–such as the obligation to ensure access to affordable medicines[52], access to adequate food[53] and access to educational materials[54]. The situation is worsened by the patent rule of the TRIPS[55] because it has caused monopoly situations[56], imposed various costs on developing countries including the cost of importing the drugs and its technology, as according to TRIPS, not only is the medication itself subject to patenting, but the processes and the technology used to implement the processes are patented as well.

Although the TRIPS Agreement allows countries to use certain key flexibilities[57], such as the granting of compulsory licenses in order to make cheaper generic versions of patented medicines or the parallel importation of patented medicines that are sold more cheaply in other countries, yet these flexibilities were not clarified and the monopoly situation was allowed to continue. Argentinean government, relying on these flexibilities, developed its intellectual property (IP) laws in a way that facilitated access to cheaper, generic medicines than the patented versions of the same medicines. But in June 2002, in response to US demands and subsequent to a complaint brought by the US to the WTO Dispute Settlement Mechanism (DSM[58]), Argentina revised its IP legislation in such a way as to curtail national production of generic medicines[59]. The threat of trade sanctions made Argentina cave in precisely at a moment when its people most needed low-cost medicines, following the severe economic crisis that started in late 2001[60]. Similar laws in South Africa and also Brazil which designed to facilitate access to generic medicines-which is the only factor that has resulted in sustainable price reductions for essential medicines - were challenged by giant pharmaceutical companies in 2001 before the national courts of these countries. However, these companies back down due to the public out cry[61].

The public outcry occasioned by the above cited cases also provided the impetus for the adoption, at the WTO's Fourth Ministerial Conference in Doha in late 2001, of the Declaration on the TRIPs Agreement and Public Health (Doha Declaration[62]). The Doha Declaration, *inter alia*, acknowledges that the TRIPs Agreement does not and should not prevent Members from taking measures to protect public health, and recognizes Members' right to protect public health and to promote access to medicines for all[63]. Later, on 30th August 2003, the WTO General Council decided to implement paragraph 6 of the Doha Declaration on the TRIPS Agreement[64], which aimed at enabling countries without pharmaceutical manufacturing capacity to obtain generic medicines under compulsory license[65].

In spite of the Doha Declaration, "stringent IP laws are still being implemented around the world in a way that makes it harder for the needy to access medicines, i.e. in a way that is inconsistent with human rights"[66]. Even certain developing and least developed countries have been indirectly forced by WTO to agree to implement the stringent rules of the TRIPS and halt immediately their use of affordable generic versions of new medicines[67]. These countries had to pay this price in order to gain WTO membership and this means they are indirectly forced to halt immediately the use of such medicines. The compulsion is made despite the fact that the Doha Declaration allows Least Developed Countries (LDCs) to wait until 20016 to halt the use of such medicines[68]. Cambodia, for example joined the WTO under such a compulsion[69]. Although a WTO Deputy Director-General later on said that Cambodia could maintain its 2016 deadline in its patent law[70], yet "the basic concern about pressure to adopt stringent IP requirements remains"[71]. Nepal, a least developed country, joined the WTO in 2003 and had to agree to implement the TRIPs agreement by January 1st 2007[72]. Other countries that are undergoing negotiation to join the WTO "are also being asked to make stringent IP commitments and thus negatively affect a range of human rights including the rights to health"[73].

The situation is worsened by certain bilateral and regional trade agreements. For instance, "the US and its pharmaceutical industries have made access to antiretroviral therapy for HIV/AIDS harder by pushing for more stringent IP requirements in regional trade agreements like the Free Trade Area of the Americas (FTAA) and the US-Central American Free Trade Agreement (CAFTA), which would restrict competition from generic medicines"[74]. The US entered into parallel agreements with Morocco, Thailand, and some southern African States, imposing similar restrictions on them. These free trade may trade away the lives of millions for commercial profit, put lifesaving treatment out of reach of all but the wealthy[75], undermine the Doha Declaration and contradict human rights obligations.

Thus, the stringent trade-related intellectual property rules of the TRIPS Agreement still remains a major source of concern for those who really cares about human rights, particularly the right to health. These rules have made access to essential medicines difficult for all and increasingly more so for many of those who most need them and by doing so it hinders the realization of the right to health in so many countries, particularly in the developing and least developed ones. A careful analysis of the TRIPS rules on patents has lead Amnesty International to say that the strict enforcement of TRIPS general rules, particularly rules on pharmaceutical patents, can and often do hinder access to essential medicines for all, especially for poor[76], and if this is the case, which surely is, governments which implement these rules risk violating the right to the highest attainable standard of health.

The TRIPS Agreement undoubtedly allow certain latitude in patent policy by making certain exceptions in its Articles 7[77], 8[78] and 27[79], but the applicability of these exceptions to a broader range of human rights concerns depend on how these exceptions are interpreted. It is sad to note, however, that the DSM of WTO often ignored the wordings of the TRIPs Agreement about balance and mutual advantage by interpreting its patent provisions largely from the perspective of intellectual property rights holders rather than from the perspective of competing social interests (such as, e.g., protection of life and health)[80].

In interpreting the TRIPS Agreement the DSM must follow the interpretative methodology provided by the relevant provisions of the Vienna Convention on the Law of Treaties (VCLT), as these methods may help the WTO to assess the human rights applicability of the exceptional clauses of the TRIPS[81]. TRIPS Agreement is a treaty and according to the VCLT every treaty "shall be interpreted in good faith in accordance with the ordinary meaning to be given to the terms of the treaty in their context and in the light of its object and purpose."[82] The term "human life or health", as appeared in the TRIPS' exceptional clauses, has an ordinary meaning which is broad and may include a number of human rights, including the right to life, right to health, and other social, economic and cultural rights. Article 25 (1) of the Universal Declaration of Human Rights provides that:

> Everyone has the right to a standard of living adequate for the health and well-being of himself and of his family, including food, clothing, housing and medical care and necessary social services, and the right to security in the event of unemployment, sickness, disability, widowhood, old age or other lack of livelihood in circumstances beyond his control."

These wide range of economic, social and cultural rights are surely connected to the concept of "human life and health" and they must be protected even if their protection requires taking of necessary trade measures. Article XX of the GATT allows a state to protect public health in its own country by imposing trade measures[83]. For instance in the *EC - Asbestos case*[84], where the goal of the import ban for asbestos containing substances was the protection of the health of workers in France[85]. Although in the case involving restrictions on the import of foreign cigarettes into Thailand the WTO dispute settlement Panel held that the ban on cigarette imports was not justified under article XX (b) of the GATT since such a measure could not be shown to have actually reduced the level of smoking in the country, yet the Panel noted that this provision clearly allowed contracting parties to give priority to human health over trade liberalization" as long as the measure taken to promote such an aim was necessary. The Panel noted that a ban on cigarette advertising was, in general, warranted on public health grounds and could be justified under article XX (b) of the GATT[86]. These cases clearly indicate that States have a broad discretion to take trade related measures to protect the life or health of their own population in their own country provided they are able to show a genuine health risk and a trade measure that genuinely tackles that risk.

4. UNILATERAL OR COLLECTIVE TRADE RELATED MEASURES *VIS-À-VIS* HUMAN RIGHTS

The question here is whether a State can take 'unilateral' trade related measures 'to improve human rights situation' in another country. Are such measures, which include prohibition or restriction of economic relation that are common nowadays, legal under international law? Are they effective? Do they really improve human rights situations? Or do they back fire? If it is the later, which surely is, why then they are taken in the name of human rights? Are such unilateral measures allowed by the United Nations (UN) Charter or by the WTO law? Well neither the UN Charter nor the WTO law allows such a unilateral measure in the name of human rights. Although the WTO law allows a State to protect public health in its own country by imposing trade measures[87], it does not allow such a State to take trade related measures or impose trade sanctions in the name of human rights against another country. For instance, the *US–Tuna case I* stated that measures with extraterritorial effects are prohibited, as they would allow Member States to unilaterally determine the life and health policies of other Member States[88]. In *Tuna Dolphin* II, the WTO Dispute Settlement Panel considered the application of a national standard extraterritorially as too strict, and thus in violation of criteria set forth under Article XX (b) and (g) of the GATT, as it forced other countries to adopt the US policy[89]. In the *Turtle Shrimp case,* the conservation measure for sea turtles was accepted, as there was at least a potential territorial effect, because sea turtles are a migratory species. However, it did not fulfill the criteria of the chapeau of Article XX, as the conservation measure was again too restrictive[90]. This jurisprudence is consistent, because it addresses the concern of the Dispute Settlement institutions in preventing States from using trade-restrictive measures to force other WTO Members to apply the imposing State's national standards, which may make a product more expensive. Similar concepts would most likely be applied, if Member States tried to force other States to implement certain health, social, and/or labor standards.

Surely, the collective security system under Chapter VII of the United Nations Charter allows the UN Security Council to impose trade restrictions or sanctions against a country that grossly violate the human rights of its population to the extent that threatens world peace. The collective trade related human rights measures are legal under both the UN Charter and the WTO law[91]. But are they effective? The answer to the last question appears to be no because in a number of situations where the Security Council imposed trade related sanctions[92] most of them backfired or failed to improve human rights situation in the targeted country[93]. Such measures instead of improving human rights situation or help the protection of them inflicts grave hardships upon the people of the countries at which they are aimed and as such they should not be imposed even by the UN Security Council.

5. CONCLUSION

Protection of human rights ensures world's peace which is a condition for the success, prosperity and the effectiveness of international free trade. International free trade if regulated, managed, conducted, and interpreted fairly it would enable the international community, particularly the Members of the WTO, to observe, respect and fulfill their obligations under international human rights law. No State should be coerced to enter into unfair international trade agreement as coercion vitiates consent. The WTO as a responsible international organization must avoid pressuring States, particularly the developing and the least developed nations, to adopt trade agreements that would reduce the ability of such States to observe their international human rights obligations. States, with the help of international human rights institutions or organizations, such as the Human Rights

Council and the World Health Organization, should carry out human rights impact assessments before signing on to trade agreements. They should sign only those trade agreements which would ensure respect for the enjoyment of all human rights, irrespective of whether these rights fall within the category of civil, political, social, economic or cultural rights as these rights are universal and indivisible. In other words, trade agreements, which States would adopt, must be human rights compliance.

The provisions of the existing international trade agreements, like AoA, TRIPS and GATS, that are apparently not human rights compliance should be interpreted by the WTO's dispute settlement body in good faith so as to ensure that they too are receptive to human rights values or that they respect the enjoyment of human rights. Trade, as the driving engine of globalization, must be governed by at least rules that do not violate human rights but rather promote and protect them. Human rights are legally binding rights as the WTO agreements are and they both are enforceable. In case of conflict, human rights have legal priority over trade agreements because human rights are included as one of the main purposes of the UN Charter. Article 103 of the Charter provides that the obligations created under the Charter prevail over the obligations created under all other international agreements. For these reasons, the provisions of the WTO/GATT should be interpreted in a fashion receptive to human rights values.

Human rights are not only legally binding rules but they are also ethical principles having moral force. Both, as ethical principles and legal obligations, human rights play important role in furthering the cause of fairness, justice, reasonableness *vis-à-vis* trade negotiations. The developing and least developed States may invoke human rights principles to balance the unrestrained economic and political power of the powerful states that are at play in international trade policy makings. They may remind their powerful counter parts at trade negotiations that they have legal and moral obligations to protect the human rights of their populations and as such they may not be able to compromise these rights with unfair trading policies. At the same time, human rights must not be abused, as some States do by taking unilateral trade related measures or imposing sanctions against developing and least developed States in the name of promoting human rights. Such measures do not promote human rights but are rather the cause of violation of human rights. Therefore, such measures should be avoided at all time.

Notes

1. Human rights are divided into three generations: 'first generation of rights' (civil and political rights), 'second generation of rights' (social, economic or cultural rights); and 'third generation of rights' (or peoples rights including the right to development). See Abdul Ghafur Hamid @ Khin Maung Sein, *Public International Law: A Practical Approach*, Pearson Prentice Hall, 2006, at 366.
2. The entire human rights corpus is based on the Universal Declaration of Human Rights, the International Covenant on Civil and Political Rights, and the International Covenant on Economic, Social and Cultural Rights, the trio of documents referred to as the International Bill of Human Rights. See below notes 6-8.
3. General Agreement on Tariffs and Trade, Oct. 30, 1947, Art. XX (e), 61 Stat. 5, A3, T.I.A.S. 1700, 55 UNTS. 187, *available at http://www.wto.org* [hereinafter GATT].
4. GATT was established on a provisional basis in 1947 in the wake of other new multilateral institutions dedicated to international economic cooperation - notably the "Bretton Woods"- institutions that are now known as the World Bank (WB) and the International Monetary Fund (IMF).
5. *See* Agreement Establishing the World Trade Organization, Apr. 15, 1994, 108 Stat. 4809, 4815, 33 I.L.M. 1125, 1144 (1994) [hereinafter WTO Agreement].
6. UNGA Res. 217A (III), Dec. 10, 1948 (hereinafter 'UDHR'). The UDHR consist of 30 articles proclaiming therein civil and political rights as well as economic, social and cultural rights. Articles 3-21 of the UDHR establishes the civil and political rights including the rights to life, liberty and the security of the person; the prohibition against slavery, torture and cruel, inhuman or degrading treatment; freedom from arbitrary arrest and detention; the presumption of innocence and the right to a fair trial; and the freedom of speech, thought, religion, belief, conscience, assembly, movement and association. Articles 22-27 of the UDHR provides for economic, social and cultural rights, including the right to social security, the right to work, the right to equal pay for equal work, the right to education, the right to rest and leisure, the right to security in the event of disability and unemployment, the right to health and the right to take part in the cultural life of the community. All these civil, political, social, economic and cultural rights are important as the UDHR makes no distinction and creates no hierarchy among them. These rights are universal and are meant to 'everyone'. 'All persons' are entitled to enjoy them and 'no one' shall be denied of these rights.

7. See Henry J. Steiner, 'Political Participation as a Human Right', 1 *Harv. Hum. Rts. Y. B.* 77, 79 (1988), has described the UDHR as the "spiritual parent" of other human rights treaties.
8. UNGA Res. 2200 (XXI), Dec. 19. 1966, entered into force March 23, 1976 (hereinafter cited as 'ICCPR').
9. UNGA Res. 2200 (XXI), Dec. 19. 1966, entered into force March 23, 1976 (hereinafter cited as 'ICESCR').
10. *See Vienna Convention on the Law of Treaties, 1969* 1155 UNTS 331 (hereinafter: "the 1969 Vienna Convention), Art 26. Article 26 of this Convention provides: "Every treaty in force is binding upon the parties to it and must be performed by them in good faith". Article 26 of he 1969 Vienna Convention is based on the doctrine of *Pacta Sunt Servanda* or the customary rule that treaties are binding on the parties and must be performed in good faith.
11. The principle of Good faith, which requires fairness, reasonableness, integrity and honesty in international behaviour, is of fundamental importance for the conduct of international relations in general and is therefore recognized as an international principle under the 1969 Vienna Convention on the Law of Treaties. See the Preamble to the 1969 Vienna Convention, *ibid.*
12. One of the main causes of such a devastation and insecurity in Europe was perceived to be the practice of 'Beggar-thy-neighbour' economic policy. This policy was blamed for the rise of fascism, and ultimately, the outbreak of WWII. The prevention of the reoccurrence of such a destructive event necessitated the adoption of a fair international trading regime.
13. Akehurt's *Modern Introduction to International Law*, 7th ed., Routledge, London, 2000, at 212.
14. *Ibid.*
15. See M. Tsamenyi, "Papua New Guinea and the West Irianese Border Crossers" (Paper presented at the 39th Annual AULSA Conference, University of Queen land, 26-29 Aug. 1984) 16-18. Tsamenyi is cited in D. Rickard, 1985, "Papua New Guineas's Obligations under Customary International Law Towards West Papuan Refugees Within Its Territory" Law-Asia, 1984, 48 AT 67.
16. Caroline Dommen, 'Raising Human Rights Concerns in the World Trade Organization Actors, Processes and Possible Strategies', *Human Rights Quarterly 2001.*
17. *Ibid.*
18. "To a great extent, the rationale for the creation of the GATT in 1947 was to prevent a repeat of the trade wars of the 1930s, not to mention the World War II that followed." Bernard, M. Hoekman & Michael M. Kostecki, *The Political Economy of the World Trading System* 2 (1995).

19. *Ibid.*

20. In the human rights field, governments must, for instance, ensure that there is a trained judiciary, that laws protecting against arbitrary detention are in place, or that public health policies exist. Likewise, in the trade field governments must ensure that institutions allowing for the review of administrative decisions affecting trade are established and maintained, and must publish their trade regulations.

21. Ernst-Ulrich Petersmann, *The WTO Constitution and Human Rights*, 3 J. INT'L ECONOMIC L. 19, 19 (2000).

22. As one of the WTO's Ministerial Declaration reads: "We believe that economic growth and development fostered by increased trade and further trade liberalization contribute to the promotion of [core labour] standards". See *Singapore Ministerial Declaration*, 13 December 1996, on the web at *<www.wto.org/english/thewto_e/minist_e/min96_e/wtodec.htm>*

23. The GATT 1994 is an updated version of the original GATT, revised and refined before its incorporation into the WTO framework. The GATT 1994 regulates ***trade in goods***, and is complemented by a host of smaller agreements that also apply to trade in goods. GATT 1994 reflects many of the developments that occurred under the original GATT since 1947. Therefore, it is the most developed of the three "pillar" agreements.

24. *See* General Agreement on Trade in Services, Apr. 15, 1994, 108, Stat. 4809, 4815, 33 I.L.M. 1167 (1994), *available at http://www.wto.org* [hereinafter GATS Agreement]. GATS Agreement, which is a new international trade agreement, setting out the rules for trade in services, pose significant danger for the campaign to realize universal human rights.

25. *See* Agreement on Trade-Related Aspects of Intellectual Property Rights, Apr. 15, 1994, Marrakesh Agreement Establishing the World Trade Organization, Annex 1C, Legal Instruments—Results of the Uruguay Round vol. 31, 33 I.L.M. 81 (1994), *available at* http://www.wto.org [hereinafter TRIPs Agreement].

26. "It has been part of UN doctrine that the entire family of rights—civil and political as well as economic, social and cultural—are indivisible....At the UN World Conference on Human Rights, which was held in Vienna in 1993, over 180 countries affirmed that all human rights are "universal, indivisible and interdependent and inter-related." The Vienna Declaration and Programme of Action goes on to assert that "while the significance of national and regional particularities and various historical, cultural and religious backgrounds must be borne in mind, it is the duty of states regardless of their political, economic and cultural systems to promote all human rights and fundamental freedoms", Considering the opposition of some states to the notion of universality, the strength and clarity of this wording is significant" . Robert Howse and Makau Mutua, Protecting Human Rights in a Global

Economy: Challenges for the World Trade Organization, 2000, available at *http://lic.law.ufl.edu/~hernandez/Trade/Howse.pdf*

27. Most of the WTO agreements are the result of the 1986–94 Uruguay Round negotiations, signed at the Marrakesh ministerial meeting in April 1994. There are about 60 agreements and decisions totaling 550 pages. Negotiations since then have produced additional legal texts such as the Information Technology Agreement, services and accession to protocols.

28. Market access, which aims to reduce border obstacles to imports of agricultural products, such as taxes and duties, is commonly known as tariffs. Also, countries had to abolish restrictions on the quantity of agricultural goods entering their markets. All other barriers that were not tariffs, known as 'non-tariff barriers' and including health standards or packaging requirements, had to be converted into tariffs, a process known as "tariffication." The Special Safeguard (SSG) is a tariff mechanism that provides temporary protection against sudden import surges or falls in world prices. However, only countries that underwent tariffication can apply the SSG. Many countries, particularly developing countries, did not undergo tariffication because they did not have a significant amount of non-tariff barriers. In Asia, only Korea, Malaysia, the Philippines, Taiwan and Thailand are eligible to use the SSG – the rest are left with no mechanism to protect themselves from floods of food imports.

29. Domestic support refers to the subsidies which governments give to farmers for specific agricultural products, or for agricultural infrastructure and research. Developed countries are the major providers of domestic support for their farmers. Its objective was to reduce the amount of money going into production of farm goods that are subsequently exported or reduced subsidies that distort the otherwise free trade of agricultural products.

30. The AoA's approach to export subsidies is to list the export subsidies that WTO Members have to reduce, and to ban the introduction of new subsidies. Export subsidies are harmful because they directly support exporters, most commonly agribusinesses or transnational commodity traders, enabling them to displace local producers – most commonly small-scale farmers in the countries to which they sell their goods – with artificially cheap products.

31. *The Agreement on Agriculture and Food Agricultural Policy Options of Developing Countries*, paper presented at ACICI conference on the Uruguay Round Agreements (September 22-23 1998).

32. There is no guarantee that food produced for export to rich countries will be accepted. Access to developed country markets for developing country products depends on producers being able to meet specific international standards, such as on food safety or packaging. Many developing countries do not have the capacity or infrastructure to meet

these standards, which are high and result in limiting developing country exports.

33. Carin Smaller *et al.*, 'Planting the Rights Seed: A human rights perspective on agriculture trade and the WTO', Backgrounder No. 1 in the THREAD series, available at *http://www.3dthree.org/pdf_3D/Backgr1webEn.pdf*

34. *Ibid*. See also The Realization of Economic, Social and Cultural Rights, Written Statement Submitted by the Centre Europe Tiers-Monde, Sub-Commission on Promotion and Protection of Human Rights.

35. "The AoA ...aims to address dumping by decreasing State subsidies that affect production and prices, but this does not stop dumping for a number of reasons. On the one hand, the complex box system has enabled developed countries to keep a large portion of their State subsidies. On the other hand, the AoA rules do not address the root causes of dumping, namely excess production and the market power of corporations. In addition, it is complicated and time-consuming for countries to take action against dumping. For instance, a country must have domestic anti-dumping laws in place in order to impose import duties on dumped products, and many developing countries have no such laws, and their only recourse is then to turn to the WTO dispute settlement system, which can take up to four years to issue a ruling. This is further complicated by the fact that WTO Members are still struggling to define which payments to farmers should be allowed by WTO rules. Dumping is a human rights issue because farmers in developing countries are unable to protect themselves against dumping. Coupled with the lack of social safety nets, this has caused serious human rights concerns since the implementation of the AoA, particularly for small-scale farmers who lose their livelihoods due to competition from subsidized, dumped imports. The human rights framework calls for governments to implement safety nets, and requires of States that they implement policies that pay particular attention to the needs of the poor.17 Whilst there are certainly cases where governments are simply unwilling to implement such policies, liberalization commitments made at the WTO (and at the World Bank and the IMF), also prevent countries from being able to design and determine their own national policy strategies which might address the problems at the border, for instance through raising tariffs, or imposing import quotas to protect against import surges". Carin Smaller *et al., ibid.*

36. See Sophia Murphy, Ben Lilliston and Mary Beth Lake, 'WTO Agreement on Agriculture: A Decade of Dumping', published by The Institute for Agriculture and Trade Policy, 2005. This publication is available at *http://www.un-ngls.org/cso/cso7/library.pdf*

37. "In 2003, agriculture exports continued to be sold well below the cost of production: Wheat was exported at an average price of 28 percent below cost of production. Soybeans were exported at an average price of 10 percent below cost of production. Corn was exported at an average price

of 10 percent below cost of production. Cotton was exported at an average price of 47 percent below cost of production. Rice was exported at an average price of 26 percent below cost of production", *ibid*.

38. See the Gender and Trade Network in Africa © 2006: By Elijah Wachira.

39. See *The Agreement on Agriculture and Food Agricultural Policy Options of Developing Countries*, paper presented at ACICI conference on the Uruguay Round Agreements (September 22-23 1998).

40. Food Security is defined as having the means as an individual, family, community, region or country adequately to meet nutritional needs on a daily and annual basis. It includes freedom both from famine and chronic malnutrition. Food security is best assured when food is locally produced, processed, stored and distributed, and is available on a continuous basis regardless of climatic and other variations. *(NGO Treaty, the United Nations Conference on Environment and Development, 1992).*

41. UN, Millennium Development Goals, 2000, available at www.un.org/millenniumgoals. The *Millennium Forum Statement* reads: "The Millennium Forum reiterates the call to realize "all human rights for all" and reaffirms the positions taken at the many World Conferences of the 1990s, that: all human rights are universal, indivisible, interdependent and interrelated; women's rights are human rights; special recognition and protection must be given to the rights of children, indigenous peoples, minorities, elderly persons, persons with disabilities, people with different sexual orientations, persons living with HIV/AIDS, and refugees and internally displaced persons; and greater attention needs to be paid to economic, social and cultural rights, including the right to development, because these have been largely neglected in the past. We also reaffirm the need for universal ratification of all international human rights instruments; the need for universal fulfillment of the human rights commitments and obligations set out in the *Vienna Declaration and Programme of Action*, and in declarations and programmes of action of the UN Global Conferences from Rio to Rome" (*Millenium Forum Statement*, p. 1.)

42. FAO, Voluntary Guidelines to Support the Progressive Realization of the Right to Adequate Food in the Context of National Food Security, 2004. <*www.fao.org/righttofood*>

43. *See* Anne Orford, *Contesting Globalization: A Feminist Perspective on the Future of Human Rights, in* The Future of International Human Rights 157, 157 (Burns H. Weston & Stephen P. Marks eds., 1999) (noting human rights law was not designed to consider as human rights violations those abuses that take place in the private sector).

44. See GATS Agreement, *supra* note 24, Arts. I:2 (d), II:1. National treatment is a specific obligation and only applies to service sectors in which a country has made a GATS commitment. GATS member must "grant foreign services and service supplies treatment no least favorable" that

domestic services and suppliers. This measure outlaws any regulations which would give preference or competitive advantage to the domestic service industry and means that "certain foreign suppliers would also be entitled to receive any subsidies given to competing domestic suppliers" (WTO).

45. See GATS Agreement, GATS, Article VI (4) (b).

46. The TRIPS Agreement, which is one of the three pillars of the WTO (the others being trade in goods and trade in services), covers *inter alia* copyright, trademarks, geographical indications, patents, plant variety protection and it sets out the procedures and remedies which should be available in Member States to enforce intellectual property rights (IPRs). The TRIPS Agreement, like the other parts of the WTO Agreement, is subject to the WTO's Dispute Settlement Mechanism (DSM). It incorporates the WTO principles of non-discrimination (most-favoured nation and national treatment) and transparency, and establishes minimum standards of protection to creators of intellectual property (IP). Unlike other WTO Agreements, the TRIPs Agreement imposes obligations on its Members to pursue specific, similar policies. The standards established under the TRIPs Agreement are *minimum* standards in the sense the Members can introduce stricter, or other forms of protection that are not included in the Agreement.

47. See An overview of the World Trade Organization (WTO) Agreement on Trade-Related (Aspects of) Intellectual Property Rights (TRIPS), *http://www.wto.org*

48. See WTO Agreements and Public Health, a joint study by the WHO and the WTO Secretariat, 2002, p. 23; Carlos M. Correa, Implementing National Public Health Policies in the Framework of WTO Agreements, 34 The Journal of World Trade, 2000, p. 89. Normally, "public health" refers to all organized measures (whether public or private) to prevent disease, promote health, and prolong life of the population as a whole.

49. *General Comment No 14 (XX00), The Right to the Highest Attainable Standard of Health,* Committee on Economic, Social and Cultural Rights, E/C.12/XX00/4, 11 August XX00.

50. See generally Keith E. Maskus, Intellectual Property Rights in the Global Economy, Institute for International Economics,XX00; Carlos M. Correa, Intellectual Property Rights, The WTO and Developing Countries: The TRIPs Agreement and Policy Options, Zed Books Ltd., XX00; Jayashree Watal, Intellectual Property Rights in the WTO and Developing Countries, Oxford University Press, XX01; W. Leaster, The Effects of TRIPS-Mandated Intellectual Property Rights on Economic Activities in Developing Countries, WIPO Research Paper, XX01.

51. See Virginia A. Leary, *Justiciability and Beyond; Complaint Procedures and the Right to Health,* 55 International Commission of Jurists Review 105, 106, 107 and 118-119 (1995).

52. The right to health is enshrined in article 12, International Covenant on Economic, Social and Cultural Rights (ICESCR) article 24 of the Convention on the Rights of the Child (CRC). It is further interpreted by the Committee on Economic, Social and Cultural Rights' (ICESCR) General Comment No. 14 (2000) and the Committee on the Rights of the Child (CRC) General Comments No. 3 (2003) on HIV/AIDS and the rights of the Child and No.4 (2003) on Adolescent Health.

53. The right to food is enshrined in article 11 ICESCR and article 27 CRC. It is further developed in ICESCR General Comment No. 12 (1999).

54. The right to education is enshrined in article 13 ICESCR and article 28 CRC, and is further interpreted by General Comment No. 13 (1999).

55. A patent is a set of exclusive rights granted by a state to a patentee (the inventor or assignee) for a fixed period of time in exchange for the regulated, public disclosure of certain details of a device, method, process or composition of matter (substance) (known as an invention) which is new, inventive, and useful or industrially applicable. It is defined by the WTO as providing "the patent owner with the legal means to prevent others from making, using, or selling the new invention for a limited period of time, subject to a number of exceptions."

56. According to WHO "patents are by no means the only barriers to access to life-saving medicines, but they can play a significant, or even dominant, role in that they grant the patent holder a monopoly on a medicine for the number of years the patent is in force". See WHO/UNAIDS/MSF, "Determining the patent status of essential medicines in developing countries", *Health Economics and Drugs*, EDM Series, No. 17, 2004 (WHO/EDM/PAR/2004.6), p. 7.

57. The flexibilities include: (a) In applying the customary rules of interpretation of public international law, each provision of the TRIPS Agreement shall be read in the light of the object and purpose of the Agreement as expressed, in particular, in its objectives and principles. (b) Each member has the right to grant compulsory licences and the freedom to determine the grounds upon which such licences are granted. (c) Each member has the right to determine what constitutes a national emergency or other circumstances of extreme urgency, it being understood that public health crises, including those relating to HIV/AIDS, tuberculosis, malaria and other epidemics, can represent a national emergency or other circumstances of extreme urgency. (d) The effect of the provisions in the TRIPS Agreement that are relevant to the exhaustion of intellectual property rights is to leave each member free to establish its own regime for such exhaustion without challenge, subject to the MFN and national treatment provisions of Articles 3 and

58. In the WTO, dispute settlement is the responsibility of the Dispute Settlement Body (DSB or the General Council in another guise). The DSB establishes panels of experts to consider the case, and then accepts or rejects panels' findings. The final appeal is to a permanent Appellate

Body (AB) consisting of seven independent expert members. Both the dispute settlement panels and the Appellate Body have a fairly wide discretion to receive submissions from interested third parties. These submissions are known as *amicus curiae* ("friend of the court") briefs.

59. Julien Reinhard (2003) 'Santé en Argentine–Dépression locale et pressions globales,' 169 *Solidaire*. For similar cases, see Sarah Joseph (XX03) 'Pharmaceutical Corporations and Access to Drugs,' 25 *Human Rights Quarterly*.

60. Caroline Dommen, 'The WTO, international trade, and human rights', available at *http://www.3dthree.org/pdf_3D WTOmainstreamingHR.pdf*

61. *Ibid*

62. WTO, the Doha Ministerial Declaration on the TRIPS Agreement and Public Health, WT/MIN(01)/DEC/2, 14 November XX01.

63. *Ibid*.

64. WTO, Implementation of Paragraph 6 of the Doha Declaration on the TRIPS Agreement and Public Health, Decision of the General Council of 30 August 2003, WT/L/540, 1 September 2003.

65. Paragraph 6 of the Doha Declaration provides: "We recognize that WTO members with insufficient or no manufacturing capacities in the pharmaceutical sector could face difficulties in making effective use of compulsory licensing under the TRIPS Agreement. We instruct the Council for TRIPS to find an expeditious solution to this problem and to report to the General Council before the end of 2002".

66. Caroline Dommen, supra n. 60.

67. "[A]s a price for being allowed to join the WTO in 2003, Cambodia had to agree to immediately halt use of affordable generic versions of new medicines.... In negotiating the country's accession to the WTO, Cambodia's delegates had asked for a 2009 deadline for TRIPs compliance but were bargained down to January 1st 2007". Ibid.

68. Caroline Dommen, *supra* n. 60.

69. Oxfam International (XX03) Cambodia's Accession to the WTO - How the law of the jungle is applied to one of the world's poorest countries.

70. See Caroline Dommen, *supra* n. 60.

71. *Ibid*.

72. *Ibid*.

73. *Ibid*

74. *Ibid*.

75. Médecins sans frontiers, *Top ten list of the year's most underreported humanitarian stories*, Media release, 6 January 2004.

76. "Tough as it is today to get cheap drugs to the poor, it is likely to get

tougher still in the future". See *Who Owns the Knowledge Economy?*, *The Economist* 17 (8 April 2000).

77. Article 7 of the TRIPS Agreement provides that the protection and enforcement of intellectual property rights (IPRs) should contribute ...to "transfer and dissemination of technical knowledge to the mutual advantage of producers and users of technological knowledge and in a manner conducive to social and economic welfare, and to a balance of rights and obligations."

78. Article 8 provides that WTO Members may "... adopt measures necessary to protect public health and nutrition, and to promote the public interest in sectors of vital importance to their socio-economic and technological development, provided such measures are consistent with [the TRIPs] Agreement."

79. Article 27, which specifies possible exceptions to the obligation of providing patent protection, says that Members can exclude inventions from patentability if inventions are contrary to *ordre public* or morality. Article 27 specifically allows the exclusion of inventions from patentability in order to protect human, animal or plant life or health or to avoid serious prejudice to the environment.

80. Caroline Dommen, *supra* n. 60.

81. Such an approach to interpretation is mandated under the WTO Dispute Settlement Understanding, article 3.2, which states that WTO agreements need to be interpreted in the light of "customary rules of interpretation".

82. See Article 31 (1) of the VCLT. This Article further provides that the "context" for the purpose of interpretation include the preamble, annexes and any subsequent practice in the application of the treaty which establishes the agreement of the parties regarding its interpretation. Article 32 allows recourse to supplementary means of interpretation, including the preparatory work of the treaty, where the interpretative process under article 31 leaves the meaning of the terms ambiguous or obscure, or leads to a result which is manifestly absurd or unreasonable.

83. See Gudrun Monika Zagel, 'WTO & Human Rights: Examining Linkages and Suggesting Convergence', *Idlo Voice of Development Jurists Paper Series*, Vol. 2. No.2, 2005.

84. *EC–Measures affecting asbestos and asbestos-containing products*, Report of the Appellate Body (WT/DS135/AB/R), 12 March XX01, para. 168.

85. In the *EC–Asbestos* case it was held that "...it is undisputed that WTO Members have the right to determine the level of protection of health that they consider appropriate in a given situation." Ibid, at para 168.

86. Thailand–Restrictions on importation of and internal taxes on cigarettes, Report of the Panel (DS10/R – 37S/200), 7 November 1990, in particular paras. 72–73 and 78.

87. See Gudrun Monika Zagel, 'WTO & Human Rights: Examining Linkages and Suggesting Convergence', *Idlo Voice of Development Jurists Paper Series*, Vol. 2. No.2, XX05.

88. United States-Restrictions on Imports of Tuna (DS21/R - 39S/155), GATT Panel Report, circulated on 3 September 1991 (not adopted), paras. 5.25 et seq.

89. United States-Restrictions on Imports of Tuna (DS29/R), GATT Panel Report, circulated on 16 June 1994 (not adopted), paras. 5.16 and 5.31.

90. United States-*Import Prohibition of Certain Shrimp and Shrimp Products* (WT/DS58), Appellate Body Report, adopted on 6 November 1998, para. 133 and paras. 164 et seq.

91. "Under WTO law, such sanctions would qualify as discriminatory trade restrictions, which are prohibited according to Art. I and XI GATT.8 They are however covered by Art. XXI (c) GATT, which allows deviating from GATT obligations, if in pursuance of a Member State's obligations under the UN Charter": Gudrun Monika Zagel, 'WTO & Human Rights: Examining Linkages and Suggesting Convergence', *Idlo Voice of Development Jurists Paper Series*, Vol. 2. No.2, XX05.

92. Examples of economic sanctions imposed by the UN Security Council are sanctions issued against Iraq, Sierra Leone, or Somalia. An overview about the existing sanctions can be found at http://www.un.org/Docs/sc/committees/INTRO.htm.For a detailed discussion of the UN Security Council Sanctions cf. M. P. Doxey, International Sanctions in Contemporary Perspective (2nd edition), London (1996); V. Gowlland-Debbas (ed.), United Nations Sanctions and International Law, The Hague, Boston, London (XX01) with further reference.

93. Gross violations of human rights were specifically targeted by the sanctions against Haiti, Rwanda, and Congo. See R. S. Taylor, Security Council Action in the Name of Human Rights, 11 African Yearbook of International Law (2003) 263-298.

UN SECURITY COUNCIL RESOLUTION 678 (1990) REVISITED: FARCE, *SUI GENERIS* OR PRECEDENT?*

*Myint Zan***

INTRODUCTION

On 29 November 1990 the United Nations Security Council (UNSC) adopted Resolution 678 (1990). Resolution 678 (1990) can be considered as a 'climax' of Resolutions adopted by the UNSC in what was then contemporaneously called the 'Gulf crisis' –and before the 'Gulf War' broke out17 January 1991. These series of Resolutions[1] were adopted by the UNSC as a consequence of the invasion, occupation and subsequent annexation of Kuwait by Iraq. Among, others, UNSC Resolution 678 (1990) authorized the use of 'all necessary means' should Iraq not withdraw its forces from Kuwait by 'January 15, 1991'. At the time the UNSC Resolution was adopted it was generally considered as very significant resolution in UN Security Council history[2]. The imputation of such significance was based on the fact that arguably it is only the second time in UN history that an authorization of 'all necessary means'–though couched in diplomatic terms - against another State (which also happened to be a member of the UN) has been made.

In the light of the significance of the UNSC Resolution the author of this article gave a presentation/seminar at the Faculty of Law of University of Malaya on 11 January 1991 entitled 'UN Security Council Resolution 678 (1990); Farce, *Sui Generis* or

* This article is an update and retrospective analysis of a seminar the author gave at the Faculty of Law, University of Malaya, in 1990.

** BA, LLB, (Rangoon), LL.M. (Michigan), M.Int.Law (Australian National University), Ph.D. (Griffith), Principal Lecturer, School of Law, Multimedia University, Malacca, Malaysia.

Precedent'. In mid-2008 it is more than 17 years since the resolution was adopted and also more than 17 years than since the 'first' Gulf war ended with the 'forced' withdrawal of Iraqi forces from Kuwait at the end of February 1991.

This article will take mainly a retrospective look at what this author stated in the seminar and also the analyses and projections the author made then in the light of relevant subsequent developments.

The author did not develop the points that he made into an article (at the time in early 1991) but retains the hand outs of the synopsis of the seminar. Since 1991, there have been developments in UN Security Council jurisprudence (so to speak) on the issue of the use of force, military intervention in general and particularly relating to Iraq. The subsequent Iraq war (of March-April 2003) and the subsequent occupation or at the very least presence of a large number of occupation or foreign forces (an overwhelming majority –if not (by August 2008) almost exclusively those from the United States) in Iraq is likely to continue, for some time. In the light of these developments a 'revisit' on Resolution 678 (1990) based on the synopsis of the seminar that the author presented will be made. Some if not most of the points that the author made will be restated with comments both in the light of subsequent developments and in the light of the author' s subsequent views and analysis pertaining to the statements the author had made in early 1991.

A retrospective look at Resolution 678 (1990) should give more pointers on 'answering' the author's query (of 1991) as to whether Resolution 678 (1990) was a 'farce, *sui generis* or precedent' or indeed a mixture of all these elements can be discerned.

In order not to 'clutter' the discussions that will follow and inasmuch as reference will have to be made to what the author stated in the seminar of January 1991 the author will use the word 'I' at least at times. Though it is generally the case that the use of the word 'I' is, in most occasions, to be eschewed or avoided in academic articles it is submitted that the use of this personal pronoun might be advisable in this particular context and the author requests the editors' and readers' indulgence on this matter.

THE ISSUE OF 'FARCE'

'The Cons'

UNSC Resolution 678 (1990) was adopted by 12 votes in favor, two against (Cuba and Yemen) and one abstention. In the immediate aftermath of the adoption of Resolution 678 (1990) there were allegations of 'farce' or that the United States as the main superpower has manipulated or cajoled members of the Security Council including its non-permanent members to vote for the Resolution. Hence statements to the effect of the UN Security Council being an 'American Security Council' in that the UNSC was dominated by the United States and therefore the Resolution was a 'farce'. In my presentation of January 1991 I took a skeptical view of that claim. Stating (in my 1991 synopsis) that there could be 'pros' and 'cons' against the claim that the UN Security Council was in effect an 'American Security Council' I started with the 'cons' (i.e. I had countered the claim that the Resolution is a 'farce') and in fact in the particular category of farce I did not address the issue of the 'pros' (i.e. there may be some elements of if not truth arguably some justifications in the claim that the Resolution was somewhat 'farcical' and that the United States has pressured some of the members of the UNSC to toe its line).

I will cover the issue of the 'pros' subsequently but on the issue of 'cons' (i.e. my critique of the claims that Resolution 678 was farcical) will be summarized and commented on. As a first argument that Resolution 678 (1990) was not farcical at least in the full sense of the claim made by the Iraqi government I pointed out that there has been unanimous or near-unanimous agreement that the Iraqi invasion of Kuwait was a violation of international law. Moreover I argued that Iraq, in August 1990, not only invaded and occupied Kuwait but annexed it as one of its provinces. I argued that the annexation of Kuwait by Iraq was the first instance since the end of the Second World War where one country Iraq-a member of the United Nations- invaded *and annexed* another country which is also a member of the United Nations.[3]

It was widely stated in newspaper reports as well as in academic discussion in the immediate aftermath of the adoption of the resolution that it was arguably only the second time in history that the United Nations was involved in either directly or indirectly in the defense of a State invaded or attacked by another.

The first instance was the UN Security Council response to the attack by North Korea against South Korea in June 1950 and subsequent (direct) involvement of the UN whereby forces (at least nominally) under United Nations command and United Nations flag fought the North Korean (and later) Chinese troops.

Without going into too much details during my 1991 seminar I presented a brief comparison and contrast as regards the process and (to borrow a mainly domestic legal term) the 'constitutionality' (as per the United Nations Charter) of the UNSC resolutions that were adopted prior to the UN involvement in the Korean War (in June 1950) and the process that led to the adoption of Resolution 678 (1990) (in November 1990) in the 'Gulf Crisis' of 1990 more than forty years later.

In the year 1950 the United States–which played an instrumental role in the United Nations- had more influence– compared to forty years later- in the United Nations in that both in the UN General Assembly[4] and in the UN Security Council[5] there are more of its allies. On that account it could be argued that the United States would be able to exert pressure more easily and its political positions and interest would have been more easily achievable.

The absence of the Soviet Union from the meetings of the UN Security Council due to its boycott of the then UN Secretary-General Trygve Lie[6] facilitated the passing of (what can be termed as) 'Korean Resolutions' in the first few months after late June 1950 when North Korea attacked 'Republic of Korea'.[7] Hence in the UN Security Council Resolution 83 (1950) of 27 June 1950 the Security Council '[h]aving determined that the armed attack from the forces of North Korea constitutes a breach of the peace [according to Chapter VII of the United Nations Charter] ..[r]ecommends that Members of the United Nations furnish such assistance to the Republic of Korea as may be necessary to repel the armed attack and to restore international peace and security in the area'.[8] Further due also to the absence of the Soviet Union the UNSC was able to pass subsequent resolutions including Resolution 84 (1950) which '[r]ecommends that all Members providing military and other assistance [to the Republic of Korea] pursuant to the aforesaid Security Council resolutions make such forces and other assistance available to a unified command under the United States of America' and 'requests the United States to designate the commander of such forces'. The Resolution also '[a]uthorizes the unified command at its discretion to use the United Nations flag in the course of its operations against North Koreans forces concurrently with the flags of the various nations participating'[9] Hence the initial Resolutions which called upon the member States to 'repel the armed attack' against the Republic of Korea as well as the authorization that the Member States cooperating with the government of Republic of Korea to use the United Nations flag as well as putting the 'unified command' under the United States of America was adopted due to the crucial fact that the Soviet Union boycotted the Security Council meetings and was 'absent' from those meetings when the Resolutions were adopted.

The armed assistance given to South Korea by member States and subsequently the use of the United Nations flag under the 'Unified Command' in 'repelling the armed attack by North Korea' would appear to have the imprimatur of Security Council authorization. However 'constitutional' questions can be raised as to whether the absence of a veto-wielding Permanent Member would or should deprive the 'legality' of the Security Council resolutions that was adopted during the initial stages of the Korean War.

In the presentation of 1991 I argued that such 'constitutional queries' cannot be discerned in the adoption of Resolution 678 (1990) since the Soviet Union was present in the Security Council meeting and voted for the adoption of the Resolution.

I also mentioned the point that the UN Security Council has become more active (since about 1988) in matters concerning peace and security and in conflict-solving and it is in accordance with those recent trends that the Security Council's pro-active stance in the then Gulf crisis should be seen. I did acknowledge that (the then) recent ending of the Cold War and the era of (relative) cooperation between the (then) two super-powers, the Soviet Union's changed stance in international affairs[10] helped bring about the Resolution. I did give a passing acknowledgment to the importance of oil (i.e. of securing the oil supplies from the Gulf region) as an important fact[11] but did not think and duly stated that these factors are sufficient or strong enough to support or accept the claim that Resolution 678 (1990) was a 'farce'.

Under-emphasis on the 'Pros'

Looking back, I am now of the view that it was remiss of me not to give any consideration to the 'pros' on the issue of 'farce'. I still believe that though the Security Council Resolution was not completely 'farcical' to the extent that its (then) vociferous detractors make it to be but I acknowledge that at the time I have not taken into account the tactics and pressure used by the United States on both permanent members and non-permanent members of the UN Security Council to agree to this mainly US-sponsored Resolution.[12]

Moreover the United States has already mentioned that it sought the Resolution mainly for political reasons and not for legal reasons in that it believe that even without the Resolution the United States and its allies do have the right to repel Iraqi occupation of Kuwait as a matter of 'collective self-defense'. The resolution was sought to confer legitimacy and the added imprimatur of legality. [13]

In 1991 when I gave the seminar it could not have been envisaged that Resolution 678 would be used as a legal justification at least by one of the members of the 'coalition of the willing' (United Kingdom)[14] to attack Iraq 12 years later in March 2003. But that did occur. I do not intend to elaborate on my strong disagreement that Resolution 678 (1990) provided a legal justification for attacking Iraq more than 12 years later in 2003 since it does not fall fully within the ambit of this 'revisit'. It will only be stated here that even if in the early days of 1991 and before the Gulf War actually started the claim that the Resolution 678 (1990) was 'farcical' can be dismissed as indeed I have done in my seminar. However I am of the view that subsequent invocations of this Resolution to legally justify the invasion of Iraq do have at least some elements of 'farce'. It is mainly in this sense that the addition of the 'pros' (i.e. elements that would support the claim of the farcical nature pertaining to the process of adopting Resolution 678) is added here in retrospect.[15]

THE ISSUE OF '*SUI GENERIS*'

There are quite a few definitions of the Latin *term sui generis* covering a range of disciplines in law, political science and sociology. In the context of this article the implication and application of the term *sui generis* would generally be in line with this exposition:

> In law, it is a term of art used to identify a legal classification that exists independently of other categorizations because of its uniqueness or due to the specific creation of an entitlement or obligation ... When referring to case citations and authorities, lawyers (and Judges) may refer to an authority cited as being 'sui generis', meaning in that context, it is one confined (or special) to its own facts, and therefore may not be of broader application.[16]

Even though the above definition is made mainly in the context of a municipal law context in that 'authorities', lawyers and Judges are being referred to the general meaning of a situation or in this case a UN Security Council Resolution being 'one confined (or special) to its own facts, and therefore may not be of broader application' can be used to contrast the features, characteristics and precedential value of Resolution 678 with comparable (not necessarily similar situation) of the Korean Resolutions of 1950. Hence the focus in this section would be whether the Resolution 678 (1990) is similar to or differs from the Korean Resolutions which was the focus of my seminar given in 1991. The 'revisit' would be on my retrospective views or analysis of what I had stated in 1991 on the *sui generis* or otherwise nature of Resolution 678 (1990). A brief narration of what I said in 1991 and analysis of whether they need to be modified in the light of subsequent developments will also be stated.

My presentation of 1991 dealt with the *sui generis* or otherwise nature of Resolution 678 (1990) in contrast to the Korean resolutions 40 years earlier as international law text books published quite some time before the 1990 Gulf crisis stated that the Korean resolutions of 1950 were initially adopted and implemented due to the absence of the Soviet Union from the meetings of the UN Security Council and that such a configuration of events and UN involvement 'is unlikely to take place in the future'.[17] In the immediate aftermath of the adoption of Resolution 678 (1990) contemporaneous report states or 'hails' its adoption as only the second occasion whereby it 'marked only the second time—the Korean war was the other instance—that the Security Council has invoked its power to sanction the use of force to counter aggression'[18]

To discern whether the (apparent) similarity and more significantly differences between the Korean Resolutions in 1950 and Resolution 678 (1990) are such that a designation of *sui generis* can perhaps be attributed to Resolution 678 will be analyzed in this section.

As excerpted above Resolution 84 (1950) 'all Members providing military and other assistance [to the Republic of Korea] pursuant to the aforesaid Security Council resolutions make such forces and other assistance available to a unified command under the United States of America' as well as authorizing 'the unified command at its discretion to use the United Nations flag in the course of its operations against North Koreans forces.'[19]

In the case of Resolution 678 (1990) and all subsequent resolutions passed in relation to the Iraqi occupation of Kuwait there was no specific or implied 'authorization' by the UN Security Council to 'fly the United Nations flag' by the 'multinational forces'[20] in using 'all necessary means' to end the Iraqi occupation of Kuwait. In that sense both in terms of symbolism (the use of the United Nations flag) and that of substance (the actual involvement of the United Nations) one can argue that the United Nations was more 'involved' in the Korean War than in the Gulf War 1991. I clearly remember hearing on radio the then United Nations Secretary-General Javier Perez de Cuellar stating that (the Gulf war) 'was not a United Nations war'.[21]

On the other hand the author has argued in 1991 that its operations against the North Korean forces' was adopted 'constitutional reservations' concerning the Korean resolutions of 1950 can be made. This is due to the fact that the Soviet Union boycotted the UN Security Council meetings and was also absent when the Korean Resolutions especially Resolution 84 (1950) which authorized the 'unified command under the United States .. to use at its discretion the United Nations flag in the course of the war [22] was adopted. The Soviet Union did challenge (though not in a juridical manner)[23] the legality of the Korean resolutions passed in is absence[24]

In contrast the Soviet Union, then a permanent Member of the UN Security Council was not only present but also voted for the adoption of Resolution 678 (1990). Hence based on this factor I had expressed the statement that the Resolution 678 (1990) was on firmer constitutional ground than the Korean resolutions adopted (in the absence of the Soviet Union) forty years earlier.

One issue that may need to be addressed on 'constitutional' or procedural grounds regarding the adoption of Resolution 678

(1990) is the abstention of the representative from the People's Republic of China. However I stated during the seminar that even though Article 27 (3) of the UN Charter states that 'Decisions of the Security Council on ... shall be made by an affirmative vote of nine members including the concurring votes of the permanent members' from subsequent UN state practice as well as in contrast with Article 108 of the UN Charter[25] an abstention by a permanent Member of the UN Security Council would not nullify the constitutionality or validity of the adopted Security Council resolution. In any case both in academic writings as early as the year 1969[26] and in an advisory opinion given by the International Court of Justice in 1971[27] it has been stated that a permanent Member abstention would not negatively effect the validity of UN Security Council resolutions as long as all the other requirements stated in Article 27 (3) are met.[28]

In addition to lack of constitutional reservations a la Korean resolutions I also mention the status of 'China' as a permanent member of the UN Security Council during the Korean resolutions. It was the 'Republic of China' or Taiwan which had taken the permanent Member seat and 'Communist China' or in its official designation of the People's Republic of China was not even a member of the United Nations. In fact later on in the Korean war the 'United Nations' forces led by the United States commander fought the forces from the People's Republic of China. Moreover one of the reasons of the boycott by the Soviet Union of the Security Council meetings was to protest the refusal of the Security Council to seat the representative from the People's Republic of China. Though I did not specifically state in the seminar the point I had wanted to make was that since a government in power and at least in *de facto* control of Chinese mainland with a population (then in 1950) about 600 million people is not represented in the Security Council and since the representative of 'China' in the UN Security Council in 1950 was a staunch American ally the composition of the Security Council at least as far as one permanent Member was concerned would indicate that it was more of an 'American Security Council' in 1950 than it was in 1990. The People's Republic of China can at that time in 1990 and even now be at best described as a 'strategic competitor' of the United States. Hence and apart from the arguments that the Resolution 678 (1990) ('the Kuwait resolution') was on firmer constitutional grounds the 'identity' of a permanent Member of the UN Security Council in 1990 in contrast to its 1950 predecessor also facilitates the view that that the Kuwait resolution is *sui generis* in that it could be substantively and substantially distinguished from the Korean resolutions.

I also raised the issue of the status of both Koreas being not members of the United Nations at the time of the Korean resolutions. In the case of the Iraqi occupation of Kuwait both are members of the United Nations. The fact that both Koreas were not members of the United Nations at that time of the Korean resolutions and that both of them did not become UN members long after the armistice of July 1953[29] should not be a material factor in and by itself to expunge the United Nations (apparent) enforcement action'. Article 2 (6) of the United Nations Charter states 'The Organization shall ensure that states which are not Members of the United Nations act in accordance with these Principles so far as may be necessary for the maintenance of international peace and security' and it is arguable that the Security Council action can be justified under this Article notwithstanding that both Koreas were not members of the UN. Hence though not of a material one the lack of United Nations membership of both the attacking and attacked States distinguishes the Korean resolutions with that of the Kuwait resolutions.

One other factor that I mentioned during the seminar was that in the Korean War there was an absence of annexation which was a prominent feature in the Iraq-Kuwait conflict of 1990. Needless to say in a hypothetical world and as a 'counter-factual' if the United Nations did not intervene the North Koreans could have 'reunified' under its 'Great Leader' the divided peninsular.[30]

I also pointed out that there was swifter United Nations (Security Council action) within days after the North Korean invasion of South Korea on 25 June 1950 United States troops were already fighting the invading North Koreans and the Security Council had by 7 July 1950 already urged the UN member States contributing to the war efforts against the North Koreans to 'unify under the UN command'. In contrast Resolution 678 (1990) was passed on 29 November 1990 nearly four months after the invasion and occupation of Kuwait by Iraq. In addition, prior to the adoption of Resolution 678 (1990) there were numerous resolutions which (prior to the Gulf War breaking out in 17 January 1991 'culminated' in the Resolution 678 (1990). In contrast, in the case of the North Korean invasion immediate 'enforcement action' was taken by the UN Security Council. Moreover an 'ultimatum' a la Resolution 678 (1990) was not given to North Korea in 1950 and a 'grace period' was given to Iraq (in the words of the Resolution itself 'to allow Iraq one final opportunity and as a pause of good will') to withdraw its forces from Iraq.[31]

Hence the *sui generis* nature of the Resolution 678 (1990) is argued mainly by distinguishing it from the previous and alleged 'enforcement action' of the UN Security Council. I had used the phrase enforcement action in quotation marks since the nature of the claimed enforcement action of both the Korean resolutions and Resolution 678 (1990) need to be canvassed as to whether they fell within the enforcement action stipulated in Chapter VII of the United Nations Charter especially Articles 42 and 43 in the following section on 'precedent'. Just as the issues and arguments of 'farce' or the alleged farcical nature of Resolution 678 (1990) overlapped and is restated in a different way on the section of '*sui generis*' there would be certain overlap and restatement of the issues discussed in the earlier sections from a somewhat different perspective when discussion of the precedential nature ('precedent') of Resolution 678 (1990) is made.

THE ISSUE OF 'PRECEDENT'

Precedent is not used in the legal, technical or municipal law sense but in the sense of whether the Resolution which apparently was passed to counter aggression and unprovoked attack by a powerful neighbor to a smaller State would act as a 'a 'warning' and a precedent to deter to attack by stronger countries against weaker countries like Saddam Hussein did when he launched an attack against Kuwait. In my presentation. I did state and draw attention to the fact that the passing of this significant resolution was facilitated by the fact that the Cold War had recently ended and the and there was less hostility perhaps even in some aspects cooperation between the then two super powers

I even (in retrospect) naively raised the hope whether some form of collective security if not exactly in the form and mode as envisaged by the drafters of the UN Charter then at least in a modified one can be implemented in the aftermath (of the then) Gulf crisis. I mentioned that the international community could, partly depending on the aftermath or outcome of the Gulf crisis, turned it into a window of opportunity to endeavor to implement some form of collective security arrangements. I did state this window of opportunity and hence the 'precedential value' of Resolution 678 (1990) would be dependent on how the Gulf crisis was resolved. Some of the points that I raised in my seminar of 11 January 1991 is the listing of possible scenarios on the outcome of the Gulf crisis.

Within a week of my seminar the Gulf war (of 1991) broke out hence some of the points that I raised had become moot. However, for the sake of the record these should be briefly mentioned in the sub-sections 'The Precedential Value of Resolution 678 (1990): Some Moot Points'. Some of the points I mentioned contained suggestions especially in relation to Articles 42 and 43 of Chapter VII of the UN Charter. These issues would be addressed under the sub-section 'Suggestions Mooted in 1991 to enhance the precedential value of Resolution 678 (1990)'. The third sub-section would deal with a brief retrospective look at some of the subsequent Security Council resolutions and the checkered United Nations practice in the fields that can (roughly) be categorized as 'enforcement actions' or (in a generic sense) matters involving aggression and international peace and security. A retrospective look at these subsequent resolutions and UN practice is made to gauge and evaluate the predictions that I have made in 1991 and to retrospectively assess as to whether it has been appropriate to consider Resolution 678 (1990) as a possible source of 'precedent' in the first place and secondly if that were to be so what was the precedent that it had set and how it was followed, ignored or violated in the subsequent years.

Precedential Value of Resolution 678 (1990): Some Largely Moot Points

Since Resolution 678 (1990) was directed to the withdrawal of Iraq from Kuwait I stated that an 'effective precedent' depends on whether or not Iraq effectively withdraws from Kuwait together with the perception of the international community would, in the future cases of aggression, effectively 'deter' aggression. I also make the statement that such a potential would depend on the continued cooperation of the two super-powers the United States and the Soviet Union.[32]

I stated that as far as the implementation of the 'demands' made to Iraq in Resolution 678 (1990) was concerned there were three possible outcomes which are (a) war (b) compromise and (c) fully compliance by Iraq of Resolution 678 (1990).

As far as the possibility of war is concerned[33] I stated that the precedent could be 'bloody' and it could also split in the support given by at least Third World countries as well as at least some Islamic countries and especially if the war resulted in a stalemate[34] then the resolve of the coalition of the countries that rallied against Saddam Hussein could be weakened. In fact though the alliance did not weaken a few persons who initially supported the Resolution 678 (1990) began to express doubts for supporting it including Malaysian Prime Minister Mahathir Mohamad.

The second possibility that I raised was a 'compromise' where Saddam Hussein agreed to withdraw from parts but not all of Kuwait[35] and then would claimed to have 'abided' the demands made by the Security Council in Resolution 678 (1990). I stated that this could amount to attempt for a 'dilution' of the resolve of the Security Council and that it is unlikely to be accepted. In any case this option of 'compromise' did not occur neither did the full Iraqi withdrawal from Kuwait as demanded by the Resolution.

Another point which I mentioned during the seminar which became moot as soon as the 1991 Gulf War broke out on 17 January was whether or not Resolution 678 (1990) can be considered as authorizing, at least implicitly, to attack Iraq rather than Iraqi-occupied Kuwait (only) in order to meet its objectives of securing an Iraqi withdrawal from Kuwait. I raised the issue of whether a separate and additional UN Security Council Resolution is necessary or not for the US-led multinational forces to attack Iraq itself in order to evict Iraqi forces from Kuwait. I did–again-raise the comparison with the Korean war where United Nations General Assembly[36] Resolution 376 (V)[37] could be construed to authorize the attack on North Korea after the United Nations forces under the United States command repelled the North Korean attack and the 'Untied Nations troops' began to cross the North Korean border and attack North Korea itself.[38]

I stated that the military need to attack Iraq might even be more crucial than to attack North Korea in the Korean war of 1950-53. I expressed my view then that perhaps a specific Security Council authorization or a 'retrospective approval by the Security might be necessary. These statements made about a week before the Gulf War broke out became 'moot' as it did since events on the ground (or more appropriately in the air) took place when the hostilities started by the bombing of Baghdad. I did mention and emphasize during my presentation though that even if Resolution 678 (1990) can be considered to authorize the 'necessary' attacks on Iraq it needs to be directed only for the purpose of ending the Iraq occupation of Kuwait and not to destroy Iraq but to restore Kuwait's sovereignty.

Precedential Value of Resolution 678 (1990): Some Suggestions and Projections of 1991 and a Retrospective Analysis

Some of the suggestions that I made in the seminar were restricted to the particular issues of the Gulf crisis and they include (1) the United Nations should work closely with nations of the 'Gulf' and also with regional organizations in matters of collective security and (2) made a feasibility study regarding the logistics and structure of a United Nations led or semi-autonomous United Nations led multinational forces in the Gulf region and elsewhere to deal with or if possible to preempt similar crises in the future. None of what I suggested or 'mooted' in 1991 have materialized[39]. My suggestion for the United Nations to play a more pro-active or cooperative role was predicated, in part, on some of the provisions of Chapter VIII of the UN Charter. For example Article 52 (3) which states 'The Security Council shall encourage the development of pacific settlement of local disputes through such regional arrangements or by such regional agencies either on the initiative of the states concerned or by reference from the Security Council' and Article 53 (1) which in part states 'The Security Council shall, where appropriate, utilize such regional arrangements or agencies for enforcement action under its authority. But no enforcement action shall be taken under regional arrangements or by regional agencies without the authorization of the Security Council'. My suggestion (or hope) then was that the cooperation that was shown or appears to have been shown by many States including those in the Gulf region could facilitate cooperation between regional organizations and the United Nations (Security Council) in matters affecting international peace and security. Not only has this cooperation not materialized a regional (defense or security) organization North Atlantic Treaty

Organization (NATO) has acted unilaterally (rather than cooperatively) in the Kosovo crisis in March and April of 1999.[40]

The other suggestion that I raised concerns the formation of the Military Staff Committee especially as envisaged in Article 42 and 43 of the UN Charter. Article 43 (1) states that:

> [a]ll Members of the United Nations, in order to contribute to the maintenance of international peace and security, undertake to make available to the Security Council, on its call and in accordance with a special agreement or agreements, armed forces, assistance, and facilities, including rights of passage, necessary for the purpose of maintaining international peace and security.

Article 43 (3) further stipulates that

> [t]he agreement or agreements shall be negotiated as soon as possible on the initiative of the Security Council. They shall be concluded between the Security Council and Members or between the Security Council and groups of Members and shall be subject to ratification by the signatory states in accordance with their respective constitutional processes.

Article 47 of the UN Charter deals with the formation and functions of the Military Staff Committee. The stated 'enforcement action' in the Korean war of 1950-53 and the 1991 Gulf War though apparently waged under the imprimatur or authorization of the Security Council it did *not* adhere to or involve the procedures as laid down in Article 42, 43 and Article 47 of the UN Charter Article 47 is reproduced in full here:

> 1. There shall be established a Military Staff Committee to advise and assist the Security Council on all questions relating to the Security Council's military requirements for the maintenance of international peace and security, the employment and command of forces placed at its disposal, the regulation of armaments, and possible disarmament.
> 2. The Military Staff Committee shall consist of the Chiefs of Staff of the permanent members of the Security Council or their representatives. Any Member of the United Nations not permanently represented on the Committee shall be invited by the Committee to be associated with it when the efficient discharge of the Committee's responsibilities requires the participation of that Member in its work.
> 3. The Military Staff Committee shall be responsible under the Security Council for the strategic direction of any armed forces placed at the disposal of the Security Council. Questions

relating to the command of such forces shall be worked out subsequently.

4. The Military Staff Committee, with the authorization of the Security Council and after consultation with appropriate regional agencies, may establish regional sub-committees.

As a matter of historical record the very first Resolution of the Security Council deals with the issue of the 'Military Staff Committee'[41]. It is now (in mid 2008) more than 62 years since the Security Council in its very first Resolution requested the Member States of the UN to conclude agreements with the Security Council to make available to it 'on its call armed forces, assistance and facilities'. Four years and 5 months after the Security Council in its first resolution urged the Member States to make agreements with the Security Council when the Korean conflict broke out on 25 June 1950 there was no such forces or agreements made as stipulated in a combined reading of Article 43 and Article 47. Neither is Article 42 or 43 'invoked' in Resolutions 82, 83 and 84 (1950) where Security Council requested assistance from Member States and also to put the 'United Nations forces' under the command of the United States.

When the Korean war broke out in 1950 there was no Military Staff Committee and no agreements made between the Permanent Members of the Security Council (the Cold War being at its height in 1950) and no troops under the 'disposal' or Command of the UN. Hence even if the UN Security Council 'authorizes' the (apparent) or alleged enforcement action against North Korea it was not in accordance with the provisions of Articles 42, 43 and 47 of the UN Charter. An admittedly weak argument or (it would seem) 'special pleading' that could be made is that even if there has not been, prior to the Korean resolutions, agreements between members of the United Nations to provide to the Security Council armed forces under its command the 'impromptu' call of the Security Council was heeded by many States and there can be said (in 'spirit' though not to the letter) instant[42] or ad hoc[43] conclusion and implementation of 'special agreements' as envisaged in Article 43 even if the Military Staff Committee was non-existent.

Be that as it may I did point out that unlike in Korea, the 'multinational troops' were sent to Saudi Arabia and the Gulf region before the Security Council called for assistance. Moreover under no circumstances could the multinational troops be considered 'United Nations troops' as in the Korean War. Therefore the lack of United Nations supervision and involvement in the Gulf war of 1991 which apparently had the imprimatur of UN Security Council authorization via Resolution 678 (1990) made it very different from that of the Korean war and the non-conformity of it to Articles 42 and 47 of the UN Charter is even more marked than the Korean Resolutions and the action taken by the United Nations Security Council in the initial phases of the Korean war.

The mechanics and the 'constitutional' procedures –or non-adherence to them- in the UN Security Council's adoption of the Resolutions during the Korean war and the 1991 Gulf war were different. Even so I suggested that the end of the Cold War and the era of cooperation between the superpowers provided an opportunity for the Permanent Members of the United Nations Security Council to seriously work towards formation of the Military Staff Committee as stated in Article 47 of the UN Charter and to make arrangements under Article 43. I did state that these or similar suggestions have been made before but in the midst and –eventual aftermath- of the Gulf crises of 1990 there should be better or at least less daunting prospects for achieving those goals and all the more reason towards working for it. This sentiment, 'hope' or suggestion is felt, at least in the early 1990s by many students and observers of international law and is reflected in a proposal made by the (at that time) new Secretary-General of the United Nations Boutros Boutros-Ghali. In a United Nations document entitled *Agenda for Peace* and dated 17 June 1992 less than 16 months after 1991 Gulf war ended Secretary-General Boutros-Ghali proposed that:

> [I]t is the essence of the concept of collective security as contained in the Charter that if peaceful means fail, the measures provided in Chapter VII should be used, on the decision of the Security Council, to maintain or restore international peace and security in the face of a "threat to the peace, breach of the peace, or act of aggression". The Security Council has not so far made use of the most coercive of these measures-the action by military force foreseen in Article 42. In the situation between Iraq and Kuwait, the Council chose to authorize Member States to take measures on its behalf. The Charter, however, provides a detailed approach which now merits the attention of all Member States.[44]

> Under Article 42 of the Charter, the Security Council has the authority to take military action to maintain or restore international peace and security. While such action should only be taken when all peaceful means have failed, the option of taking it is essential to the credibility of the United Nations as a guarantor of international security. This will require bringing into being, through negotiations, the special agreements foreseen in Article 43 of the Charter, whereby Member States undertake to make armed forces, assistance and facilities available to the Security Council for the purposes stated in Article 42, not only on an *ad hoc* basis[45] but on a permanent basis. Under the political circumstances that now exist for the first time since the Charter was adopted, the long-standing obstacles to the conclusion of such special agreements should no longer prevail. The ready availability of armed forces on call could serve, in itself, as a means of deterring breaches of the peace since a potential aggressor would know that the Council had at its disposal a means of response. Forces under Article 43 may perhaps never be sufficiently large or well enough equipped to deal with a threat from a major army equipped with sophisticated weapons. They would be useful, however, in meeting any threat posed by a military force of a lesser order. I recommend that the Security Council initiate negotiations in accordance with Article 43, supported by the Military Staff Committee, which may be augmented if necessary by others in accordance with Article 47, paragraph 2, of the Charter. It is my view that the role of the Military Staff Committee should be seen in the context of Chapter VII, and not that of the planning or conduct of peace-keeping operations.[46]

Sixteen years after the sixth Secretary-General recommended to member States in June 1992 'that the Security Council [should] initiate negotiations in accordance with Article 43, supported by the Military Staff Committee' neither the Article 43 arrangements nor the Military Staff Committee as stated under Article 47 has materialized under the United Nations system.

More than thirteen years after Secretary-General Boutros-Ghali's report of *Agenda for Peace* in September 2005 the United Nations held 'Millennium + 5 Summit' of major world leaders. The Draft Outcome Document of the summit[47] mentioned briefly (i.e. in comparison with Secretary-General Boutros-Ghali's 1992 *Agenda for Peace* report 13 years earlier it was not as detailed) under the sub-heading 'Use of Force under the UN Charter' from paragraphs 54 to 56 which did not specifically mention either Article 43, 47 or the (desirability of forming the) Military Staff

Committee. Under paragraph 168 and last paragraph of the Draft outcome it was stated that the Heads of State which participated in the Summit 'request the Security Council to consider the composition, mandate and working methods of the Military Staff Committee and to submit a recommendation for further action to the General Assembly'.

And nearly sixty years before September 2006 Millennium + Summit of major world leaders requesting the Security Council to 'consider the composition, mandate and working methods of the Military Staff Committee' in its (very) first resolution, Resolution 1 (1946) the Security Council in its second meeting on 25 January 1946 '... directs as its first tasks to draw up proposals for its organization (including the appropriate secretarial staff and procedure and to submit these proposals to the Security Council'

The track-record of the Security Council including the various Secretaries-General and the 'international community' towards the formation of a functioning Military Staff Committee suggests that this has been mooted as early as January 1946. Cold War antagonisms and super and regional power politics prevented the formation of a functioning Military Staff Committee as well as the effective implementation of the arrangement as stated in Article 47 of the UN Charter during the first forty-five years of the United Nations. It is perhaps understandable if–in retrospect over-optimistic- to envisage, propose or suggest in the immediate aftermath of the 'end' of the Cold War in the early 1990s that Chapter VII arrangements would or should come into operation. Notwithstanding the recommendations of the (now former) Secretary General Boutros-Ghali's serious proposal about the Military Staff Committee in 1992 and the reiteration of the substantially similar proposal in UN summit of world leaders proposals in September 2005 an effective and functioning Military Staff Committee has not been realized. The 'bench mark' or criteria proposed in my seminar of January 1991 also expressed the desirability of the establishment of a Military Staff Committee in order for the 'spirit' of Resolution 678 (1990) (standing up to aggression) to establish a 'good precedent'. The precedential value of Resolution 678 (1990) is at best anomalous and the hopes (or suggestion) that I then made that the 'Gulf Crisis' should ease some of the 'technical' and geo-politics based intricacies and difficulties that had hitherto prevented the formation of Military

Staff Committee seem –in retrospect- to be premature. And this is notwithstanding the fact that many persons including a former UN Secretary-General has periodically raised this issue in the post-1991 period and within the United Nations.

Precedential Value of 'all Necessary Means' in Terms of Security Council action Regarding 'Threats to the Peace'

Resolution 678 (1990) employed a term that is pregnant with meaning in terms of the threat it imposes to the 'target audience' which is the then Iraqi government: if Iraq did not implement Resolution 660 (1990) and did not withdraw its forces from Kuwait by 15 January 1991 then the Security Council authorizes 'all member States cooperating with the government of Kuwait' to use 'all necessary means' to 'uphold Resolution 660 (1990) and all subsequent resolutions [pertaining to the Iraqi occupation of Kuwait]'. The enigmatic at the same time potent (with threats) and 'operative' phrase of Resolution 678 (1990) is the phrase 'all necessary means' which in effect authorizes and gives a legal imprimatur to use military force to evict Kuwait from Iraq. On the day of the 'deadline' set by the Security Council then Secretary-General Javier Perez de Cuellar made a reference to the phrase 'all necessary means' in what can be described as an ironic tone. The Secretary-General stated that '[n]o one and no nation can—except with a heavy heart—resort to the other "necessary means" implied by Resolution 678, knowing in advance that tragic and unpredictable consequences can follow'.[48]

There could have been earlier occasions when similar phrases or 'euphemisms' were used in United Nations discourse to warn that recalcitrant members of the United Nations or non-State actors which (in the determination of the Security Council) had caused 'threats to the peace, breaches of the peace or acts of aggression' to 'cease and desist' (to use a municipal law term) and if not 'all necessary means' could be employed towards stopping or reversing such actions.

Still, the frequency of the use of phrase 'all necessary means' or terminology to that effect indicating the authorization of the use of force or 'other forcible measures'–in its various permutations- became more frequent in the aftermath of Resolution 678 (1990). This 'invocation' of the threat to use forcible measures did become more marked in subsequent United Nations

Security Council resolutions when it deemed it fit on selective occasions[49] to determine that certain actions of States and non-State actors[50] constitute a threat to international peace and security. For example in Security Council resolution 836 (1993)[51] concerning Bosnia and Herzegovina it decided that 'Member States acting nationally or through regional organizations or arrangements may take, under the authority of the Security Council and subject to close coordination with the Secretary-General and UNPROFOR [United Nations Protection Force] *all necessary measures* through the use of air power, in and around the safe areas of Republic of Bosnia and Herzegovina, to support UNPROFOR in the performance of its mandate [to protect the safe areas]'[52]

Similarly in relation to Somalia, the Security Council in Resolution 794 (1992)[53] '[a]cting under Chapter VII of the Charter of the United Nations, authorizes the Secretary-General and Member States cooperating .... to use *all necessary means* to establish as soon as possible a secure environment for humanitarian relief operations in Somalia'[54]

During the time of the Rwanda genocide which took place in the period of April to July 1994 the Security Council did pass a Resolution[55] where again the phrase 'all necessary means' was mentioned. Acting under Chapter VII of the United Nations it authorizes Member States 'to use all necessary means'[56] 'in order to achieve the objectives of the United Nations in Rwanda through the establishment of temporary operation under national command and control aimed at contributing in an impartial way, to the security and protection of displaced persons, refugees and civilian at risks in Rwanda on the understanding that the costs of implementing [such an operation based on what the Member of the United Nations had] offer[ed] will be borne by the Member States concerned'[57]

The Security Council, in 1994, even went to the extent of authorizing the use of 'all necessary means' to ensure the departure of what it termed an 'illegal de facto regime'. In Resolution 940 (1994)[58] the Security Council 'determine[d] that the illegal de facto regime in Haiti ... is in breach of its obligations under relevant resolutions of the Security Council'[59] and '[a]cting under Chapter VII of the Charter of the United Nations authorizes Member States to form a multinational force under unified command and control and, in this framework, to use all necessary means to facilitate the departure from Haiti of the military leadership ... [and] the prompt return of the legitimately elected President and the restoration of the legitimate authorities of the government of Haiti ... on the understanding that cost of implementing the temporary operation will be borne by the participating Member States'.[60]

Subsequent to Resolution 678 (1990) there have actually been occasions when the Security Council using the term 'all necessary means' or 'all necessary measures' implicitly or euphemistically authorized the threat or use of force, under the parameters established by relevant resolutions, to recalcitrant States or non-State actors whose acts or actions are deemed by the Security Council to involve threats to international peace and security. In that sense, it is arguable that Resolution 678 (1990) did set a precedent in relation at least to the use of that particular term. Additionally and substantively the Security Council (rightly or wrongly) became more 'pro active' in the post Gulf-crisis/Gulf-war period in that the threat to use force for actions which affect international peace and security becomes more frequent than in the preceding years.

If one looks at the selected instances where the Security Council had authorized the use of all necessary means/ all necessary measures it would be seen that (needless to say) the factual situations and also the international legal dimensions in the above instances are different from that of the Gulf crisis of 1990.

For example, UNSC Resolution 836 (1993) can be said to be taken mainly against the Bosnian-Serb faction for its violations of international humanitarian laws. Even though issues of possible aggression or at least unlawful armed attacks (under international law) are prominent features of the war in and against Bosnia-Herzegovina (during the period of 1991 to 1995) it did not involve the whole sale annexation of a member of the United Nations (Kuwait) by another larger neighboring State (Iraq) as it did in the 1990 Gulf crisis. Moreover the actions taken by 'Member States of the United Nations' in response to the Security Council Resolution requesting them to assist the United Nations Protection Force (UNPROFOR) vis-à-vis the security of safe havens in Bosnia-Herzegovina is nowhere near as 'intense' as the US-led coalition's actions during the 1991 Gulf war which did use 'all necessary means' and perhaps substantially more 'means' than those that were actually necessary in their efforts to 'liberate' Kuwait from

Iraq.[61] And whereas the wording of Resolution 678 (1990) is open-ended and in a sense can be construed to give almost a 'carte blanche' Resolution 836 (1993) carefully hedged its authorization to use 'all necessary measures' to a specific and narrow objective: 'to support UNPROFOR in the performance of its mandate [to protect the safe areas]'[62]. Further, the use of 'all necessary measures' by Member States is 'subject to close coordination with the Secretary-General and UNPROFOR'.[63]

Similar observations can be made as regards the 'Somalia Resolution' where the Security Council authorized member States 'to use *all necessary means* to establish as soon as possible a secure environment for humanitarian relief operations'.[64] Compared to the Gulf War during the Somalia crisis of 1992 the use of force was minimal and the target relief was couched in humanitarian terms.

The authorization of the use of 'all necessary means' in the Somalia resolution above can be argued not to have involved trans border or inter-State violence and armed conflict. In the case of Bosnia-Herzegovina since it was previously part of the then Federal Republic of Yugoslavia it can be described at least initially as a civil war. In both cases the Security Council used very similar phrases to authorize its Members the requisite or 'necessary' measures or means to achieve its aims. Hence it can be argued that the 'precedent' of authorizing 'all necessary means' have been expanded in that the Security Council's authorization covers instances where there is no inter-State armed conflict.

In terms of the enormity of the lives lost the Rwanda genocide of April to July 1994 would easily exceed the deaths caused and the lives that were 'disrupted' by Saddam Hussein's invasion of Kuwait (on 2 August 1990) and its continued occupation by Iraqi forces till the start of the 1991 Gulf War on 17 January 1991. Many critiques have been made of the United Nations inaction in the Rwanda genocide. About two months after the genocide started in April 1994 the UN Security Council did pass a resolution where 'all necessary means' are authorized to achieve the 'United Nations objectives' in Rwanda. The fact that no effective action to prevent, stop or even 'ameliorate' the genocide in Rwanda by the United Nations and indeed by its Member States makes the invocation by the Security Council of 'all necessary means' to 'achieve its aim in Rwanda to be an exercise in futility.

The Security Council Resolution on Haiti[65] openly states that the then ruling Haitian military junta is. 'an illegal de facto regime'[66]. The use of 'all necessary means' were also authorized in order to 'facilitate the departure from Haiti of the military leadership'.[67] The author submits that the wording and orientation of this Resolution is quite significant in that the Security Council deemed it fit to determine that a military takeover and an overthrow of a legitimate government can, in certain circumstances, amount to a 'threat against peace and security' under Chapter VII of the UN Charter. In addition the military takeover and its consequences as well as the refusal of the 'illegal de facto regime' in Haiti to relinquish power is considered grave enough for the Security Council to invoke the phrase 'all necessary means': a term which was previously used in connection with the arguable first instance of invasion and annexation of a member of the United Nations by another Member. This occurred less than four years earlier when Iraq invaded and annexed Kuwait in August 1990.

The author does not suggest that the Security Council necessarily 'equates' the situation in Haiti at the end of July 1994 which, in the words of Resolution 940 (1994) was 'deteriorating, complex and extraordinary … [which] requir[ed] an exceptional response'[68] with the even graver and even more 'extraordinary'– indeed much more shocking and appalling- genocide that had occurred in Rwanda and which had just tapered off at the end of July 1994 when it adopted the Resolution concerning Haiti. Still, the phrase, the authorization of 'all necessary means' to Member States of the UN in their efforts to achieve the objectives laid down in the Resolutions appeared in both the Rwandan resolution and Haitian resolution adopted less than seven weeks apart from each other.[69] Both Resolutions contained a declaration by the Security Council of an understanding 'that the costs of each operation' authorized by the Security Council will be borne by the Member States'[70]. In the aftermath of the Haitian resolution and the eventual departure of the Haitian military junta as demanded by the resolution there were 'murmurs' from some international lawyers of 'the legality of pro-democratic invasion' with a possible imprimatur from the Security Council.

The Haitian resolution which deplored the military takeover and eventually authorized the use of 'all necessary means' to 'facilitate the departure of the military regime' was itself, in my opinion, not facilitated or caused by an ethical and legal standpoint taken by the Security Council on the 'illegality' (even in international law) of military coups and the need for the Security Council to 'stand up' to them. It is instead a by-product of a congruence of geo politics and the cooperation which the sole super power was able to obtain from Permanent Members of the Security Council at that particular period in relation to its small island neighbor. Due to its geographical proximity in the earlier days –and perhaps even in recently modern times- Haiti can be considered within the United Nations sphere of influence. The Haitian resolutions did not set a precedent for Security Council censure of most military coups that took place after its adoption. And it certainly did not set a precedent or led to any subsequent Security Council 'imprimatur' for the legality of 'threatened' or actual 'pro-democratic invasion'.

In comparison with the pre Resolution 678 (1990) days or the Cold War period the Security Council did play a comparatively pro-active role even if it is a selective and non-consistent or at least non-uniform. The involvement of the Security Council in terms of authorization of the threatened or actual use of force has in mixed results: in success as in the departure of the military regime in Haiti in 1994. It is noted though that the resolving of the crisis was mainly due to former United States president Jimmy Carter's intervention backed up as it were by the possibility of 'pro-democratic invasion' by the United States . In 1994 the Haitian military junta was warned to aide by the UNSC resolution or else faced the consequences of 'all necessary means'. In other cases like in the Security Council's failure to prevent or ameliorate the Rwandan genocide not only 'all necessary measures' were not taken but the Security Council even did not take 'minimal' measures. The 'precedent' that the Security Council has apparently set through its inaction or at least lack of effective actions like that in the Rwandan genocide is indeed deplorable. This 'bad' precedent should act as a warning for the Security Council in similar situations not to dither and to take all necessary measures through all politically and legally possible means to avoid a repetition of such events.

An Almost Farcical Misuse of Resolution 678 (1990) to Justify the Iraq War of 2003

One final issue that needs to be briefly mentioned and rebutted is that of what can only be described as a misuse of Resolution 678 (1990) to justify the 2003 Iraq War and its attack on Iraq in 2003 by the United States and United Kingdom-led 'coalition of the willing'. The factors that could be considered either way on the issues of 'farce', *sui generis* and precedent have been discussed above.

The subsequent misuse by certain circles in stating that Resolution 678 (1990) amounted to an authorization and United Nations approval of the invasion of Iraq in 2003 is, if not a farcical argument, and then it amounts to 'special pleading'. It needs to be pointed out that the authorization or imprimatur given by the Security Council in Resolution 678 (1990) was in the context of the invasion and occupation of Kuwait by Iraq and former President George H. W. Bush himself has written in his memoirs (written jointly with former National Security Advisor Brent Scowcroft) *A World Transformed*[71] that '[g]oing in and occupying Iraq thus *unilaterally exceeding the United Nations mandate* would have destroyed the *precedent* of international response to aggression we hoped to establish.'

In the context of the 1991 Gulf War one of the main protagonists of it-the President of the United States at the time-has written that in 1991 the invasion of Iraq with the purport of overthrowing Saddam Hussein would have 'unilaterally exceed[ed]' the United Nations as specifically stated in Resolution 678 (1990). And it would have set a 'bad' precedent.

John C. Yoo in his article[72] has made this line of argument. Yet the fact is that both the United States and United Kingdom before they invaded Iraq in 2003 did try very hard to obtain another Resolution which would have given an 'imprimatur' to its 2003 invasion of Iraq as it did for the 1991 Gulf War and they failed to obtain that.[73]

There was strong opposition to the 2003 Iraq war around the world and by a significant majority of international lawyers. In the light of the statement by the UN Secretary-General Kofi Annan that he hoped that 'we do not see another Iraq-type operation for a long time - without UN approval and much broader support from the international community'[74] and inasmuch as certain circles mainly those government officials from the protagonists of the 2003 Iraq war had misused Resolution 678 (1990) as a cover, excuse or justification for a war which among others the Secretary-General of the United Nations has termed 'illegal' and from the perspective of post 2003 war Iraq, Resolution 678 (1990) though arguably not farce-at least not to the extent that its detractors and critiques had asserted at the time the Resolution was adopted in 1990- and *sui generis* in the sense indicated in an earlier section has been misused as a bad precedent in the 2003 Iraq war. UN Secretary-General Kofi Annan had 'hoped' in his BBC interview of September 2004 that 'we do not see another Iraq style operation in a long time'. To put the (now) former Secretary-General's sentiments in the context of the theme of this article one also hopes –but one can never vouchsafed-that circumvention of the authority of the UN Security Council in the 2003 Iraq war and its contemporaneous as well as retrospective justification by reference to Resolution 678 (1990) would not set a (bad) precedent which the world's sole super power or other States for that matter feel that they are 'bound' to follow.

CONCLUSION

This article is an expansion, update and retrospective look back at the author's contemporaneous observations of and comments on UN Security Council resolution 678 (1990) based on a seminar the author gave in January 1991. The analysis and projections then made were in considerable detail commented on in this article to gauge, in part, as to whether and to what extent the author's analyses and predictions were borne out or proven wrong by future developments.

In terms of the 'farcical' issue pertaining to the adoption of Resolution 678 (1990) I would state that, in 1991, I have been entirely or almost entirely dismissive of the possible–or at least alleged by some- as to its farcical nature. Still, the self-critique that I have been dismissive of the contrived-if one is to abjure from using the term farcical again-nature pertaining to the adoption of Resolution 678 (1990) would be more of *a posteriori* argument or admission. It is *a posteriori* obviously in the sense that the analysis here is made–more than 17 years after the events pertaining to the adoption of Resolution 678 (1990). Subsequent assertions by some scholars as well as government officials to justify the invasion of Iraq in 2003 by referring to Resolution 678 (1990) has been, the primary reason for my statement *a posteriori* that the 'invocation' of Resolution 678 (1990) as support for the 2003 invasion of Iraq can be considered farcical.

On the issue of *sui generis* analysis was made retrospectively and prospectively on the peculiar or unique nature, as the case may be, of Resolution 678 (1990). In 1991 the closest comparison to this Resolution was the Korean resolutions of 1950 and the differences as regards the adoption of the Resolutions as well as future action were highlighted. The issue of developing better 'enforcement action' arrangements as envisaged mainly in Chapter VII of the United Nations Charter was also raised. Both the Korean resolutions and the Kuwaiti resolution 678 (1990) authorized the use of force against the States which had attacked their neighbors. And as far as the implementation of these Resolutions was concerned they were not done in accordance with the provisions of Chapter VII of the United Nations Charter. This particular aspect of the issue of *sui generis* is linked to the issue of precedent in that as stated in 1991 and as still relevant in the first decade of the 21st century an effective precedent to deter aggression is dependent on the United Nations being able to develop and enhance the collective security measures in accordance with the provisions of the Charter. Though in recent years measures have been taken in that direction the expectations articulated in my seminar as well as during the time of the 1990 Gulf Crisis in the immediate period preceding to and in the aftermath of the adoption of Resolution 678 (1990) has proven to be optimistic.

The major aspect of the article concerns the issue of 'precedent'. The issue of the imprimatur of 'all necessary means' being authorized to be employed by the Security Council to wrong-doing States such as that of Iraq in 1990 is remarkable. Later the targets were warned that actions could be taken not only against wrong-doing or recalcitrant States but have extended to non-State actors within a State[75] First, it is notable semantically in that this phrase finds its way into various Security Council resolutions pertaining to various regions after its ostensible and first ground-breaking use[76] in 1990 in regard to the Iraqi invasion of Kuwait. Secondly, it is also notable-perhaps even significant-in that at least compared with the four decades preceding 1990 the UN Security Council role in its primary function of dealing with 'threats to the peace, breaches of the peace and acts of aggression' have become if not more proactive then at least less crippled. In the subsequent decade and a half after 1990 the UN Security Council did intervene or did act with some frequency to stem, reverse or counter what it deems to consider threats against international peace and security from Bosnia to Haiti. The checkered results of the varying UN involvement is to be expected though the United Nations inaction especially in the Rwandan genocide is a precedent that needs to be avoided and which it is hoped[77] will not be repeated.

In the context of Iraq which provided the foregrounding, so to speak, of Resolution 678 (1990) it is also not a positive precedent that what was decided by the UN Security Council in 1990 is used as a legal justification for an invasion of Iraq which the then UN Secretary General belatedly and some what coyly described as 'illegal according to the United Nations Charter'. One realizes though that the legal justifications were made in a sense of attempting to provide legitimacy of a *fait accompli*: the invasion and occupation of Iraq and therefore the issue is 'academic' Neither the United Nations nor the massive demonstrations of hundreds of thousands of people prior to the forthcoming Iraq war of 2003 was able to stop it and –again- *a posteriori* legal justifications do not change the reality of the invasion and occupation of Iraq in 2003.

One realizes though that international law and its uses and misuses in official rather than primarily academic discourse[78]and actions is only one part of equation in the complexities of international relations and politics. In that sense I would state that the analysis and projections I made in 1991 in relation to the significance and future projections and permutations incidental to and consequence of Resolution 678 (1990) was (in the not too complimentary sense of the words) 'legalistic' where I have not fully considered other aspects of international relations pertaining to the subject.

Nevertheless in the matrix of power politics and of international relations international law is not always irrelevant[79] and what one believes to be a politico-legal analysis of one of the most significant UN Security Council resolutions in recent history is a worthwhile task. With that thought in mind a retrospective analysis of matters pertaining to, arising from or have connotations with UN Security Council Resolution 678 (1990) in the field of international law and international relations have been made in this article.

Notes

1. Prior to the adoption of Resolution 678 (1990) the UNSC has adopted, a series of Resolutions which in summary consist of: Resolution 660 (1990) which, among others, ' condemn the Iraqi invasion of Kuwait'; Resolution 661 (1990) which (among others) 'affirm[s] the inherent right of individual and collective self-defence in response to the armed attack by Iraq against Kuwait; Resolution 663 which, among others, [d]ecides that the annexation of Kuwait by Iraq under any form and whatever pretext has no legal validity and is considered null and void'; Resolution 664 (1990) which, among others, '[d]emands that Iraq permits and facilitates permits the immediate departure from Kuwait and Iraq of third-State nationals and grant immediate and continuing access of consular officials to such nationals'; Resolution 665 (1990) which, among others, '[d]etermined to bring an end the occupation of Kuwait by Iraq which imperils the existence of a Member State, and to restore the legitimate authority, sovereignty, independence and territorial integrity of Kuwait,: Resolution 666 (1990) which, among others, 'reaffirms that Iraq remains fully responsible for [the] safety and well -being of [third-State nationals] in accordance with international humanitarian law'; Resolution 667 (1990) which, among others, expressed is 'outrage[ ] at recent violations of Iraq of diplomatic premises in Kuwait and the abduction of personnel enjoying diplomatic immunity and foreign nationals who were present in these premises'; Resolution 670 (1990) which, among others 'condemn[ed] Iraq's continued occupation of Kuwait, its failure to rescind its action and end its purported annexation of Kuwait and its holding of third-State nationals against their will, in flagrant violation of Resolution 660 (1990), 662 (1990), 664 (1990) and of international humanitarian law; Resolution 674 (1990) which among others, 'stress[ed] the urgent need for immediate and unconditional withdrawal of all Iraqi forces from Kuwait and the restoration of Kuwait's sovereignty, independence and territorial integrity and of the authority of its legitimate government' ; Resolution 677 (1990) which, among others, stated that it was '[g]ravely concerned at the ongoing attempt by Iraq to alter the demographic composition of Kuwait and to destroy the civil records maintained by the legitimate Government of Kuwait'. Hence prior to the occurrence of the Iraq war there were series of Resolutions adopted by the UNSC which 'culminated' in Resolution 678 (1990) and which, among others, '[a]uthorizes member States co-operating with the government of Kuwait, unless Iraq on or before 15 January 1991 fully implements ... the above mentioned resolutions [which the UNSC has previously adopted in relation to the invasion, occupation and annexation of Kuwait by Iraq] 'to use all necessary means to uphold and implement Resolution 660 (1990) and all subsequent relevant resolutions and to restore international peace and security in the area'.
2. Compare this contemporaneous report in the 30 November 1930 issue of the New York Times 'The resolution authorizing force was supported

by 12 of the Council's 15 members, including the United States, Britain, France and the Soviet Union, which are permanent members and have a veto over decisions....The vote marked only the second time—the Korean war was the other instance—that the Security Council has invoked its power to sanction the use of force to counter aggression. To underscore the importance of the vote, all the Council members were represented by their Foreign Ministers, with the exception of Yemen and the Ivory Coast. The Soviet Union also cast the resolution as a turning point in international affairs that could lead to a more credible role for the United Nations in preserving international peace and resolving conflicts.' Paul Lewis 'MidEast Tensions: UN Gives Iraq Until January 15 or Face Force,; Hussein Says He Will Fight', New York *Times*, 30 November 1990, From New York Times Archive search *http://query.nytimes.com/gst/fullpage.html* (accessed 2 June 2008).

3. The author is aware of other instances of annexation which took place after the Second World War namely the Chinese invasion, occupation and annexation of Tibet in the early 1950s and the Indonesian invasion, occupation and annexation of East Timor in the 1975. But in both instances there was a factual and therefore an arguable political as well as legal distinctions which can be made vis-à-vis those two annexations and the Iraqi annexation of Kuwait in 1990. The status of the territories or 'entities' of Tibet and East Timor as independent States at the times of their annexations by China and Indonesia is disputable or unclear. In any case, both Tibet and East Timor, unlike Kuwait in 1990, were not members of the United Nations. (It is realized that membership of the United Nations is not necessarily a *sina qua non* for an entity to be recognized as a 'State' in international law. The author also realizes that in the case of East Timor the United Nations General Assembly as well as Security Council (in the immediate aftermath of the annexation of East Timor) adopted resolutions that deplored the invasion and annexation of East Timor. It is also realized that Israel annexed both the Golan Heights and East Jerusalem in the aftermath of the 1967 Six Day War. However the author contended I in 1991 and still contends that the Iraqi annexation of Kuwait in 1990 can be factually and legally distinguished from those annexations in that the Iraqi annexation of Kuwait was the annexation of the whole country which also a member of the United Nations–an arguable first instance since the end of the Second World War.

4. For example in relation to the Korean War itself when the Soviet Union ended its boycott of the UN Security Council and began vetoing the Resolutions in the Security Council the United States and its allies 'engineered' to bring the issues deadlocked in the Security Council to the General Assembly. And the UN General Assembly in the early 1950s mainly constituted of allies of the United States were able to pass the resolutions for example to condemn the (what was then called)'Red' Chinese intervention in Korea (General Assembly Resolution 498 (V) of

14 December 1950) and to recommend economic sanctions against it (General Assembly Resolution 500 (V) of 18 May 1951.

5. For example it is stated that in the first ten years of its existence the (former) Soviet Union exercised its veto powers in the UN Security Council 79 times : nearly half of the vetoes used during that period, 'United Nations Security Council Veto Power' *Wikipedia www.en.wikipedia.org/wiki/United_Nations_Security_Council_ Veto_Power*. That would indicate that in the early years of the United Nations, allies of the United States predominate in both the Security Council and the General Assembly. By 1990 as far as the General Assembly is concerned due to the influx of admission of many developing countries the geo-political interests of the United States will not generally – if not most of the time- be served by referring a matter deadlocked in the UN Security Council to the United Nations as it has done in the early days of the 1950s through the mechanism of the 'Uniting for Peace Resolution'.

6. In his memoirs *In the Cause of Peace[:] Seven Years with the United Nations* (1954) the first Secretary-General of the United Nations.Trygve Lie recounted how the delegates of the Soviet Union to the United Nations boycotted him. Trygve Lie also related about the Korean war in his memoirs.

7. Even though both countries from the then (1950) and now (2008) still divided peninsular were not members of the United Nations at the time the Korean resolutions were adopted it is significant that South Korea was mentioned in the UNSC resolutions of 1950 as 'Republic of Korea' and Democratic People's Republic of Korea (formal designation) as 'North Korea'.

8. UNSC Resolution 83 (1950). At the end of the Resolution it was stated that 'Adopted at the 474th meeting by 7 votes to 1 Yugoslavia). In foot note 12 it was also mentioned that '[t]wo Members (Egypt, India) did not participate in the voting, one member Union of Soviet Socialist Republics was absent.'

9. UN Security Council Resolution 84 (1950) of 7 July 1950. The footnote to the Resolution again stated that 'one member (the Union of Soviet Socialist Republics) was absent'.

10. Compare this note from a contemporaneous report from the New York *Times*:' By collaborating in the sanctions against Mr. Hussein, Moscow stands not only to secure its candidate membership in the club of civilized nations, but to greatly enhance its relations with the rich Gulf states and moderate Arab countries like Egypt.... Soviet leaders have been pressing to give the U.N. a wider role, and multilateralism has become more urgent to Moscow with the withering of the Soviet bloc in Europe.' Bill Keller, 'Confrontation in the Gulf, In Moscow Gulf Crisis Ranked Second' New York *Times* , 1 September 1990 (accessed from New York *Times* archive).

11. The author was aware of the importance of oil in the intense reaction especially of the United States during the Gulf crisis of 1990. In my article

'A Survey of International Law Aspects of the Gulf Crisis' which was published only a few days before the Gulf War (of 1991) broke out on 17 January 1991 I wrote that 'though there are other extra-legal factors such as the end of the Cold War, the era of cooperation between the two super-powers and the importance of oil this article will concentrate on its international legal aspects', Myint Zan, 'A Survey of International Law Aspects of the Gulf Crisis' (1991) *Current Law Journal* i. During the Gulf war in February 1991 the author had attended a seminar that was held at the University of Colombo, Sri Lanka on the Gulf war. One of the speakers a Professor from the University mocked the United States (in his view) (feigned) concern for 'poor little Kuwait' and the Gulf War (in his words) was 'all about oil, oil and again oil'.

12. To illustrate the points of the various political, economic and other pressures exerted by the United States so that both the permanent and non-permanent members of the Security Council would agree to its draft resolution one contemporaneous report states that 'The Security Council resolution, and the follow-up strategy now unfolding, were largely the product of month long travels by [former US Secretary of State] Mr. Baker and daily phone calls by President Bush to fellow heads of state, including one that involved tracking down the Malaysian Prime Minister in a Tokyo restaurant to browbeat him into getting his foreign minister to listen to Mr. Baker's arguments ...With America's place in the world, not to mention Mr. Bush's political future, riding on the outcome of the gulf crisis, the Administration never hesitated to let other nations know that their support for this resolution was vital to Washington, which would remember its friends, and its foes. Minutes after the Yemeni delegate joined the Cubans in voting against the resolution at the Security Council on Thursday, a senior American diplomat was instructed to tell him: "That was the most expensive no vote you ever cast" — meaning it would result in an end to America's more than $70 million in foreign aid to Yemen. More than American-Soviet diplomacy, of course, went into producing Resolution 678. Equally important to the effort, officials said, were less visible strategies, like the Bush Administration's decision to encourage Saudi Arabia to give $1 billion in aid to help the Soviets through the winter; its decision to let the Chinese know that if they did not veto the resolution their Foreign Minister would be received at the White House after 18 months of isolation; and arguments with smaller coalition members in which the President and the Secretary emphasized that every small state would be at the mercy of larger predatory neighbors if the United Nations failed to dislodge Iraq from Kuwait' Thomas L. Friedman' MIDEAST TENSIONS; How US Won Support to Mideast Forces the Iraq Resolution: A US-Soviet Collaboration- A Special Report; 2 December 1990 (accessed 4 June 2008 from New York *Times* archives)

13. The author cannot provide sources for this claim that in 1990 the United States sought the Resolution mainly for political reasons in the sense

indicated above. The 'counter-factual argument' that the United States and its allies would have proceeded in counter-attacking and 'liberating' Kuwait even if there has not been Resolution 678 can be made *a posteriori* from what subsequently happened in the Iraq war of 2003. The United States and its main ally in the 2003 Gulf War the United Kingdom tried very hard to obtain a Security Council authorization for its attack on Iraq in March 2003 but when it failed the 'coalition of the willing' attacked Iraq any way. Significantly–and to this author- and without legal justification the supporters of the 2003 Iraq war claimed that Resolution 678 (1990) read with Resolution 1441 (2002) gave them the 'legal' basis for the 'coalition' attack against Iraq in 2003.

14. See for example Attorney General Clarifies Legal Basis for Use of force against Iraq (18/03/2003) and Statement by the Attorney General, Lord Goldsmith, in answer to a Parliamentary question, tuesday 18 March 2003 and also see Attorney General's Advice on Legality of Iraq war: Straw Statement (26/03/2005) Statement by the Foreign Secretary Jack Straw, House of Commons, 24 March 2005 *www.fco.gov.* uk (archives search) (accessed 9 June 2008).

15. That does not necessarily mean that I am (from the perspective of 2008) ot the view that Resolution 678 (1990) is fully legitimate even if it is not entirely farcical. In 1991 though I would admit of less equivocation as regards both the legality and legitimacy of Resolution 678 (1990). For an expression of the 'precarious legitimacy' of the Resolution 678 published in the early days of 1991 Gulf War see Burns H. Weston 'Security Council Resolution 678 and Persian Gulf Decision Making: Precarious Legitimacy' (1991) 85 *American Journal of International Law* 516-35.

16. 'Sui generis', *Wikipedia, http://en.wikipedia.org./wiki/Sui_generis* (accessed 9 June 2008).

17. For e.g. D.J.Harris in the 1983 edition of *International Law; Cases and Materials* stated that UN Security authorization of a UN command to fight the North Koreans is 'unlikely to take place' D. J. Harris *International Law[:] Cases and Materials* (1983).

18. Paul Lewis 'MidEast Tensions: UN Gives Iraq Until January 15 or Face Force, Hussein Says He Will Fight', New York *Times*, 30 November 1990, From New York Times Archive search ***http://query.nytimes.com/gst/ fullpage.html*** (accessed 2 June 2008).

19. See text and notes accompanying above n 9.

20. During the time of the Gulf Crisis of August 1990 to January 1991 and the Gulf War of January to February 1991 the term that was used by the countries to repel the Iraqi invasion of Kuwait was 'the multinational forces'. The term the 'coalition of the willing' was used by the main protagonists and supporters of the 2003 invasion of Kuwait to refer to the few countries (fewer than the 31 counties which constituted the multinational force in 1991) during the US-UK led invasion, in 2003, of Iraq.

21. Due to passage of time I cannot provide the exact source of the Secretary-General Perez de Cuellar's comments but I did hear it on radio. For the Secretary-General's own account of events concerning the Gulf War see Javier Perez de Cuellar, *Pilgrimage for Peace [:] A Secretary-General's Memoir* (1997) *par tim*. Compare the categorical statement of the fifth Secretary-General of the United Nations that the 1991 Gulf War was 'not a United Nations war' with the belated statement–given almost under pressure or at least under repeated though gentle questioning by the interviewer- in a British Broadcasting Corporation (BBC) interview on 21 September 2004 that the March-April 2003 US-UK invasion was 'illegal according to the United Nations Charter' by Kofi Annan the seventh Secretary-General of the United Nations (again I could not give the exact time of the interview though it was broadcast or re-broadcast on 21 September 2004.) UN Secretary-General Kofi Anan was responding to the question of the BBC interviewer whether the 2003 US-UK invasion of Iraq was 'illegal'. After being gently asked twice Kofi Anan replied that it was 'illegal according to the United Nations Charter'. The fifth Secretary-General Perez de Cuellar did try to pre-empt the 1991 Gulf War when he visited Baghdad and met the late Saddam Hussein just about a week before war broke out on 17 January 1991 and as the 'January 15, 1991' deadline for Iraq to withdraw from Kuwait approaches. The fifth Secretary-General's mediation efforts did not succeed due at least in part to the stubbornness of Saddam Hussein. In the months leading to the 2003 invasion of Iraq due also (equally) to the stubborn 'determination' of the leaders of the 'coalition of the willing' the United States and United Kingdom to invade Iraq-and after failing to achieve or manufacture a resolution to attack Iraq-the hundreds of thousands of people demonstrating–in advance- against the war also failed to prevent it.

22. The author is aware that the United Nations Charter is not a 'World Constitution' and did not and does not intend to use the phrase 'constitutional reservations' in a municipal law sense. Even though in 1991 the Korean Resolutions were more than 40 years old the Soviet Union's absence in the Security Council meetings could, at least in the academic sense, raise some 'constitutional' or 'procedural' issues vis-à-vis the Korean resolutions. Compare 'The constitutionality of the Security Council resolutions on Korea question is uncertain' in Abdul Ghafar Hamid@Khin Maung Sein, *Public International Law [:] 'A Practical Approach* 445.

23. International Law text books (see for e.g.) Bowett below n. 24 mentioned that the Soviet Union 'challenged' the legality of the Korean resolutions but it never did challenge them in a juridical manner : that is before the International Court of Justice ((ICJ), the judicial organ judicial 'arm' or 'branch' of the United Nations. The closest occasions that would come to where some Judges of the ICJ expressed views on the 'legality' or constitutionality of the decisions of the UN Security Council can be found in the dissenting opinion of Judge Weeramantry in what is known as

the *Lockerbie* case (1992) ICJ Reports 3 and observations of Judge Lauterpacht in the *Genocide Convention (Provisional Measures)* case 1993 ICJ Reports 3. For an academic discussion of the possible 'review' of the Resolutions of the UN Security Council see T.D. Gill 'Some Legal and Political Limitations on the Power of the UN Security Council to Exercise its Enforcement Powers under Chapter VII of the Charter' (1995) 26 *Netherlands Yearbook of International Law* 33-138.

24. See for e.g. D. W. Bowett, *The Law of International Institutions*, (1982) 32.

25. 'Amendments to the present Charter shall come into force for all Members of the United Nations when they have been adopted by a vote of two thirds of the members of the General Assembly and ratified in accordance with their respective constitutional processes by two thirds of the Members of the United Nations, including *all* the permanent members of the Security Council' (emphasis added). The argument is that in the case of amendments in the UN Charter as stated in Article 108 *all* the permanent members are required to approve it whereas Article 27 (3) did not mention the word 'all'.

26. See for e.g. Goodrich, Hambro and Simons, *Charter of the United Nations: Commentary and Documents* (3rd edition, 1969) 230.

27. *Legal Consequences for States of the Continued Presence of South Africa in Namibia*, (1971) ICJ Reports 16, 24.

28. In the adoption of Resolution 678 (1990) twelve members of the UN Security Council (including four permanent and eight non-permanent members voted for the Resolution, one permanent Member (People's Republic of China) abstained and two non-permanent Members (Cuba and Yemen) voted against the Resolution.

29. Both the Democratic People's Republic of Korea and the Republic of Korea became members of the United Nations after the Security Council recommended in Resolution 702 (1991) (of 8 August 1991) to the General Assembly that both 'be admitted to membership in the United Nations'.

30. '[Soon after the invasion of South Korea by North Korea on 25 June 1950 and] [a]s the ground attack continued, the North Korean Air Force conducted bombing of Kimpo Airport near Seoul. North Korean forces occupied Seoul on the afternoon of June 28. However, North Korea's hope for a quick surrender by the [then South Korean President Sygman] Rhee government and the reunification of the peninsula evaporated when the United States and other foreign powers intervened with UN approval' 'Korean War' from *Wikipedia http:// www.en.wikipedia.org/wiki/ Korean_War* (accessed 11 June 2008). Of course even in this hypothetical counter-factual if the North Korean had succeed in 'reunifying' the Korean peninsular that process could not, in international legal terms, be expressed as 'annexation' but possibly 'forcible unification'.

31. I am aware that the military and strategic factors pertaining to the North Korean invasion of or attack on South Korea in June 1950 is quite different

from and cannot be fully analogized far less equated with the Iraqi occupation and subsequent annexation of Kuwait in August 1990. Kuwait is a much smaller country than South Korea and even though the North Korean forces were in the initial stages of the Korean war stronger at least in terms of (to use the now politically incorrect but at least factually correct) having more manpower and firepower than the South Koreans in the initial stages of the Korean war. Still, unlike the Iraqi invasion of Kuwait even at the height of the initial North Korean success the North Koreans were unable to have effective control of the Koran peninsular. In contrast, the domination and complete occupation of Kuwait by Iraq within a day or so of its attack was so swift that the Security Council, even if it had wanted to, would not be able to respond in the same mode as it had responded in the early stages of the Korean War. Inasmuch as the newspaper reports–and to a certain extent- academic commentary as well focus on the claim that the response of the Security Council to the Gulf crisis of 1990 was 'only the second time in UN history' a fairly detailed statements of the differences of the 'second time' with that of the 'first time' in UN Security Council history are being mentioned.

32. I could not, together with many others, including area experts (those of the Soviet Union) envisaged in January 1991, that the Soviet Union would collapse or at least most of its Constituent states would be transformed into the Commonwealth of Independent States before the year 1991 ended. It is true though that as long as there are two superpowers the cooperation or reduction of antagonisms among the two superpowers could facilitate the smoother functioning of the Security Council in its primary role of maintaining international peace and security.

33. When I gave the seminar on 11 January 1991 war had not broke out in the Gulf as yet though there was at that time a slim chance that the then UN Secretary-General Perez de Cuellar could still tried to reason out or negotiate a compromise with Saddam Hussein. I recall that when I wished the Secretary-General 'well' one of the persons attending the seminar pointed out to me that the Secretary-General has just returned 'empty-handed' from Baghdad.

34. The 1991 Gulf war which broke out on 17 January 1991 ended on 27 February 1991 when the United States led coalition evicted Iraqi forces from Kuwait.

35. Compare this contemporaneousness report from the New York *Times* 'Secretary of State James A. Baker 3d told America's NATO allies today that he expected President Saddam Hussein of Iraq to take a dramatic step, like a partial withdrawal from Kuwait, just before a United Nations resolution authorizing force to evict Iraq goes into effect in mid-January. Addressing foreign ministers at the North Atlantic Treaty Organization's annual winter meeting, Mr. Baker urged his colleagues to stand united against any such "ploy." "We should anticipate," Mr. Baker said in his remarks to the ministers, "that as we draw close to Resolution 678's Jan. 15 deadline, and as the choices are presented starkly, Saddam Hussein

is likely to try to undercut the collective will of the international community to use force... he may take a dramatic step on or around Jan. 15. He could withdraw partially' 'Standoff in the Gulf: A Partial Pull out by Iraq is feared as Deadline Ploy', Thomas l. Friedman, 18 December 1990, from New York *Times* archive *www.query.nytimes.com* (accessed 13 June 2008).

36. It is to be emphasized that this is a General Assembly rather than a Security Council resolution. The Security Council did not pass any more Resolutions on the Korea after July 1950 when the Soviet Union ended its boycott of the Security Council.

37. The relevant phrases of the General Assembly Resolution 376 (V) [1950] read '.. *Having* in mind that the United Nations armed forces in Korea are operating in accordance with the recommendation of the Security Council of 27 June 1950 [Resolution 83 (1950)] ... *Recommends* that all appropriate steps be taken to ensure conditions of stability throughout Korea'. I realize that the 'recommendation' made by the General Assembly has less legal effect and import than that of a Security Council resolution. One notes though that the phrase 'all appropriate steps' did appear in this General Assembly resolution of 7 October 1950 it preceded by more than forty years the potent as well as intended to be 'foreboding' phrase 'all necessary means' in Security Council Resolution 678 (1990).

38. Around the time the General Assembly resolution 376 (V) was adopted on 7 October 1950 'The United Nations troops drove the North Koreans back past the 38th parallel... The UN forces crossed into North Korea in early October 1950'. 'Korean War' *http//en.wikipedia.org/wiki/Korean_war* (accessed 13 June 2008). The General Assembly Resolution appeared either to retrospectively justify or authorize such an action as mandated by the Security Council resolutions.

39. Even though some of the points or issues that I raised in the seminar such as that of whether a separate Security Council resolution authorizing to attack Iraq (in the efforts of the multinational forces to evict Iraq from Kuwait) is necessary becomes moot (based on facts on the ground and on the air strikes against Baghdad and other places)s some issues that I have proposed and which would seem–at that time-to have some chance of implementation did not at all occur.

40. For an eclectic commentary on NATO's unilateral actions vis-à-vis Kosovo and also Yugoslavia in the immediate aftermath of the NATO's intervention see for e.g. Ruth Wedgwood, 'Nato's Campaign in Yugoslavia' (1999) 93 (4) *American Journal of International Law* 828-34; Christine Chinkin 'Kosovo: A "Good" or "Bad" War?' 1999 93 (4) *American Journal of International Law* 841-47; W. Michael Reisman 'Kosovo's Antimonies' 93 (4) *American Journal of International Law* 860-62.

41. On its meeting on 25 January 1946 the UN Security Council adopted Resolution 1 (1946). The Resolution was entitled 'Military Staff

Committee'. *www.un,org* (archives search under Security Council resolutions).

42. Ostensibly, Professor Bing Cheng first used the terms (in a related sub-field of international law) the phrase 'instant customary international law': see Bing Cheng, United Nations Resolutions on Outer Space: Instant Customary International Law? (1965) 5 *Indian Journal of International Law* 36. Here the word 'instant' is used in the context of the heeding of the UN Security Council Resolutions by some of the States to send their forces to the assistance of the government of South Korea.

43. The phrase 'ad hoc' is taken from sixth UN Secretary-General Boutros Boutros-Ghali report *Agenda for Peace* (1992) note 45 below.

44. Paragraph 42 of Boutros Boutros-Ghali, *An Agenda for Peace* (United Nations Document A/47/277 - S/24111 17 June 1992.

45. Emphasis added and foot note inserted. Compare the use of the word 'instant' application of Article 43 vis-à-vis the Security Council resolutions during the Korean war in text accompanying above n. 42.

46. Agenda for Peace above note 44 at paragraph 43.

47. *Revised Draft Outcome Document of the High Level Plenary Meeting of September 2005 submitted by the President of the General Assembly* UN Document A/59/HLPM/CRP.1/Rev.2

48. Confrontation in the Gulf: The Secretary-General: Text of Statement by UN Chief in Appeal to Iraq, New York *Times*, 16 January 1991 (from New York *Times* archives). Even though this comment was mentioned in a matter-of-fact manner in the Secretary-General's statement it does, in my view, bore an 'ironic' tone in that several days after the 1991 Gulf War broke out after the United States (mainly) and its allies with or without 'a heavy heart' implemented all those 'necessary means' to attack both Iraq and Iraqi-occupied Kuwait I have heard the Secretary-General stated on radio that the war was 'not a United Nations war'. Whether 'the necessary means' employed by the coalition (during the 1991 Gulf War) were conducted (to quote from Perez de Cuellar's phrase) with a 'heavy heart' or not the loss of civilian lives in the aftermath of the American-led bombing of Baghdad and other areas in Iraq in the 1991 Gulf War was indeed heavy. An international law scholar in an article written in the aftermath of the Gulf War stated that '[t]he enormous devastation that did result from the massive aerial attacks [in Baghdad and other places] suggested that the legal standards of distinction and proportionality did not have much practical effect', Oscar Schachter, United Nations Law in the Gulf Conflict (1991) 85 *American Journal of International Law* 452, 466.

49. The occasions in which the Security Council deemed that a certain situation affects or threatens international peace and security can only be 'selective'. When the protagonists or culprits which caused such consequences are Permanent Members of the Security Council or even

if that is not the case when any of the Permanent Member's direct or indirect national interests are affected the veto will be exercised which would prevent the adoption of the Resolution.

50. Not all the 'actors' to which the Security Council warns that all necessary measures or means may be taken against them if they do not abide by its resolutions are States. At the least they could not be unambiguously considered as States. For example, in the Security Council resolutions authorizing (albeit with qualifications) the use of 'all necessary measures' in relation to the safety and security of safe areas during the Bosnian conflict of the 1990s the main protagonist against whom all necessary measures may be taken is in the words of Security Council resolution 836 (1993) (see text and note accompanying n.51 below) is the 'Bosnian Serb party'–a non-State actor.
51. UN Document S/RES/836 (1993) 4 June 1993.
52. Ibid paragraph 10. Emphasis added.
53. UN Document S/Res/794 (1992), 3 December 1992.
54. *Ibid*, paragraph 10.
55. UNSC Resolution 929 (1994) UN Document S/RES 929/1994, 22 June 1994.
56. *Ibid* paragraph 3.
57. *Ibid* paragraph 2.
58. UN Document S/RES//940 (1994), 31 July 1994.
59. *Ibid* paragraph 3.
60. *Ibid* paragraph 4.
61. See for .e.g. *Report on the Gulf War* (Amnesty International) (1991), *Needless Deaths in the Gulf War* (Human Rights Watch) (1991). For a contemporaneous journal article and (at least) implicit critique of the loss of non-combatant civilian lives in the 1991 Gulf War see Judith G. Gardam 'Noncombatant Immunity and the Gulf Conflict' (1992) 22 (4) *Virginia Journal of International Law*, 813-16, 827-34.
62. UNSC Resolution 836 (1993), paragraph 10.
63. *Ibid*.
64. UNSC Resolution 794 (1992) paragraph 10.
65. UNSC Resolution 940 (1994).
66. Third paragraph of preamble of Resolution 940 (1994).
67. *Ibid*. Paragraph 4.
68. *Ibid*. Paragraph 2.
69. UNSC Resolution 929 (1994) on Rwanda was adopted on 22 June 1994 and UNSC Resolution 940 (1994) was adopted on 31 July 1994.

70. Paragraph 2 of Resolution 929 (1994) (concerning Rwanda) and paragraph 4 of Resolution 4 of Resolution 940 (1994) (concerning Haiti). As stated earlier Secretary-General Perez de Cuellar soon after the 1991 Gulf War commented that it was not 'a United Nations war'. More than three years later the Security Council in its Resolutions 929 (1994) and 940 (1994) did authorize the use of all necessary means to achieve its objectives as stated in the respective Resolutions. However the expenses must be borne by Member States and it is not at–to paraphrase Perez de Cuellar- 'United Nations' costs' or expense should they deemed it fit to act (in accordance with their national self-interests) based on the authorization and guidelines stated in the Security Council resolutions.
71. George H. W. Bush and Brent Scrowcroft, *A World Transformed* (1998) Chapter 19.. Emphases added. See also *Public Papers* (1992-93) 548.
72. John C. Yoo, 'International Law and the Iraq War', *Public Law and Legal Theory Research Paper Series*, No. 145 (2004) Text and notes accompanying foot note 25 to 27. For a more compelling and legally and morally valid argument see Carsten Stahn 'Enforcement of Collective Will after Iraq' (2003) 97 *American Journal of International Law*, 804, 806.
73. For one contemporaneous report of the failed efforts to get the approval of the Permanent Members of the UN Security Council see *Joint Declaration by Russia, Germany and France*, 10 February 2003, *Web Site of France Diplomatie*, www. pastel.diplomatie.govu.fr./editorial (accessed 8 July 2008). See also 'Latest US-Britain Draft Resolution in the UN', New York Times, 2 October 2002; Julia Preston & Eric Smith, 'US-French Split on Iraq Deepens' New York *Times*, 15 October 2002 at A1. For only a few among many others critiques of the United States and the United Kingdom's actions in the 2003 Iraq war published just before and in its aftermath see Rainer Hoffman 'International Law and the Use of Force against Iraq' (2002) *German Yearbook of International Law*, 33, Thomas M.Franck, 'What Happened Now? The United Nations after Iraq' (2003) 97 *American Journal of International Law*; Carsten Stahn 'Enforcement of Collective Will After Iraq' (2003) 97 *American Journal of International Law* 804; Sean D. Murphy 'Assessing the Legality of Invading Iraq' (2004) *Georgia Journal of International and Comparative Law* 173.
74. 'Iraq war illegal says Annan', *www.bbc.news.co.uk* Thursday 16 September 2004, 09:21 GMT (accessed 8 July 2008).
75. See for e.g. Security Council resolution 836 (1993) parts of which were directed towards the 'Bosnian Serb party'. See text and notes accompanying above n.4.
76. It is of some interest and perhaps legal significance as to how some terms first used by judges in judicial decisions or in politico-legal documents such as United Nations Security Council resolutions entered the corpus of domestic or international legal usage. See for. e.g. the author's tribute to the late Lord Denning in Myint Zan, 'Obituary: Lord Denning (1899-1999), 73(5) *Law Institute Journal of Victoria*, (May 1999),

p.37 where he credited Lord Denning for 'devising' the term 'legitimate expectation' in Administrative law. This term has been adopted and the concept has also been subsequently employed by some apex courts in the British Commonwealth. For the author's commentary on the term 'parallel wife' in the context of Burmese customary law –its first use being in a Chief Court decision of 1971- see Myint Zan, 'Of Consummation, Matrimonial Promises, Fault and Parallel Wives; The Role of Original Texts, Ideology and Policy in Pre and Post-1962 Burmese Case Law (2000)' 14 (1) *Columbia Journal of Asian Law* 153, 193-94, 196-97. See also above n. 42 concerning Bing Cheng's ostensible devising of the term 'instant customary international law'.

77. At least one international law scholar has used the term 'hope[s]' in the title of a book. See Julius Stone, *of Law and Nations: Between Power Politics and Human Hopes* (William S Hein & Co., 1974).

78. Though this would not always be the case the dichotomy between academic and official discourse can be discerned in relation to analysis of international affairs and the application of international law. See for example, Dean Acheson 'The Arrogance of International Lawyers' (1968) 2 *International Lawyer* 591. The late Dean Acheson, a former US Secretary of State was primarily castigating the (academic) international lawyers Myers S. McDougal and W. Michael Reisman's for the contents of their article 'Rhodesia and the United Nations: The Lawfulness of International Concern' (1968) 62 *American Journal of International Law* 1. Dean Acheson was very critical of McDougal and Reisman for supporting the United Nations Security Council resolutions imposing economic sanctions against the then Rhodesia for its unilateral declaration of independence and for the then Ian Smith regime's white minority rule. This is only one example of a dichotomy between (arguable) official and academic discourse. It is true that Dean Acheson being a former US Secretary of State (at the time of publication of article in 1968) cannot be 'officially' designated. However Professors the late Myers McDougal and Michael Reisman can be described as academic international lawyers and their writings would form part of academic discourse. And even if Dean Acheson cannot be described as an official he cannot be described as primarily an academic international lawyer. It was evident from Dean Acheson's article that he had directed his criticism –if not scorn- against 'arrogant' academic international lawyers.

79. I would like to end this article with a personal anecdote and recall of an event. Seven months after I gave the seminar on Resolution 678 (1990) at the University of Malaya Law Faculty on 11 January 1991 Professor C. G.Weeramantry, a Judge of the International Court of Justice (as he then was) gave the inaugural Tun Hussein On (third Prime Minister of Malaysia) memorial Lecture on 23 August 1991 in Kuala Lumpur, Malaysia. The title of Professor Weeramantry's Lecture was 'Does International Law Matter?' I invited a senior colleague of mine from the History Department of University of Malaya to attend the Lecture. My

colleague replied perhaps mischievously but also perhaps with some degree of belief or conviction that he did not want to since he was already of the view that international law does not matter. Notwithstanding my colleague's–at times-justified skepticism, perhaps even cynicism- on the role and functions of international law, international law at least at times does matter or should matter. Parts of this article are devoted to this theme in both a general basis and more particularly in relation to UN Security Council actions.

THE WTO TRADE POLICY REGIMES AND THE WELFARE DISCOURSE: SEARCHING FOR THE SYMBIOSIS

Haniff Ahamat*

In principle, the WTO (and GATT) has a neo-liberal origin. Nevertheless it can be argued that what is reflected in its treaty instruments which allow WTO Member States to impose trade policy measures does not necessarily promote free trade or reduce protectionism. Hence WTO trade policy regimes like anti-dumping, TBT and SPS regimes do have negative impacts on efficiency and economic welfare. However, in Section II, this paper finds that such measures have been justified on notions other than efficiency including those of fairness, communitarianism and sustainability. It is the interaction between efficiency and its competing notions that the welfare discourse on WTO trade policy regimes is built upon. At the same time, Section III shows that while the WTO Agreement and its annexes do contain provisions and measures which are not restricted to the maximisation of economic welfare, it is still difficult for those legal instruments to fulfill the realisation of social welfare goals. While such goals may be used to defend the use of 'WTO-consistent' trade policy measures, the social effects of such measures are marginal because the existing legal framework is less accommodative of the social considerations arising from the use of trade barriers. Consequently social rationales of trade policy measures were used to mask protectionism. This paper finds that the symbiosis between economic and social welfare is necessary and possible as shown in the discussions undertaken in Section IV which espouse the linkages between economic and social welfare considerations and the prioritisation of the latter in cases of persistent deprivation. The invocation of symbiosis in such context can minimise the abuse of trade policy for social reasons. In Section V, two mechanisms are proposed to institutionalise the symbiosis between economic welfare and social welfare in the context of the application of trade policy measures – revitalisation of the Special and Differential Treatment (SDT) regime and expansion/balancing of the interests considered in the relevant decision-making process.

I. INTRODUCTION

The welfare implications of the use of trade policy measures have long been subjected to debates. Drawing upon such implications,

* Assistant Professor, Ahmad Ibrahim Kulliyyah of Laws, International Islamic University, Malaysia

trade policy measures which are imposed by States to restrict imports can be beneficial to domestic producers if, as a result of the measures, they are protected from foreign competition. However, they can deleteriously affect consumers who would have to pay high prices for goods or foreign producers who are denied access to local markets. This paper discusses the implications of welfare on the use of trade policy measures which are 'sanctioned' by the World Trade Organisation (WTO). It also analyses how the notion of (economic) welfare interacts with other competing notions that justify the use of such measures which for the purpose of this paper are encapsulated in the term 'social welfare' as espoused by Amartya Sen. Such dichotomy explains the gap between the legal and economic aspects of the WTO trade policy regimes. This paper investigates whether the gap can be reduced through possible symbiotic relationship between the economic and social considerations underlying such regimes which can later address the concern that the WTO system is not capable of incorporating social welfare considerations.

The paper will first discuss the justifications of trade policy measures in the context of the dichotomy between 'welfare' and its competing notions. This is followed by an examination of the problems arising from the approach of the WTO towards the welfare discourse. Then, the paper explores the possibility of between economic and social welfare complementing each other to provide a solution to the notional gaps within the application of WTO trade policy rules. This will be followed by a discussion on the proposed mechanisms to realise the objectives of the envisaged symbiotic relationship.

II. JUSTIFICATIONS OF TRADE POLICY MEASURES–'WELFARE' VS OTHER COMPETING NOTIONS

The WTO rules allow importing countries to use trade policy measures including anti-dumping, countervailing and safeguard measures. To the welfarists, these measures are trade barriers. They prevent penetration of imports into local markets, reduce competition or even increase the prices for consumers. Hence they reduce the economic welfare of at least the importing country, which use and are supposed to benefit from them. The emphasis here is the economic welfare of consumers in the importing country not the welfare of domestic producers, workers or other economic agents. With free flows of goods in and out of the market, there will be competition between domestic and foreign players. The domestic players will have to adjust and remain competitive in order to continue their market presence.

The conceptual justification underlying the emphasis on the (economic) welfare arguments for reducing or eliminating barriers to international trade is the notion of efficiency. Welfare is measured in terms of utility-based Pareto-optimality (economic efficiency). Greenawalt explains Pareto-optimality in the following situation-'if someone is made what he or she regards as better off, and no one is made worse off, the situation is Pareto-superior to that which has preceded it'.[1] If there is a free market with perfect information and no transactions costs, exchanges between the players will continue until they reach a Pareto-optimal level.[2]

The notion of efficiency also places emphasis on efficient allocation of resources, maximisation of production and maximisation of welfare. The notion of efficiency also rejects barriers to trade because they make information between the players imperfect and contribute to transactions costs. Trade barriers are seen as causing a net loss to the economy (of the user of the tariff) by distorting the economic incentives of both producers and consumers[3] or allowing rent-seeking by special interest groups (which relates to capturing of trade measures by special interest groups).[4] Efficiency is also associated with the need for perfect competition in a market. Other salient features linked to efficiency are the achievement of greater economies of scale, the stimulation of technological innovation and the acceleration of diffusions of ideas and processes.[5]

The notion of efficiency, if applied to trade policy measures only erodes their economic rationales. One good example is anti-dumping policy which is the response to the practice of dumping. Dumping is selling in the export market at a price below normal value. Only when dumping leads to inefficiency (which is rare if the concept of predatory dumping is assumed), the state can intervene in the market by imposing anti-dumping measures. Otherwise anti-dumping measures will protect inefficient producers and reduce the economic welfare of the importing country.

Anti-dumping measures are still allowed within the WTO and General Agreement on Tariffs and Trade (GATT) systems. Together with countervailing measures which are aimed at subsidies, they are justified by the unfairness stemming from the trade practices that the measures address. There are also other trade policy measures whose objective derogates from economic welfare enhancements. These would include agricultural subsidies in the EC which protect farmers from cheap imports by subsidising production even if these measures benefit inefficient producers. In Japan, tariffs are used against imports of certain sensitive products particularly rice ostensibly to protect the interest of the farmers.

Consequently, alternative concepts were put forward to counter the critiques against anti-dumping and anti-countervailing measures. The concept of fairness was used to justify anti-dumping and countervailing measures taken against dumping and subsidies respectively. Dumping and subsidies become actionable not because they cause inefficiency but because they are associated with market asymmetries that give foreign producers an advantage over domestic producers. Market asymmetries are contemplated in the closure of the dumping/subsidising market due to high tariffs, restrictive business practices or government aid and these conditions facilitate foreign producers to cross-subsidise their export sales which in turn cut down prices in the importing market leading to the demise of the domestic producers.[6] The 'fairness' theorists of anti-dumping and countervailing measures argue that such unfairness is the reason for the domestic producers not being able to produce efficiently and hence driven out of the market.[7] Fairness has also been argued to justify anti-dumping measures when there are asymmetrical environmental and labour conditions between the exporting and the importing countries and such asymmetries give advantage to producers in the former to dump their products in the latter.[8]

Apart from fairness, communitarianism can be used as a justifying concept. Communitarians do not believe in the right of a rational individual to choose freely.[9] To them, human behaviour can only be understood by referring to individuals in their social, cultural and historical contexts.[10] Arguments propounded by individualism, such as achieving a genuine community is impossible, some ideas of good life that should be sustained by the state should be neglected *etc.*, do not lead to morally unsatisfactory consequences and at the same time constitute an unjust distribution of goods.[11]

Communitarianism is another basis to counter efficiency-based assaults on trade policy measures which have the effect of reducing economic welfare. The Pareto-optimality standard does not adequately address communitarian concerns arising from trade because it merely emphasises on transfers between individuals and once the individuals are better-off the society, it is assumed will be automatically better-off (this still depends on the level of indifference between the players).[12] Competition resulting from the quest for efficiency can cause distress to the community which may take the form of damaged ties of affection and kinship or disappearance of a common purpose and tradition. Apparently, such concerns are not adequately addressed by the notion of economic welfare measured according to the Pareto-optimality standard.

In their explanation of the different approach of the communitarians to anti-dumping measures, Hutton and Trebilcock state:

> 'The (communitarian) theory recognises that personal identity derives in large part from various social and community attachments. To disturb too much of these attachments, or to radically alter the nature of a community, may impair the welfare of individuals as *social beings*. In our modern, rapidly-changing society, individuals are often left with comparatively few traditional attachments to institutions such as family and religion, and job displacement may be particularly traumatic to the individuals and communities concerned.'[13] (Emphasis added)

It is always possible to expand the ratio of the above statement to other types of trade policy measures or other indirect measures aimed at curbing the influx of cheap imports. The EC's Common Agricultural Policy (a subsidy mechanism) has been used to protect some French farmers in the name of preserving their unique traditional and rural way of life[14] while steel tariffs were used by the US for the protection of steel producers which have been an integral part of the "industrial belt" communities in states like Ohio and Pennsylvania.[15] In Asia, agricultural tariffs against imported rice have been used by South Korea to protect its dwindling paddy-farming communities which are threatened by urbanisation, industrialisation and penetration of imports.[16]

These measures might not be only about the free choice of each individual which is normally geared towards the realisation of pecuniary aims. Some concerns which are linked to a particular attachment of individuals to their community and help realise non-pecuniary aims of those individuals and their surroundings may give a different account of such measures. For example, jobs that are lost due to cheap imports may be few or workers may migrate to other areas to find jobs so that such consequences of free trade continue to enhance the aggregate welfare of the country concerned. Besides, adjustments could be made by the economic agents in accordance with their comparative advantage.

Yet a communitarian will consider the fact that since those unemployed will no longer be able to purchase or use goods and services from other local industries, these industries will also be affected.[17] This is even more serious if such industries are unique to a particular country for their historical, cultural or even nationalistic values. Their inability to compete with foreign producers means they will be out of business. This will be not just an end to an industry which can be replaced by another more viable industry but a loss to the community or the nation as a whole.

Another alternative justification of trade policy measures is sustainability. It may be argued that such measures are justified if they prevent unsustainable production practised by foreign producers which leads to environmental damage, poverty, health problems, unemployment, human rights violation, social problems *etc.*[18] Ekins identifies three categories of sustainability – economic sustainability, social sustainability and environmental sustainability which interact with one another in a complex way embedded in the variable ethical, environmental, economic and social influences on those categories of sustainability.[19] A holistic approach is what is needed to achieve sustainability[20] although the meaning of holism might be highly subjective. Thus the notion of sustainability may encompass other concepts like fairness and communitarianism.

However, what is economically, socially and environmentally sustainable does not necessarily means that welfare or efficiency is increased. The increase in welfare (as well as growth and development) which is indicated by increase in production and consumption may prove unsustainable not only to the environment and the society but also to the economy.[21] To see whether something is economically sustainable, the maximisation of the value of consumption must not only be at present but also for the future.[22] The economic welfare of future generations as well as environmental preservation and maintenance of social well-being are not addressed by the Pareto-optimality standard.

Finally, trade policy measures can be justified based on development. It must be noted that economic efficiency does not necessarily spur economic growth and development in a particular country. Hence there is a thin line between development and the preceding concepts. For instance, development can reinforce the efforts to promote fairness and counteract imbalances between an exporting country and importing country. The latter could be a developing country with weak legal infrastructure, high unemployment, limited skills and technology, small market, high proportion of agriculture in the Gross Domestic Products (GDP), weak social safety nets, low tax revenues *etc.*[23] These conditions put developing countries in a disadvantageous position when competing with developed countries in international trade giving foreign producers (from developed countries) an advantage over domestic producers (from developing countries) in the absence of trade barriers.[24]

III. THE WELFARE DISCOURSE WITHIN THE WTO LEGAL FRAMEWORK

The WTO and its predecessor (GATT) are neo-liberal institutions whose main function is to liberalise world trade. The reason behind the formation of GATT had much to do with the Great Depression in the 1930s which was partially triggered by escalations of protectionism following the introduction of the protectionist Smoot-Hawley Tariff Act by the US Congress in 1930. The effect of such disaster had prompted the international community to establish GATT which promoted non-discrimination (through the Most Favoured Nation (MFN) and National Treatment rules) and progressively reduced tariffs and made non-tariff barriers more transparent and subject to international scrutiny.[25]

The economic welfare objectives of the GATT are stated in its preamble. The preamble to the GATT 1994 (which reinforces the GATT 1947) recommends the objectives of trade and economic relations which include 'raising standards of living, ensuring full employment and growing real income and effective demand, developing full use of the resources of the world and expanding the production and exchange of goods'. It thereby commits GATT's Members to enter into 'reciprocal and mutually advantageous arrangement directed to the substantial reduction of tariffs and other barriers to trade and to the elimination of discriminatory treatment in international commerce'. These objectives and commitments are symptomatic of the special position of the economic welfare within the GATT.[26] But does this mean that other concerns apart from that of economic welfare based as it is on the Pareto efficient should be discarded from such framework?

As will be seen below, the corpus of GATT rules is not restricted to achieving economic efficiency in world trade through trade liberalising measures. A broader dimension has been envisaged in the world trading legal framework post Uruguay Round where the overall objectives of the GATT/WTO system are no longer confined to enhancing economic welfare. The following has been added to the preamble to the Agreement Establishing the WTO which reaffirms the GATT preamble:

> "while allowing for the optimal use of the world resources in accordance with the objective of sustainable development, seeking both to protect and preserve the environment and to enhance the means for doing so in a manner consistent with their respective needs and concerns at different levels of economic development".

When sustainability is also included as a major factor for the optimal use of resources, the measures taken should be tailored to the different levels of development of each WTO Member. One could then argue that the symbiotic relationship between economic welfare and social welfare is at least recognised theoretically. WTO Members should not limit their deliberations on merely optimising production which could result in enhancing the quality and quantity of consumption (the engineering aspect of economy). They must also pay attention to how the exchange process promotes the well being of all economic agents in the society for now and the future (the ethical aspect of economy).

While social factors are spelt out in the preamble to the WTO Agreement, the WTO system itself is not necessarily pro-free trade. In general, the WTO creates two types of measures - measures which impose an obligation on Member States to refrain from having recourse to trade barriers,[27] and measures which regulate Member States in their use of trade policies which can produce the same effect as trade barriers. It is the latter which normally depart from the neo-liberal philosophy of the GATT promoting free trade.[28] For example, the WTO anti-dumping rules (found in Article VI of GATT and the WTO Anti-Dumping Agreement) are grounded on the need to counteract dumping which causes injury to domestic industry. In other words the prime concern is attaining fairness rather than economic efficiency. Thus the basic standards created by the framework do not reflect the concerns of the economic welfare of the importing country. It is the domestic industry that the policy or law protects competitors not competition in the domestic market as such.

The problem is that the WTO's anti-dumping regime is not so amenable to having social inputs in determinations made within the various decision-making processes. As discussed in the previous section, social reasons can justify anti-dumping measures especially when one alludes to the notion of sustainability and that social dumping should be actionable and be subjected to anti-dumping measures because the practice of dumping though involves low pricing and it can adversely affect workers in the importing country (anti-dumping user) or contribute to low labour and environmental standards in the exporting country (target of anti-dumping measures).

Nevertheless the substantive rules within the current WTO anti-dumping regime (which include national regimes) can determine whether or not actions taken accommodate elements of social dumping. Only economic indicators (which translate into the price strategies of foreign exporters and the consequential performance of the domestic producers) are considered and assessed before dumping is determined to be injurious to domestic industry and the corresponding measures are recommended. Even if attempts are made to introduce such social indicators, they can only succeed if the scope of international labour and environmental standards is properly defined. At the moment, it is not. This makes it difficult for the inclusion of such indicators to achieve the required objectives including addressing poor human rights, labour and environmental standards in production of goods and provision of services. Worse still, it will merely justify proliferations of protectionist measures by WTO Member States.

Other than anti-dumping measures, there are trade policies regulated by the WTO system which obviously promote non-economic objectives. These policies allow WTO Member States to use domestic regulations imposing health and safety standards (and to a certain extent, environmental standards) against imports and they are the Agreement on Sanitary and Phytosanitary Measures (SPS Agreement) and the Agreement on Technical Barriers to Trade (TBT Agreement).

These two instruments are among the offshoots of Article XX of GATT which lays down the exceptions to the general obligations for trade liberalisation within GATT. The grounds of Article XX exceptions include 'protection of human health or safety, animal or plant life or health, or the environment' and even the prevention of depletion of natural mineral resources.

The TBT Agreement governs technical regulations, standards and conformity assessments which include packaging, labelling, water and electricity efficiency criteria, product noise regulation etc.[29] This regime allows WTO Member States to make and enforce regulations on products not only based on their features when they reach the end-users but also on how they were processed. For example, a WTO Member State may impose a certain tax on imported products which do meet standards protecting the environment such as the use of refillable containers or recyclable materials. However such measures cannot be more trade-restrictive than what is needed to achieve a legitimate objective which is reflected in Article XX mentioned earlier. Additionally the measures must consider what risk will entail from non-fulfilment of a particular standard, and the risk is assessed based on scientific, technical and practical considerations.[30]

The SPS Agreement, on the other hand is more specific that it allows Member States to create measures to protect human, animal or plant life or health from pests, contaminants, toxins, disease-carrying organisms etc. What the Agreement also stresses is an SPS measure must be necessary and as much possible based on scientific principles and evidence. SPS measures act as non-tariff barriers against imports of genetically-modified foods, foods treated with hormones and other chemicals or foods infested by pests.

The objectives of TBT and SPS measures centre around the promotion of non-economic welfare interests *i.e.* health, safety, life and the environment even though in practice they can act as obstacles to free trade. In other words, the establishment of the measures by the WTO denotes the prevalence of social considerations (such as sustainability) over economic considerations (economic efficiency) in the exceptional circumstances characterised by Article XX. However there are claims that SPS and TBT measures may still maximise welfare and serve efficiency purposes by enhancing allocative and technical efficiencies (as opposed to productive efficiency), promoting product compatibility and thus increasing the possibility of economies of scale and scope and even promoting innovation and long term growth.[31]

Such claims can be undermined by the fact that scientific principles and evidence on which both regimes are heavily dependent may vary and produce variable results especially when due to the risks involved, precautionary measures were taken. The question now is what standards should be applied? For most products, there are international standards setting bodies. In such cases, SPS and TBT measures which use standards inferior to those prescribed by the bodies will be GATT-inconsistent. But for products not covered by the specific international standards, there may be less objectivity as the WTO rules provide that pertinent evidence or information is sufficient, subject to some other procedural conditions.[32] It must be noted that the use of TBT and SPS measures is subject to the application of national treatment rule so that standards imposed on imports must be equally imposed on like products from domestic produces.[33] However, the WTO jurisprudence still permits 'above international standards' measures as long as they are the least trade-restrictive means to achieve the relevant legitimate objective measures.[34]

This is how the pursuit of economic welfare objectives of trade collide with the promotion of health, and safety as the use of TBT and SPS measures can be protectionist and increase the costs of production unnecessarily at the expense of consumers. Yet the pursuit of the latter objectives (health and safety) is also in the interest of consumers. For example, unsafe food if consumed will affect consumers though its production and sales are economically efficient. The problem is that the WTO rules could create grey areas in which inconsistencies and uncertainties resulting from scientific processes may allow Member States to use the measures to prevent imports in a very trade-restrictive way *i.e.* when the risk of non-compliance is exaggerated. There is further complication when TBT and SPS measures are used by developed countries against developing countries (or even least developed countries) for risks which scientists have disagreement or for those which draw upon both social and scientific explanations. Producers from developing countries may not have sufficient resources or the necessary technology to ensure that their products can meet the possibly high (TBT and SPS) standards imposed on them by developed countries. This obstacle to trade will require special consideration of the adverse effects of such measures on the economic welfare of both importing and exporting countries.

The question now, can there be a symbiotic relationship between economic and social welfare considerations? If the answer is affirmative how would the linkage present a possible solution to the notional gaps within the application of WTO trade policy rules?

IV. A SYMBIOSIS OF ECONOMIC AND SOCIAL WELFARE?

As discussed in the previous sections, the polemics between (economic) efficiency and other competing notions have explained the different attitudes towards free trade and the measures regulating it. In fact such polemics are reflected in the WTO rules despite the neo-liberal roots of WTO and its predecessor – the GATT. At this juncture, one may raise the question whether the wide gulf between efficiency and the rest can be reduced. This brings us to Amartya Sen's criticisms of 'welfarism'.[35]

Sen argues that welfare should not only be measured in terms of utility-based Pareto-optimality. Therefore in enhancing the welfare of a society factors other than economic efficiency should be involved.[36] In other words there should be social efficiency as well in order to achieve welfare. Besides, he argues that it is possible to make 'cogent aggregative judgements about the society' (social welfare judgements) which take into consideration the distribution of utilities between persons.[37] This is most apparent when a person is affected by 'persistent deprivation' such as when he lives in poverty or works under exploitative economic arrangements.[38] In such cases, the rules determining welfare will differ in their acceptance of equity and efficiency so that factors such as inequality, poverty, distribution-adjusted national income and environmental evaluation will be taken into account.[39]

In contextualising Sen's criticisms of the conflict between the economic and non-economic goals of trade expansion beyond national borders mentioned earlier, economic efficiency is seen as creating situations. And these may differ between individuals and groups of individuals. Economic efficiency is usually linked to situations where goods or services are optimally produced at the minimum cost allowing the fruits of production to be available to consumers in the best form but at the lowest possible price. However these situations may also require workers to work more hours but with lower wages, forests to be cleared for agricultural and industrial activities, natural resources to be exhausted or inefficient factories to close down creating unemployment.

At the macro level, developed countries with technological, financial, market or other capabilities can heavily subsidise their relevant economic sectors (such as agriculture) and dump their products in least developed countries at very low price. That could be disastrous for the domestic producers. However, alluding to Sen's argument that social efficiency should be promoted and take precedence over economic efficiency, the well-being of consumers (which is advanced by the promotion of the latter) must not trump the advancement of those interests which draw upon the maximisation of social (not economic) welfare.

The question now is how do economic welfare considerations which promote consumerism interact with social welfare considerations to protect workers, the environment and the poor? Interestingly Sen does not postulate a dichotomy between social efficiency and economic efficiency. He does not reject, totally, the usefulness of economic welfare rule (the Pareto optimality test). What he disapproves is the use of such rule as the sole indicator of welfare.[40] In fact he (Sen) admits that the engineering aspects of economics (which include the mechanics of economic efficiency) are still needed to serve 'useful purpose in understanding the nature of many social relations of importance in economics' and allow the 'ethical aspects of economics' (which are reflected in the social welfare rules) to tackle 'the intrinsics of consequential analysis'.[41]

The economic interests of consumers in price or other factors which characterise economic welfare can be promoted side by side with the promotion of social welfare interests such as the promotion of workers' rights and environmental protection. What if the two categories of interests do not complement but contradict each other? This leads to the possible ranking of the interests which must take into account Aristotle's saying that the end of economics is not wealth but promotion of a good quality life.[42] Accordingly, it can be said that the social welfare interests should be ranked first so as to prevail over the economic interests (of consumers) in case of conflict. But such claim must be qualified by the complexity of making interpersonal comparisons which is needed to address distributional issues. Any attempt to disregard such complexity will result in arbitrariness as the society has complex multitudes of conflicting interests and it is difficult to give effect to each individual's preferences within the society. But as highlighted by Sen, persistent deprivation can minimise the relevance of such complexity.

The question now is how the symbiosis of economic welfare and social welfare can be institutionalised within the WTO framework. As discussed in the previous section, the preamble to the WTO Agreement does mention about the so-called social welfare considerations. But one must remember that the main objective of the GATT and WTO is still liberalisation of trade. Here, drawing upon the "symbiosis" theory, the ideal situation should be that the pursuit of the main objective should take into consideration social welfare indicators.

The problem is, there is complexity in how economic and social welfare considerations interact within the context of WTO rules. As mentioned above, ranking variables relevant to the attainment of the well being or promotion of the interests of a human is not an easy task. And these are of a purely philosophical nature. The complexity is even more acute when the discussion embarks on what the WTO legal instruments have to offer.

Reference should be made to the debates on the interaction between human rights and world trade law. On one side, writers opine that human rights values should be read into the WTO corpus so that if an obligation to reduce or eliminate trade barriers is linked to a human right violation in one way or another, such obligation will not stand. In other words, there should be no right to free trade.[43] Or human rights rules are part of the same legal order as trade liberalisation rules wherein the former should take precedence over the latter. On the other side, it has been viewed that the WTO should institutionalise free trade in a constitutional framework modelled after the European economic constitutionalist system (the EC) which establishes the four free trade freedoms–freedoms of movements of goods, people, capital and services based on the principle of open competition.[44] Responding to this view, it has been counter-argued that the very purpose of the WTO (GATT) differs from the purpose of the EC. Unlike the EC which created the Common Market, the WTO does not eliminate all measures at the customs check-points of each of its Members (*i.e.* the WTO only speaks about trade liberalisation not the replacement of local markets with a single WTO market).[45]

Between the two extremes, a line is drawn separating the "spheres" of human rights rules and trade liberalisation rules.[46] As such, human rights violations should be dealt with by human rights treaties not WTO agreements. The same applies to violations of international environmental law. These are despite the "close proximity" between the violations and the application of trade liberalisation rules.

In the end, problems remain as to how to fit social welfare indicators (such as human rights and environmental protection) into the WTO framework. What more, the inclusion of these indicators will affect the balance in world trade regulation against the interests of developing countries as developed countries with higher human rights, labour and environmental standards use such indicators to prevent access of goods from the former into the latter. This is evident in the case of the TBT regime where the use of such trade policy can mask protectionist measures against developing countries which cannot meet the high technical standards imposed on their products. The measures may not be based on concrete social reasons or if they are, the use of such measures does not remedy the so-called social deprivation in the importing country, the exporting country or the world as a whole. This brings us back to Sen's thesis on the interaction between economic welfare and social welfare whereby the latter should be given priority over the former–the element of persistent deprivation should be addressed.

V. THE MECHANISMS PROPOSED FOR INSTITUTIONALISING THE SYMBIOSIS OF ECONOMIC AND SOCIAL WELFARE

Two mechanisms are proposed to institutionalise the symbiosis of economic and social welfare in the context of WTO trade policy system. First is the revitalisation of the special and differential treatment (SDT) regime for developing countries. Second is the expansion and/or balancing of the interests considered in the decision-making process of trade policy measures.

1. Mechanisms which Revitalise the Special and Differential Treatment (SDT) Regime within Non-Tariff Barriers to Trade

The concerns of developing countries arising from international trade are related to the symbiotic relationship between economic and social welfare. This is because the notion of 'persistent deprivation' is evident at inter-State (macro) level. And this can be discerned in the disadvantageous conditions in developing countries.[47] These in turn hinder their welfare-maximising participation in international trade. At the same time, the inclusion of social welfare considerations may act as a double-edge sword against developing countries as they can impinge on the natural advantages benefitting them such as low production costs and largely available natural resources.

When the concerns of the developing countries in international trade are addressed it should facilitate or allow asymmetrical commitments to be imposed on developed as well as developing countries. It also allows harmonisation of social (environmental and labour) standards between all countries. In this regard there is a need for certain degree of diversity of such standards which is driven by natural rather than artificial factors and this diversity promotes the economic welfare of developing countries.

The SDT provisions which are found in the GATT, the WTO Agreement and most of the annexed agreements[48] will now be discussed. These provisions presuppose the relaxation of certain GATT principles *i.e.* the principle of reciprocity in trade concessions and negotiations, and the principle of non-discrimination. The GATT allows non-reciprocity in the commitments undertaken by a developing country to reduce or remove tariffs and other trade barriers vis-a-vis a developed country while the developed country maintains or even increases its commitments for the same purpose with respect to the developing country.[49]

However the SDT principle remains largely unenforceable in the context of non-tariff barriers. In all agreements implementing the various GATT provisions imposing such barriers, the respective SDT provisions remain toothless. This can be seen in

Article 12 of the TBT Agreement and Article 15 of the Anti-Dumping Agreement. Both provisions only require the special needs of developing countries to be considered in the applications of those agreements but mention nothing about how the overall obligations of developed and developing countries arising from the agreements can be 'tailored' to the need of creating a level playing field between developed and developing countries.[50]

One of the strategies is for the WTO system to allow different thresholds for developing and developed countries within the substantive rules of the trade policy regimes. For example the WTO anti-dumping regime can prescribe higher *de minimis* thresholds for developing countries of 'negligible' dumping margin and import volume hence making it more difficult for imports from developing countries to be imposed with anti-dumping duties. Additionally, there can be parallel rights and duties arising from the use of trade policy measures by developed countries against developing countries. For example, the WTO TBT regime can attach to the right to impose technical standards for, say, environmental protection, an *obligation* to provide technical assistance or ensure transfer of technology to developing countries so that the legitimate objective behind the imposition of such standards can be achieved.

However, there can be an unexpected consequence if trade policy measures are used by developing countries against other developing countries which is now the trend among not only developing countries but also least developed countries (LDCs).[51] If higher thresholds are applied only in measures by a developed country against a developing country producer, such special treatment will be automatically excluded in intra-developing country trade. On the other hand, if it is applied to such trade, the use of the measures will be made difficult and this will lead to a paradox because the measures are supposed to remedy the imperfections of free trade affecting developing countries in the first place. There may also be continuing criticisms if such treatment is used by a more industrialised developing country against an LDC.

A possible solution is an intra-State (micro) mechanism which expands and balances the interests considered in the decision-making process of trade policy measures at national, regional and multilateral levels.

2. Mechanism which Expands and/or Balances the Interests Considered in Decision-Making Process

The above mechanism actually refers to the public interest clause. Many writers relate the objectives of inserting public interest clause in a trade policy regime to the improvement of the regime for the benefits of consumers in the importing country. They argue that public interest clause increases flexibility, transparency and participation,[52] and exposes the narrow attitude of favouring domestic producer interests in the regime.[53]

However, the interest-expanding and interest-balancing roles of public interest clause can be undermined by some conceptual difficulties underscoring the WTO system itself. Mavroidis, for example, argues that the foundations of the WTO rules on non-discrimination (MFN and national treatment) do not include consumer welfare concerns, let alone take a stance on whether producer and consumer interests should be balanced, in relation to non-discriminatory market access of goods although they provide for the safeguarding of producer interests.[54]

Besides, Messerlin observes that the WTO Agreement and its annexed agreements can hardly incorporate a cost-benefit analysis of welfare balances to the overall benefit of the WTO members[55] (but it must be noted that the WTO safeguards regime contains a public interest clause). The introduction of such analysis could hardly produce any difference because 'sovereign states' would still 'put different weightings on the various components of the welfare balances' even if they act in good faith.[56] WTO rules are also different from laws made by a Parliament and imposed on its citizens and that the former (WTO rules) are defined by WTO Members to be applied to themselves.[57] This makes states look for stronger terms for their partners and looser terms for themselves, thus it is difficult for rules and procedures which can loosen the grip of the importing country over a trade policy regime to the advantage of the exporting country, to be made mandatory especially when the position of each States as users and targets of trade policy measures is not equal.[58]

Even at domestic level, while some trade policy (including anti-dumping) legislation may contain a public interest clause, the prospect of such clause is very much dimmed by what is termed as 'public choice'. The public choice theory is defined by Downs who suggests that it is the private interest which motivates government to perform its social function and as such, such function is accomplished by the private motive of attaining the income, power and prestige of being in office.[59] The implication of such theory is that laws and policies will only benefit self-interested individuals (both within and outside governments) at the expense of the larger public.

Do the above assertions mean that public interest clause is not relevant? At the same time, one may wonder whether there is a need for expanding or balancing the interests affected by the use of trade policy measure. A trade officer can easily say that any Tom, Dick and Harry should not be let in so that busybodies will not make noise in the decision-making process of such a sophisticated policy as trade policy. Nevertheless, a good policy depends on what feeds it. This means that though concrete outcomes of policy-balancing are hard to realise, the expansion (if not balancing) of the interests beyond those of domestic producers can do good to the stakeholders especially if one alludes to the possible captures of trade policies.

The regulatory capture theory was first developed by Stigler who expounded his 'economic theory of regulation'[60] which is explained by Peltzman as 'an integration of the economics of regulation and the economics of politics in which transactions between self-interested suppliers and demanders determine the regulatory income'.[61] The suppliers are political actors who can be the legislators, executive etc while what they have to sell is power over the wealth of a regulated industry's buyers and sellers who are the demanders.[62] These demanders compete for access for such power and well-organised and well-resourced interest groups will prevail over poorly-organised and poorly-resourced interest groups.

Regulatory capture takes two forms – special interest capture and political capture. Special interest capture links the question of regulatory capture to the prevalence of special (producer) interest prevailing over public (consumer) interest.[63] Political capture, on the other hand is about regulation being shaped to further the interests of the political elites.[64] Lack of informed opinions outside government and absence of independent media and judiciary can further transform such capture into cronyism or corruption.[65]

Special interest and political captures of trade policy measures can create negative economic and social welfare impacts. They can reduce economic welfare by closing markets to imports, impeding competition or reinforcing monopolies. Diametrically opposed, the captures of trade policy measures can reduce social welfare by limiting the fruits of trade protection to special interest groups and political elites although the initial arguments for such protection are that they are justified on social grounds including environmental protection and job creation/protection. Worse still, social welfare will be minimised by the effects of cronyism and corruption which create both economic and social costs to be borne by the public. And these phenomena are evident in developing countries that they may reduce the effectiveness of the SDT measures used in the context of trade involving such countries.

These arguments can provide a momentum for public interest clause to foster a symbiotic relationship between economic and social welfare. The formal or informal use of public interest clause can at least increase informed opinions outside (and inside) government and this can increase transparency and deter cronyism and corruption which are rampant in some developing countries. Again, when one alludes to SDT measures, the lack of mechanisms which increase informed opinions will only make such measures prone to special interest and political captures. In the end, the impacts of such measures can hardly reach the poor and others who suffer from persistent deprivation.

The *Newsprint* case[66] is good example. It was an anti-dumping case from Malaysia on imports of newsprint, a raw material for manufacturing newspapers. The welfare-synthesising function of the public interest clause is evident in this case when 'public interest' investigation was used by interested parties to assess the impact of anti-dumping duties on the price and availability of school exercise books in Malaysia. In the Canadian anti-dumping case of *Certain Prepared Baby Foods from the US,*[67] the argument that the use of anti-dumping measures can have deleterious impact on low-income families which heavily depend on cheap baby foods imported from the US was raised in the public interest investigation.

VI. POSTSCRIPTS

The above discussions show that interaction and at times tension (or dichotomy) between economic welfare and social welfare can be used to critique trade policy measures for social reasons. The use of the measures on such grounds may take into account the unique and special conditions in developing and least developed countries. The emphasis should be on the matter of persistent deprivation as a yardstick to ensure that social welfare can be given priority over economic welfare only in real and genuine cases. Otherwise the positive effects of free trade will not materialise. Further, the restrictions on international trade to enhance social welfare may be subjected to regulatory capture and later abuse by special interest and political interest groups.

It has been shown that both economic and social welfare can be institutionalised through mechanisms which enhance the special and differential treatment for developing countries and even more important, the least developed countries. However this may only provide a solution in an inter-State context. It is still likely that while the particular developing country benefits from such treatment, the impact is not felt by the stakeholders. And one must not forget that problems facing these countries may be internally generated particularly by corruption. Again, political theories are quick at saying that organisation and resources determine whose interests will be advanced. This is how the invocation of persistent deprivation may require the next step to be taken–expand and/or balance the interests considered in trade policy decision-making process. In this regard, there should be a symbiotic relationship between the first and second mechanisms where the use of the latter complements the former and vice-versa.

Yet it may be argued that such a mechanism is difficult to enforce due to organisational and practical barriers or even due to the reality in public decision making which favour special interests over public interest. These barriers can be offset by evolving communication technologies (e.g. digital television, the internet and mobile phones). As observed by Lupia and Sin, such technologies can reduce the organisational costs of large groups[68] and maximise the 'noticeability' of the groups' members.[69] Large groups like consumers are difficult to manage due to high organisational costs which have to be spread over a large number of individuals. Some of these individuals are free riders. The groups must also bear the cost of enabling the flow of what Bartlett terms as subsidised information.[70] Such information supports what the groups want from a government policy including trade policy. Technologies like the internet can break the barriers between these individuals. This in turn expedites the utilisation of the resources needed for the advancement of the groups' interests arising from the use of the policy concerned.

Future research may expand the role of evolving technologies in facilitating the positive symbiosis between economic and social welfare in the context of trade policy regimes. The research can analyse the two proposed mechanisms–the SDT and public interest regimes. It should also look into how far such technologies contribute to making the mechanisms practicable and achieve their objectives.

Notes

1. Greenewalt, K., *Law and Objectivity* (New York: Oxford Univ. Press, 1992), p. 170.
2. *Ibid.*
3. Krugman, P.R. and Obstfeld, M., *International Economics–Theory and Policy* (Boston: Addison-Wesley, 2003), p. 219.
4. Porter, R.B., 'Efficiency, Equity and Legitimacy: The Global Trading System in the Twenty-First Century' in Porter, R.B. and P. Sauve, P. (eds), *Efficiency, Equity and Legitimacy* (Washington D.C.: Brookings Institution Press, 2001), p. 6.
5. *Ibid.*
6. Holmes and Kempton, (1997), p. 13.
7. Stewart, T. P. and Brightbill, T. C., 'Some 'Heretical' Observations on the Interaction of US Trade and Competition Laws: A Defense of US Antidumping and Countervailing Duties', *US-Mexico Law Journal* 4 (1996): 35-48, p. 38.
8. Cass, R. and Boltuck, R., 'Antidumping and Countervailing Law: The Mirage of Equitable International Competition' in Bhagwati, J.N. and Hudec, R.E., *Fair Trade and Harmonization: Prerequisites for Free Trade?* (Cambridge MA: MIT Press, Vol. 2, 1997), pp. 395-401.
9. Avineri, S. and de-Shalit A., *Communitarianism and Individualism* (Oxford: Oxford Univ. Press, Oxford, 1992), pp. 1-2.
10. *Ibid.*, p. 2.
11. *Ibid.*
12. See definitions of Pareto-optimality standard in Greenewalt, *Law and Objectivity*, (1992), pp. 170-171.
13. Hutton, S. and Trebilcock, M.J., 'The Empirical Study of the Application of Canadian Anti-Dumping Laws: A Search for Normative Rationales', *JWT* 24 (1990): 123, p. 135.

14. See *http://www.brookings.edu/opinions/2005/1115france_gordon.aspx.* (accessed on 7/11/2008).
15. See *http://www.iefd.org/articles/local_democracy_possible.php*. Also note the tariffs were imposed by President George W. Bush in 2002 but after there were declared illegal by the WTO and the EC threatened with retaliatory measures, they were lifted in 2003. See the report in the Boston Globe, December 5, 2003 available online at *http://www.boston.com/news/nation/articles/2003/12/05/bush_lifts_steel_import_tariff* (accessed on 7/11/2008).
16. See *http://yaleglobal.yale.edu/display.article?id=6196*, (accessed on 7/11/2008).
17. Leclerc, J.M., 'Reforming Anti-Dumping Law: Balancing the Interests of Consumers and Domestic Industries', *McGill Law Journal* 44 (1999): 111, p. 119.
18. Alben, E., 'GATT and the Fair Wage: A Historical Perspective on the Labor-Trade Link', *Columbia Law Review* 101 (2001): 1410; Fletcher, C. R., 'Greening World Trade: Reconciling GATT and Multilateral Environmental Agreements Within the Existing World Trade Regime', *Journal of Transnational Law and Policy* 5 (1996): 341-372.
19. Ekins, P., *Economic Growth and Environmental Sustainability – the Prospects for Green Growth*, (London: Routledge, 2000), pp. 70-71.
20. Dunphy, D and Benveniste, J., 'An Introduction to the Sustainable Corporation' in Benveniste, J., Dunphy, D. and Griffiths, A. (eds), *The Corporate Challenge of the 21st Century* (Crows Nest NSW: Allen & Unwin., 2000), p. 3.
21. Ekins, (2000), pp. 61-62.
22. *ibid.*, p. 75.
23. Stiglitz, J. and Charlton, A., *Fair Trade for All – How Trade Can Promote Development* (Oxford: Oxford Univ. Press, 2005), pp. 24 35.
24. *Ibid.*, pp. 78-79.
25. See Trebilcock and Howse, *op. cit.*, p. 20.
26. As to "full employment" mentioned in the preamble, one may allude to two different approaches–efficiency and equity approaches to the issue of employment. It can be argued here that it is the former that is contemplated in the preamble.
27. Such rules include the rule banning the use of quantitative restrictions.
28. However it is still possible for the former type of rules to prevent the fulfillment of such philosophy i.e. by not being enforced. For example, the rule banning the use of quantitative is still not enforceable. The same applies to the rules on agriculture which should have seen the tearing down of trade restrictions on imports of the relevant products but so far such objective is still not achieved.

29. See Annex 1 of the TBT Agreement.

30. See Art. 2.2 of the TBT Agreement.

31. Trebilcock, M.J. and Howse, R., *The Regulation of International Trade* (London: Routledge, 2nd ed. 1999), p. 144.

32. See Art. 2.4, 2.5 and 2.9 of TBT Agreement. Also see Trebilcock and Howse, *op. cit.*, p. 143.

33. See Art. 2.1 of TBT Agreement.

34. See for example the Appellate Body's decision in the *EC Measures Concerning Meat and Meat Products (Hormones)*, Complaint of the US, WT/DS26/AB/R (also known as the *Beef Hormone* case). See Trebilcock and Howse, *ibid.*, pp. 155-156.

35. See Sen, A. K., *On Ethics and Economics* (Oxford: Blackwell, 1987); Sen, A. K., 'The Possibility of Social Choice', *American Economic Review* 89(3) (1999): 349-378.

36. Sen, A. K., *On Ethics and Economics*, pp. 31-41.

37. Sen, A. K., 'The Possibility of Social Choice', p. 349.

38. *Ibid.*, p. 358.

39. *Ibid.*, p. 357.

40. Sen, A. K., *On Ethics and Economics*, pp. 31- 33; Sen, A.K., 'The Possibility of Social Choice', pp. 352-353.

41. Sen, A. K., *On Ethics and Economics*, p. 10.

42. Aristotle, Politics III.ix – translation by Barker, 1958, p. 117. Note that Sen alludes to that saying in his *On Ethics and Economics*, p. 3.

43. See Alston, P., 'Resisting the Merger and Acquisition of Human Rights by Trade Law: A Reply to Petersmann', 13 *European Journal of International Law* (2002) 815. Also see Howse, R., 'Human Rights in the WTO: Whose Rights, What Humanity? Comment on Petersmann', 13 *European Journal of International Law* (2002) 651.

44. Petersmann, E. U., 'Time for Integrating Human Rights into the Law of Worldwide Organization', *Jean Monnet Working Paper* 7/01 available on *http://www.jeanmonnetprogram.org/papers/01/012301.pdf.*

45. Infra note 38.

46. See Marceau, G., 'WTO Dispute Settlement and Human Rights', 13 *EJIL* (2002) 753.

47. Supra notes 23 and 24.

48. The annex agreements include the Anti-Dumping Agreement, TBT Agreement and SPS Agreement.

49. See Article XXXVI:8 of GATT. Also see Trebilcock and Howse, *op. cit.*, p. 34.

50. It is true that Art 12(4) of the TBT Agreement modifies certain substantive obligations of developing countries *i.e.* their technical regulations may not be based on international standards. However, this does not mean that the regulations of developed countries can be equivalent to or above such standards. Besides, it is the latter which will restrict trade for the benefits of developing countries.
51. See Kufuor, K. O., 'The Growing Problem of Intra-Developing Country Actions in World Trade' in Debroy, B and Chakraborty, D., *Anti-Dumping: Global Abuse of a Trade Policy Instrument* (New Delhi: Liberty Institute, 2007).
52. Stegemann, K., 'Anti-Dumping Policy and the Consumer', 19 *JWT* 19 (1985): 446-484, p. 473.
53. *ibid.*
54. Mavroidis, P.C., 'Come Together? Producer Welfare, Consumer Welfare and WTO Rules', in Petersmann, E-U. (ed.), *Preparing the Doha Development Round: Challenges to the Legitimacy and Efficiency of the World Trading System* (Robert Schuman Centre for Advanced Studies, EUI: San Dominico di Fiesole, Italy, 2004), pp. 140-149.
55. Messerlin, P.C., 'Non-Discrimination, Welfare Balances and WTO Rules: An Historical Perspective' in Petersmann, E-U. (ed.), (2004), p. 167.
56. *Ibid.*
57. *Ibid.*
58. *Ibid.*
59. Downs, A., 'An Economic Theory of Political Action in a Democracy', *Journal of Political Economy* 65 (1957): 135-50, pp. 135-138.
60. In Stigler, G.J., ' The Theory of Economic Regulation', *Bell Journal of Economics and Management* 2 (1971): 3-21.
61. Peltzman, S., 'George Stigler's Contribution to the Economic Analysis of Regulation', *Journal of Political Economy* 101:5 (1993): 818-832, p. 822.
62. *ibid.*, p. 823.
63. Cook, P., Kirkpatrick, C., Minogue, M. and Parker, D., 'Competition, Regulation and Regulatory Governance: An Overview' in Cook, Paul et al. (eds), *Leading Issues in Competition, Regulation and* Development (Cheltenham: Edward Elgar, 2004), pp. 10-13.
64. *Ibid.*
65. *Ibid.*
66. See *Newsprint from Canada, Indonesia, Korea, Philippines and the US* [Preliminary Determination], 24 May 2003 (Case No: AD01/03).
67. See *Certain Prepared Baby Food from the US*, Public Interest Investigation (November 30, 1998), PB-98-001, available on *ftp://ftp.citt-tcce.gc.ca/doc/english/Dumping/Public_Interest/Considerations/pb2a001e.pdf.*

68. This is by such evolving communication technologies improving 'collective effectiveness' and enhancing the bargaining process. See Lupia, A. and G. Sin, 'Which Public Goods are Endangered?: How Evolving Communication Technologies Affect the Logic of Collective Action', *Public Choice* 117 (2003): 315-331, pp. 319-321.
69. This is by evolving communication technologies reducing dependence of noticeability on small numbers and this may reduce the impact of free-riding. See Lupia and Sin, *op. cit.*, pp. 321-322.
70. Bartlett, R., *Economic Foundations of Political Power* (New York: The Free Press, 1973), pp. 132-137.

A BACK-TO-BASICS APPROACH TO INTERNATIONAL LEGAL PERSONALITY: NEW THINKING ABOUT THE INDIVIDUAL, THE STATE AND THE ERA OF GLOBALIZATION

Christopher Barbara*

Law is a social phenomenon which finds its genesis in helping to assure the survival of Mankind. This article seeks to explore the future of international law-via the fundamental concept of international legal personality–in the contemporary context of globalization.

In light of the newly developed 'interest based' theory of globalization, it becomes apparent that contemporary human societies will in the future no longer so readily tolerate a derivative international legal personality. The inflexible concept of 'state' is thus singled out as the main hindrance to the development of an international society which accords with the direction 'interest based' globalization is asking it to take. Thus, both globalization and the 'first principles' of legal science are militating for a system which privileges the wellbeing of Man above all else.

This direction will, at one time or another, have to be closely examined by practitioner and academic alike in order to ward off the sort of popular revolt the informational and organizational aspects of globalization facilitate.

1. GENERAL INTRODUCTION

As the builders say, the larger stones do not lie well without the lesser.

Plato

1.1 Introduction

It is a small observation of mine that most people who are not trained in international law have little understanding of what we mean when we talk about international legal personality. In

* The author welcomes and encourages correspondence 18, rue Desbarats, Montréal (Québec) H9J 2P2, Canada, *E-mail: c.barbara@umail.leidenuniv.nl*

attempting to explain our understanding of the concept, I often find myself instead forced to defend the practice of international law. The average person–or so it would seem–perceives international law to be nothing more than a game played between bickering nations, like petulant schoolboys roughhousing on the playground. Rwanda, Iraq, Darfur: Why does international law *let* them happen? Why do so many people *have* to die? These are questions that I have not been able to satisfactorily answer; or at least not to the satisfaction of my lay interrogators. It has since occurred to me that perhaps international law has in some way lost sight of what should be its essential motivation as a legal system: to assure Man's survival and wellbeing.

Through the concept of international legal personality (hereafter ILP), international law has a mechanism by which to regulate participation in the application and creation of international legal rules. My concern rests with the dominant definition of ILP in which states alone hold the exclusive title of 'supreme' legal being. Indeed, one needn't search hard to find clues that something may be amiss in the world of ILP. The very name 'international legal *personality*' portrays remarkable irony as the original 'prototype'[1] legal person–the *human being*–is only accorded a minor rank in the dominant definition of ILP. Quite unlike the situation at municipal law, where the natural person is in actual fact *supplemented* by a variety of fictional persons (corporations, municipalities, etc); the top rank of international law is composed *exclusively* of fictional persons: those being, of course, states. The exclusion of individuals from the highest orders of international law cannot be blamed on practical considerations alone (like the decentralized structure of international law) – it is an exclusion which is deeply rooted in our dominant legal theory. The supreme legal actor in effect sets the motivation for all subsequent legal activity and thus poses far-reaching theoretical concerns for us as legal scholars.

1.2 Problem and Purpose

Legal personality is perhaps the most fundamentally important concept in the totality of judicial science. The reason for this is a clear and simple one: without legal personality, an entity does not exist in the eyes of the law. Without this quality, it is impossible for an entity to participate meaningfully in legal life.[2] Of course, the objective existence of a given entity is unassailable by a mere legal conception and continues regardless of its status at law.[3] This distinction between mere factual *existence* and legal *standing* boils down to the capacity to be the bearer of rights and duties. These twin elements constitute the very foundation of international legal life as together they allow complex interaction to take place and permit the possibility of meaningful and predictable outcomes. It can thus be said that in the subjective world of modern international law, legal personality is the entry ticket to existence.

Whilst recognizing that being extensively deprived of ILP likely has only a marginal impact on people's daily lives, it is open to discussion whether the same can be said about the theoretical implications to international law as a whole. It is my essential proposition here that the current iteration of ILP centred on the state (as opposed to the individual) fails to exhibit a sufficiently robust logical consistency to serve as a basal notion of international law. By this I mean that when we superimpose the meaning and effect of state-centric ILP on our present-day globalized reality, an ideal theoretical model for the regulation of involvement in international law fails to materialize from our dominant conceptual approach to ILP. The significance of a notional solution which does not hold up against an examination of its logical foundations down to the lowest levels of abstraction is highly significant. Whilst it may not necessarily be a problem of immediate practical significance, it is without question a problem for the future development of international law. This is because a system based on assumptions which are fundamentally flawed or otherwise not adapted to the realities and tendencies of their operative context will inevitably lead to a system which both behaves in unexpected ways and ultimately falls short of expectations.[4]

The only way to mitigate these problems is to adequately understand the relationships at play and what each contextual player is asking of the other. Let me try to explain. Trying to study ILP wholly (or mostly) within the current theoretical framework would be deceptive (and counterproductive) because ILP, the state and positivist international law *do* indeed fit together nicely; but this is only because these three notions collaborate in a closed system where they share an *interdependent* logical consistency. Therein lays the problem: the system projects an illusion of logic, but it is a *discrete* and *finite* logic. Were we to step back and look at the positivist international system from outside its own little universe, would it still make as much sense? The real test is not whether concepts make sense when examined within their own systemic environment, but whether they make sense in the broader context as well.

With regard to ILP, this broader context comprehends two ideas which, in a sense, buttress ILP on both ends of the socio-legal timeline. In considering the past, we must examine the fundamental purpose of law in order to gain a clear understanding of what our essential impetus is in elaborating legal notions in the first place. This will help us in forming clear motivations and in determining what essential characteristics should be part of our conception of ILP. In considering the present and future, we must consider the changes which are occurring to our traditional understanding of society in the context of globalization. Important here is not to elaborate a list of globalization's symptoms, but rather to establish the most basic psycho-social characteristic underlying globalization, upon which we can then depend to helpfully inform the law.

In theorizing about the future of ILP, as discussed above, this article aims to approach the subject from multiple vantage points in order to capture the essential elements of the current operative context of international law. In this regard, four principle tasks shall be undertaken:

1. to establish both the effect and the meaning of legal personality generally, and determine if these conclusions can be extrapolated to the international level,
2. to determine the essential purpose of law from the perspective of Man, and to develop from this some fundamental assumptions ('first principles') on which to base our study of ILP,
3. to elaborate a working definition of globalization and determine what significance this phenomenon ought to have on influencing the future direction of ILP; and
4. to appraise the logic of a state-centric international system in an environment marked by a continually increasing ability to interact effectively at lower and lower levels of global stratum (which is a key feature of globalization).

1.2.1 A Word on Methodology

A general methodological consideration of this article is to engage in an analysis which is as free from the grips of abstraction and needless complexity as possible. In a practical sense, this means we must elaborate some *basic* definitions of the concepts that we shall explore. This process of simplification is imperative if wish to come to a *useful* understanding of the ideas under consideration. Whilst the principle topic under consideration here is ILP, a multi-faceted and comprehensive approach shall be taken to best appreciate ILP's meaning, issues and future for us–the ultimate beneficiaries of this and every legal concept. This being the case, we must look closely at these related topics too, and develop definitions of them which adequately capture their basic traits in a way that mirrors the essentialist approach we shall take with legal personality *per se*.

1.2.2 Doctrine of Progressive Interpretation

The doctrine of progressive interpretation is a fundamental principle of constitutional interpretation in Canadian law and one which provides us with a convenient way to illustrate the rational for this investigation. Originally formulated by Lord Sankey in the case of *Edwards* vs. *Attorney-General for Canada*,[5] the Doctrine posits that: '... "frozen concepts" reasoning runs contrary to one of the most fundamental principles of Canadian constitutional interpretation: that [the Canadian] Constitution is a living tree which, by way of progressive interpretation, accommodates and addresses the realities of modern life.'[6]

In considering foundational aspects of international law, it is of paramount importance to also adequately consider the context in which the law operates. The law, if it is ultimately to be respected, must be prepared to see itself adapted to the new realities which inevitably surface as society evolves.[7] It is my proposition that globalization is *prompting* us to re-evaluate the way we construe ILP (and by implication, international law generally). It is not my bid that we abandon the concept of ILP, but rather that we proceed with a fundamental and progressive reconstruction of it. The doctrine of progressive interpretation thus provides us with some further methodological guidance in approaching ILP. It is helpful, particularly, in reminding us that the evolution of existing concepts is important (indeed, imperative) to the long-term survival of the law. In this regard, the concept of

ILP must be prepared to accept new interpretations in response to a changing operative environment.

2. THINKING ABOUT LEGAL PERSONALITY IN GENERAL

If at first, the idea is not absurd, then there is no hope for it.

Albert Einstein

2.1 Introduction

As the preceding has aimed to highlight, ILP plays an important and well-accepted role in international law. Indeed, the modern, positivist, *limited* conception of ILP has become so ingrained in present-day legal thinking that rarely do we take time to consider the position of those entities *not* already bestowed with ILP. The state-centricity of modern international law is in part to blame for this.[8] The state as willing international actor is absolute and all other entities are merely supporting players with varying degrees and forms of status, all measured against that of the state but never matching it. As a result, conceptions of ILP which do not place the state at their centre are often discounted; seen as unrealistically (or needlessly) utopian or mere theoretical musings of no practical utility to modern mainstream judicial science.

This commonly adopted approach to ILP is regrettable for two reasons. Firstly, it casts a pall of absurdity over conceptions of ILP which do not reinforce the position of the state. Once shrouded in marginalism, it becomes all too easy to cast non-conventional views of ILP aside as 'only' *lex ferenda,* lumped under the rubric of 'other theories'. This is often fatal in judicial science where only the *lex lata* is seen as truly relevant, as what counts, and what is deserving of study. Once a strand of thought has been discounted by the mainstream it is an uphill battle to revive it: we need only turn to naturalists for a dramatic example of this in practice. Clearly, it must be conceded outright that not all theories deserve to live–but neither do they deserve to die because they do not dovetail neatly into the contemporary mainstream. Non-state-centric theories of ILP are therefore (partially) beholden to the realities of international legal studies; they must in turn overcome a predominating scepticism to their very existence by appealing both to logic and–perhaps ironically–to the same basic emotions which are helping to relegate non-state-centric ILP to academic obscurity.

Secondly, it creates a disincentive to examining the position of non-state actors (this term is used in the broadest sense) as the dominant positivist conceptions of ILP, for the reasons mentioned above, provides no doctrinally sanctioned room for their advancement up to the top spot in the status hierarchy. With no formal possibility of 'full' personification, non-state actors are essentially trapped in their current position. The disagreeable consequence of this–besides the obvious difficulty for the actors concerned–is an academic mindset conditioned to accept the *persistent* disenfranchisement of anything which is not a state. It is important to observe from the outset that this situation persists not only because of the doctrinal momentum surrounding the traditional limited conception of ILP. More distressingly, it persists because modern positivist international law holds the sanctity of the state, and the consequent *disenfranchisement* of the natural person, as *imperative* to the very existence of international law. Modern international law has evolved in such a way that to be part of the mainstream one must hold the state above all else.

2.2 The Technical Characteristics of International Legal Personality

Drawing a comparison between individual legal personality in municipal law and the situation of individuals under international law as it now stands, Malanczuk makes an interesting observation.[9] In municipal systems, he notes, every individual has legal personality of some measure whilst animals have none whatsoever. Personified individuals, however, pass rules which are made for the *benefit* of animals (*e.g.*: prohibiting animal cruelty) but which confer no rights to them. Under our current positivist notions, then, individuals at international law are in a position comparable to animals in the municipal system: rules are made for their benefit, but the individual is not an international legal person. This means individuals are not, *inter alia*, able to appear as a party before the International Court of Justice (hereafter ICJ)[10], become a member of the UN[11], create rules of customary international law[12] or to conclude treaties[13].

Indeed, legal personality is a relative concept whose substance is linked inexorably with the demands of a particular legal system.[14] Whilst the specifics are subject to change, a few general observations about legal personality can be made. The principle *legal effect* of legal personality is to regulate participation in the legal process. Those with legal personality are seen as legitimate creators, subjects and otherwise independent users of the law. This characteristic is however Janus-faced, as it necessarily leads us to question the standing of those *not* endowed with legal personality. Here we must recall that legal personality is a *regulatory concept*; its *raison d'être* is essentially to *limit* participation in a legal system. In fulfilling its role as regulator, legal personality engages in a process of selective personification. This is merely the flip-side of LP's technical mandate: to empower one must nessicrarily exclude as capacity can only exist as a correlative to incapacity.

2.2.1 *Black and White and Shades of Gray*

The next step in sorting out the technical aspects of ILP is in deciding who is personified? It is clear that not all entities are legal persons at international law.[15] On this score Shaw helpfully informs us that ILP is simply '...participation plus some form of community acceptance...'[16]–but what exactly do we mean by community? Our interpretation in this regard is limited as it can only make sense to assume that this *de facto* communitarian ILP jury is one composed of entities who are themselves indisputably personified to the highest attainable degree.[17] In modern international law this leaves us with only one candidate: the state.

Indeed, it can be said that the principle beneficiary (and benefactor) of ILP is at present the state, though this is not a point of conclusion *in se*. As legal personality is an entirely relative concept, the notions we use today with regard to the state are not readily assignable to other entities. This highly specific state-centric context forces us to look to the lower levels of abstraction as the exterior plane (that is, ILP as it is currently defined *vis-à-vis* the state) is not suitable for a prospective analysis: we cannot, for instance, simply shift state-centric ILP to the human person. This is all to say that the specific qualities that we *now* ascribe to ILP do not matter to us in the context of this investigation. What is important for us is the concept of ILP as a general regulatory mechanism and as a *de facto* foundational concept of international law. It is as a regulatory instrument that ILP is crucial in deciding if an entity may legitimately be part of international legal discourse in terms of both perception and in actual fact.

Indeed, ILP is not a black and white proposition: shades of gray most certainly *can* exist. International organizations may have functional legal personality and individuals, even, have standing in certain international courts. These, however, are what I consider to be secondary grants of circumscribed ILP and not equivalent to the 'full' ILP exercised by states. By this I mean that states remain the supreme international legal persons and they alone populate the influential community which Shaw invokes in his definition. For instance, the European Court of Human Rights (hereafter ECHR) has the jurisdiction to receive claims directly from individuals[18]–in pointing to ECHR one might argue that individuals are already international legal persons to a certain degree, or is this ability something other than ILP? To verify this proposition we must look closer at our definition of ILP and whether or not one chooses to admit the possibility of graduated ILP.

On one hand we may construe ILP broadly and admit to its ranks any entity which satisfies Shaw's participation-based definition. On the other hand, the theory of individual international legal *capacity* proposes a stricter view which sees ILP *per se* restricted only to states with all other entities merely exercising a grant of tightly defined international standing. To argue for the capacity thesis is to prominently recognize that individuals may see some form of international standing–but not ILP-and this only due to the positive actions of states (*e.g.*: that the individuals concerned may have standing to bring cases before the ECHR).

Some authors, like Menon, argue that the traditional doctrine is presently undergoing modification to allow individuals some measure of international personality.[19] He points particularly to an individual's *locus standi* before some international tribunals (*e.g.*: ICTY, ICTR).[20] It is important, though, not to conflate these developments with the idea of a *full* international personality for individuals which would place the human person on an equal (or superior) theoretical footing with states. The ability in certain highly defined circumstances for the individual to be party before an international tribunal is merely an expression of state consent that this be permitted–the debate on whether to call this capacity or personality is another matter. In either case, we always find our way back to the state. Let us consider for a moment the case of the ICTY, which is representative of this phenomenon. Article 1 of the Statute of the Tribunal states that the Court '...shall have the power to prosecute persons responsible for serious violations of international humanitarian law...'.[21] Article 1, if examined in isolation, might well be construed as according the individual some form of standing at international law. However, we must also consider that the ICTY is a creation of UN Security Council.[22] And furthermore, that the UN is an international organization of which membership is set aside exclusively for states. Indeed, it is no accident that this discreet opening for individuals at international law, regardless of how we chose to label it, can be traced back to the actions of states.

The debate between graduated ILP and international capacity is, however, one rooted mostly in a false distinction as they both rely on state action. Indeed, they differ mostly on nomenclature and on where to draw the line between being an international legal person and everything else. The standing accorded individuals is identical in both constructions, it is merely a distinction based on how tightly one wishes to bind ones general definition of ILP to positivist theory. Shaw's definition of ILP–which is central to our investigation-plainly allows for a graduated construction of ILP (as it has for a starting point the actual participation of an entity).[23] The state, however, remains central to our present understanding of ILP regardless of how precisely we chose to construe the various modes of involvement (graduated *vs.* restrictive ILP). In the dominant theoretical approach it can be said that the states claim on ILP has an aura of eternal legitimacy while other legal actors are in truth beholden to state for their ILP status (or indeed, their international capacity). Regardless of one's position, the dynamic of the present arrangement is one arising out of dissimilar and unequal *origins*: one eternal and one derivative.

My reading of the dominant theoretical approach thus sees multiple levels of ILP with the state taking top ranking. Beneath the state and by complicity of the state, secondary levels of ILP exist; all having a similar genesis in that they are accepted by the community of states (correlative to this, of course, is that the community of states may equally deny a grant of ILP). It is this acceptance of their claim to an ILP which grants these entities the legitimacy needed to play an independent role in international legal discourse, no matter how minor the part might be. This mechanism for allotting ILP is however problematic because it essentially depends on the goodwill and interests of states and not on maintaining clear theoretical motivations or upholding the logical consistency of the international system. The preeminent role is therefore reserved for the state-a legal fiction-rather than for the human person. In safeguarding its position, the state is motivated out of self-interest rather than concern for the wellbeing of Mankind. Having Man's interest as a goal amongst others is very different than having it as the *raison d'être* of the whole international legal system.

Regardless of the unjust appearance this process might have, we must recall for the time being that the effect of legal personality exists without an intrinsic meaning as concepts as such are qualitatively neutral. The *meaning* of legal personality is something specific to its use. The meaning of legal personality in practice is certainly related to its effect, but one must not confound its *meaning* with its *effect*.

2.3 Human Agency in Shaping the Meaning of Legal Personality

Law is a social phenomenon–its existence is due wholly to the initiatives of Man and its meaning is shaped by its elaboration and application by human beings.[24] Before looking more closely at LP's meaning to human beings, it is important to briefly explore the origin of human society. This will help us to better see the original and fundamental functions of law and thus give us an interpretive context for looking at ILP as a legal principle. In this respect, ILP should, ideally, serve these core purposes of law in an identifiable and cogent way. What we need to examine here, and in the following sections, is whether ILP serves the core functions of legal life, or whether it has strayed away and thus become a conceptual liability.

Man by his biological nature is a social creature for whom life in a collective has always served an important purpose.[25] Human society traces its origins back to nothing more than a practical necessity. Primitive Man found living in groups to be an indispensible aid in the struggle for survival against the unwavering challenges encountered in living, as they did, so intimately with the natural environment.[26] This simple purpose–*survival* of our species-has evolved and expanded over the millennia such that society now serves primarily as a mechanism for the advancement of collective *wellbeing*.[27] Pound offers up a particularly stimulating account of this more modern aspect of the law:

> For the purpose of understanding the law of today, I am content to think of law as a social institution to satisfy socials wants–the claims and demands involved in the existence of civilized society–by giving effect to as much as we need with the least sacrifice, so far as such wants may be satisfied or such claims given effect by an ordering of human conduct through politically organized society. For present purposes I am content to see in legal history a record of a continually wider recognizing and satisfying of human want or claims or desires though social control; a more embracing and more effective securing of social interests; a continually more complete and effective elimination of waste and precluding of friction in human enjoyment of the goods of existence–in short, a continually more efficacious social engineering.[28]

Indeed, a primary instrumental concern of society is maintaining order amongst the collective. Maintenance of order is both a goal *in se*–one harkening back to the initial societal purpose of survival -and a useful step towards achieving other more abstract social ends (*e.g.*: promotion of the arts). Legal rules are therefore part and parcel of the societal mechanism; law is both a product of and a servant to society.

Law is the most systematized outcome of our need and desire to maintain order amongst the group. Unlike informal social conventions and other general norms of behaviour, law ('formal social control') is a wholly conscious creation of Man meticulously engineered to serve his specific ends.[29] The social aspect of law is aptly captured by the Roman maxim: *hominum causa omne jus constitutum est*.[30] With Man as its principle beneficiary, law is an intractably social phenomenon which, as such, exists in a symbiotic relationship with its social context. Legal rules are devised by Man to achieve specific socially motivated goals, and in doing so seek necessarily to regulate some facet of a society. (This endeavour, *in extremis*, does no less than help assure the survival of the society.) The social genesis of law naturally shapes the content and thus the meaning of specific legal ideas. There can be no escaping the reality that legal rules are utterly inconsequential when viewed apart from their social context–they posses no eternal validity or relevance of their own. The *meaning* of a legal idea or rule–such as legal personality-is only discernable by observing its elaboration and the subsequent application of the concept in practice. In thinking about ILP, we surely must consider this aspect in a way that goes beyond the technical characteristics of the concept.

2.3.1 *A Selected Examination of Legal Personality in Past Municipal Practice*

With ILP having taken on an air of settled law, the true meaning of disenfranchisement is often overlooked. Here it is instructive to turn to historical examples to help elucidate the meaning traditionally associated with the concept of legal personality. In particular, we need to remind ourselves of the unfair and often cruel ends Man has sought to attain by withholding or the stripping of legal personality. On this score, let us recall that in the not too distant past full classes of otherwise capable, fit, biologically equivalent natural persons were completely deprived of (municipal) legal personality. Noteworthy in this regard are the classic examples of slaves and women. Admittedly, these two cases seem somewhat mundane today–the errors of long-ago so strikingly obvious to our modern eye that scarcely a spark of indignation is summed up. The reason for this perhaps unanticipated reaction is however clear: the affront posed to the basic precepts of human dignity in denying human beings an independent legal existence has become internalized–in law and in culture - to such an extent that regression or reversion to the previous state of affairs is now simply unthinkable, and it thus fails to stir us any longer.

Let us be under no misconceptions, these examples are ones of subjugation in a most intimate form. Indeed, the very foundation of enslavement is that slaves have no right to protest their situation: they are nothing more than chattel, subject wholly to the whims and desires of their owners–a situation unrepentantly abetted by the deprivation of legal personality. At this point we can already see the unfavourable comparisons emerging. Were we to transpose these meanings to ILP we might equate the legal capacity thesis to slavery or the graduated ILP thesis to some manner of second-class municipal personality. In any case, it remains that the state is in a dominant position *vis-à-vis* other international actors.

These two historical examples serve in particular to demonstrate the power dynamic which results from an unequal status at law of otherwise basically equal entities. Selective personification of nominally equal entities nessicrarily places one at the mercy of the other with the former having no legal right to defend them against the latter. *In concreto,* the lack of personification robs the deprived class (*e.g.*: non-personified human beings) of a legal basis on which to stake their claim and exert their rights in a legal process. In this sense, we see the effect of selective personification, a sort of systematized legal inequity which can serve no meaningful theoretic purpose other than to assist in satisfying the self-interest of the empowered class to the prejudice of the disempowered class. Yet, these examples do not succeed in completely conveying the meaning inherent in this state of affairs. For this aspect, we must cast our minds to history yet again; this time to the period spanning the fifth to sixteenth century.

For our present purposes, it is only necessary to recall that the Middle Ages constituted one of the most atavistic, socially precarious, and intellectually stifled periods in the history of modern Man. The newly invigorated cultural and academic atmosphere emerging from the dearth of the Middle Ages was aptly termed the Renaissance precisely because the contrast with the preceding era was felt to be so stark. It is not insignificant then that one of the most insidious punishments ever devised should emanate from this most brutish period of human history. Often mistaken as an innocuous synonym for a simple bandit, the classification of 'outlaw' has a much deeper significance, one with great relevance to understanding the meaning of legal personality. The term 'outlaw' itself is derived from the Old Norse word 'útlagi', which literally translates as 'laid outside'[31]. In English common law of the time a Writ of Outlawry constituted a judgement declaring an accused to thenceforth be 'laid outside' the ambit of the law[32]. In other words, the outlaw was stripped of his legal personality; his punishment was being deprived of a legal existence. Outlawry was considered a particularly harsh punishment because of the position of vulnerability it imposed on the wrongdoer. As far as the legal system was concerned, the convict ceased to exist and protections normally afforded by the law could not be sought by him. Accordingly, the convict could fall victim to an aggrieved party in search of 'private justice' who could, with absolute impunity, mete out justice as he saw fit. The significance of this scenario to us is in better isolating the meaning we associate to the deprivation of one's legal personality. It is significant that depravation of legal personality was (and is) seen with great negativity; indeed, it was one of the harshest punishments available to the courts.

2.4 Provisional Conclusions

This section has sought in particular to highlight the negative connotation associated with deprivation of legal personality generally. Indeed, the negative implications are so dramatic that the striping of one's juristic life has erstwhile only been contemplated at municipal law in the context of imposing punishment for criminal transgression and deprivation of legal personality for certain classes of people is no longer tolerated in most legal systems. In the author's estimation, the only course of action consistent with the rigors of logic dictates that a substantively parallel international concept must carry the same connotation, *cēterīs paribus*, as its municipal equivalent. Moreover, I can see no theoretical necessity or benefit which would support the deprivation or limitation of ILP for individuals at international law. Indeed, doing so has negative implications for international law in both connotative terms and with regard to maintaining a logically sound legal structure.

As legal personality has an equivalent *effect* both municipally and internationally, there is no basis to conclude that their *meanings* should be substantively divergent. The prevalent theoretical perspective restraining Man from an international legal life must, in turn, be considered profoundly prejudicial for individuals. Whilst I am not suggesting that individuals are being punished by international law in the sense of an outlaw, I do wish to make clear that from the perspective of fairness, a systematized legal inequity can serve no meaningful purpose other than to assist in satisfying the self-interest of the empowered class – which, in our case, leads straight back to the state. Indeed, were we to confer upon individuals the same species of ILP that we now construe for states, it would no doubt result in a myriad of absurd scenarios.[33] It is evident that were individuals granted a full and formal ILP on the same hierarchical level as the state, it would have to be one specially adapted for them–in other words, a new species of ILP.

3. HISTORICAL INTRODUCTION

Those who cannot remember the past are condemned to repeat it.
George Santayana

3.1 Introduction

When considering the position of the individual, it is a hazard of our theoretical habituation to straight away compare and contrast Man's position to that of the state. Surely this sort of comparison can easily and straightforwardly be done. Indeed, Malanczuk does so and concludes with a litany of acts which individuals cannot partake in. The peril in making these sorts of conclusions is in being too easily satisfied with little more than such a list as either a rational for changing the system or for maintaining the *status quo*. We must always keep in mind that the rights and duties of the state as international legal person have developed in parallel with the statist model of organizing international law.[34] Consequently, our current international legal conceptions are so entangled with the concept of state that they make little sense when shifted verbatim to the individual. There is, for instance, no reasonable basis for suggesting that an individual human person ought to have the legal ability to declare war or to join the UN. The issue for us is therefore not which elements of state-centric ILP (or 'full ILP') should be granted to individuals, but rather to think about whether the state is indeed the best reference point for the complete range of international legal conceptions?

Indeed, the concept of state and state sovereignty is not problematic *in se*. The idea that a state-centric international system ought to be made up of independent[35] and equal[36] players is certainly a sound model.[37] However, maintaining its logic consistency depends on our unqualified acceptance of the state as basal component of the international system. It is with this supposition that we run into difficulty: is the state really the best starting point for international law if the wellbeing of Man is (in theory) our principle concern? To help us gain perspective on this question, the following section proposes to briefly review the orthodox positivist view of international law as well as a selection of other historically relevant perspectives.

3.2 Traditional State-centric International Law

The orthodox positivist position was aptly summed-up by Oppenheim who wrote in 1912 that: '[s]ince the law of nations is based on the common consent of individual States, and not of individual human beings, States solely and exclusively are subjects of international law'.[38] This strict position was loosened somewhat by the *Reparation for Injuries* case in which the ICJ found that the United Nations, in its capacity as an international organization, possessed a functional form of ILP. In the same Advisory Opinion the ICJ also chose to reaffirm that only '... a state possesses the totality of international rights and duties recognized by international law.'[39] In this light, the situation of international organizations can in fact be seen as the exception that proves the rule: international organizations are the creations of states and it is only their desire as the supreme international actors to endow an international organisation with legal personality which makes it so.[40]

Lauterpacht takes a slightly different approach in cautiously pointing out that there is indeed no positive rule of international law which would preclude individuals or bodies other than states from having international legal personality.[41] This observation is especially interesting when we cast our minds to the history of international law. There we find that under natural law–previous the dominant legal theory-individuals were in fact commonly considered to have some measure of ILP. In other words, no sharp distinction was made between municipal law and international law–the equality of Man was the principle philosophical foundation for all our legal conceptions.[42] Naturalism as a legal theory undeniably gave way to positivism in the nineteenth century, and it is in relation to this fact that we find an awkward turn of events concerning ILP. As international law evolved, strove for rationality, became more mature, comprehensive and far reaching, the individual has-in one doctrinal leap-been pushed out of the philosophical underpinning of international law. Our modern positivist notions demand that international law be founded upon the consent of states, and accordingly we now see the state as our philosophical compass.

On this theoretical shift, it is important to keep in mind two points: (1) the status of the individual as an international subclass is not inalterably set–a look at the factual history of the matter shows us that it has changed once (in the move from naturalism to positivism), and logically it can change just as dramatically again; and (2) as these historical propositions have not been accepted by states–the sole creators of international law in the contemporary dominant positivist legal order - any view granting individuals full international legal personality holds weight only as a specific expression of *lex ferenda*. The following section proposes to give a brief overview of the naturalist school's take on ILP–an indispensible endeavour given the complete definitional reversal which took place on the eve of naturalisms slide into disuse.

3.3 Naturalism-de Groot, Hobbes, Pufendorf, Vitoria

As far back as Vitoria and further still to the ancient Greek author Mestriūs Plutarchus, scholars and theologians have suggested that non-state entities have recognizable international legal rights.[43] Natural law dictates that the basic principles of all law arise not out of Man's choice, but rather from principles which hold universal (or divine), which hold eternal validity and which can be discovered by reason alone.[44] The inherent breadth of natural law as a school of legal theory is well demonstrated by some of the work done by Vitoria. In attempting to establish a legal order that would encompass the 'Indians' of the American continent–a major theoretical leap for the period-he proposed establishing natural law as the universal law of all humanity.[45] de Groot considered that natural law was an automatic outflow of people living together in society, and that its rules existed regardless of the existence of God or religion, but rather as a necessity for peaceful cohabitation in society.[46] By virtue of its ostensibly universal appeal, natural law is seemingly well suited to fulsomely including individuals in any conception of international law premised on its principles.

By the sixteenth century, international law had become a well recognized discipline and scholars began systematically tackling the question of individual legal personality in international law using methodology rooted in social, political and judicial science. de Groot, for instance, saw individuals as the centre of all his legal conceptions.[47] 'He considered the law of nations as a body of rules governing the activities of individuals in international relations rather than as a body of provisions binding on States in their relation with other States'.[48] de Groot's naturalist contemporaries also found along similar lines. Hobbes, in *De Cive, Imperium,* expressed a similar view to that of de Groot[49]. Pufendorf, influenced by both de Groot and Hobbes, wrote in his *De Jure Naturae et Gentium* that he considered natural law binding on individuals as well as states.[50] More generally it can be said that the naturalist position views individuals as enjoying certain natural or human rights which ought to be protected by the world community of Mankind.[51] Equally, the individual is also bound by certain natural human obligations which ought to be similarly enforced by the world community.[52]

Classical natural law is unlikely to be able to topple the (positivist) *status quo* for several reasons, not the least of which is that has few followers amongst modern international legal scholars. Indeed, it is improbable that naturalist scholarship could forge a coherent bridge between its precepts and our current positivist notions. Positivist theories and definitions, which are premised on state-centricity, would give rise to profound problems were they used wholesale in some modern iteration of naturalist ideas. Nevertheless, naturalist ideas do put on display foundations which have aspects of a clear and valid logic (such as Man as foundational legal being), but are on the other hand diminished by over-reliance on shadowy notions of humanity, universality and divinity.

In sum, an ILP for the individual rooted solely in the realm of natural law would prove unsatisfactory when held to modern standards of legal scholarship. Whilst the allure of all encompassing universality might prove compelling for some- even if only on an emotional level-natural law remains too vaguely rooted and irrecoverably shaded in mysticism. These two elements in particular make natural law wholly unsuitable as a modern basal theory on which to base ILP. However the spirit, if not content, of natural law remained an important force in international law well into the nineteenth century. During this late period natural law was–silently–picked-up and re-worked by a group of scholars I have chosen to term as 'Progressive legal scholars'. The next section shall aim to give an overview of this strand of legal thought which is closely linked to naturalism from which it seemingly took much of its inspiration.

3.4 Progressive legal scholars-Bluntschli, Le Fur, Heilborn, Martens, Verdross, Westlake

Whilst many publicists of the nineteenth century viewed natural law as obsolete (indeed, this consideration had already started to set-in by the eighteenth century), this did not stop some authors of the period from professing an individual international legal personality.[53] Bluntschli had a great influence on international law during this period.[54] His 'modern' method of legal scholarship largely dispensed with the positivist–naturalist distinction that marked international law scholarship up until that point.[55] Rather than place ideas in categories reflecting their diametrical opposition, he constructed an international law continuum starting with 'legal ideas' and finishing with 'real' or 'binding' law confirmed by practice.[56] Bluntschli's conclusion, however, was that international law was based on the shared human nature of Mankind and was guided by humanity.[57] Human nature, to Bluntschli, was the '... firm and lasting foundation of all international law'.[58] 'This shared human nature and, accordingly, this shared legal nature bound all peoples by an inevitable necessity'.[59] This aspect of Bluntschli's thoughts have a certain semblance to those of de Groot, who in breaking from S[t]. Thomas Aquinas and the strictures of divinity gave natural law an essentially instrumental–but indispensible-role in facilitating human cohabitation in society. Both of these authors agree that Man is the essential object (or subject) of all law.

On the object-subject distinction, Heilborn gives us an interesting view of what the term 'object' can mean with regard to international personality. He posited the now widely known object theory of international law which is often employed in positivist notions of the present subject. Heilborn himself, however, considered that the individual is *either* an object or a subject of international law and ascribed the individual some degree of international legal capacity.[60] Heilborn, along with Martens, believed that individuals ought to have international protection of their human rights and in this area to have a direct legal personality.[61] [62] Clearly, authors describing a positivist notion take-up the 'object' side of the equation,[63] whereas those arguing for individual standing at international law tend toward the 'subject' side of the equation.[64]

This line of thought continued to occupy an important place in legal scholarship up until the early twentieth century. Many notable scholars of the time accepted the notion that individuals might or should have some form of ILP. Le Fur dichotomises states as 'direct' subjects of international law, whilst individuals as 'indirect' subjects who appear in international law via the state – this despite the individual being the *true* subject of international law.[65] Verdross cites a similar division, that of 'active' and 'passive' international subjects.[66] Westlake notes that the '... duties and rights of States are only the duties and rights of men who compose them'.[67]

3.5 Sociological theory-Duguit, Politis and Scelle

3.5.1 Introduction and Background

These authors, all writing in the first half of the twentieth century, posited similar accounts of human society. This is likely due, at least in part, by the local social context which enveloped them at the time they wrote. The French context during the period of the Third Republic (1870-1940) was one of constant political and constitutional drama. Coming to replace the authoritarian regime of the Second Empire, the Third Republic was an uneasy compromise forged between left-wing Republicans and right-wing Monarchist sympathizers.[68]

Under the constitutional laws of 1875 the highly ambiguous position of President of the Republic was created. The French president was on the one hand charged with little day-to-day responsibility but on the other hand was '... through the influence of the monarchists, given the powers of a constitutional king on the English or Orleanist model.'[69] The President had, for instance, the right to appoint and dismiss government ministers, and '... he tested the limits of this right with some regularity.'[70] One notable example is the political crisis of 16 May 1877 when President Mac-Mahon unilaterally dismissed the Prime Minister.[71] Another notable characteristic of the compromise constitutional laws of the Third Republic was the lack of a declaration securing fundamental individual rights, a situation resulting from the inability of the two factions to arrive at a consensus and which represented a great departure from revolutionary tradition.[72] On this score we find the Dreyfus affair–notable in its own right- was a defining moment for French society of the Third Republic. Baselessly accused and convicted of high treason, '[t]he Dreyfus affair demonstrated that the state could not only fail, but could even crush individuals by a sequence of failures. The state repeatedly failed to uphold justice, while the army involved itself in fabricating false evidence against Dreyfus and ignoring evidence against another officer. The traditionally anti-semitic catholic clergy supported the anti-Dreyfussards and the parliament, which was controlled by the liberal bourgeoisie, consistently turned a blind eye. The parliament continually refused to grant a retrial until the very end of the affair in 1906...'[73]

In sum, when faced with persistent democratic crisis in their own lived reality, these three authors endeavoured to legally secure the position of the individual. They sought foremost to protect the individual against abuses of crushing power by those in government.[74] These views on society are significant not only because they serve to remedy democratic concerns at the municipal level, but they do so at the international level as well. Indeed, these sociological theories recast international law as a true *'droit des gens'* by abolishing level divisions and adopting a wholly monist perspective.

3.5.2 *International Law*

The theories proposed by the French sociological scholars are of particular interest because they seek to reconcile modern international law with the fundamental reality of Man as a social creature and creator of all law (in contrast to the universalist position of the naturalist scholars). By placing the sociological realities of Mankind at the foundation of their theories, they seek to achieve a fairer and more representative basis on which to structure more abstract legal relations. This logical progression is well represented by the social continuum articulated by Politis. He sees no reason why social evolution should end at the state.[75] The scope which society encompasses has been continually expanding since the dawn of Man: from the single family unit, to the clan, to the city, to the nation and finally to what we consider the state.[76] Thus, progression to a universal community of human beings is in no way radical; rather, it is perfectly logical. Politis sees but one legitimate reason for the existence of law altogether: the

> [b]onheur et perfection de l'humanité, tel en effet le but de toute société, et, partant, de tout droit. Il en est ainsi de la

> société international comme de la société nationale. Elles n'existent que pour assurer a l'homme la possibilité de vivre et de se développer.[77]

Thus, the solidarity of Mankind must be respected, represented and placed as the logical foundation for all our legal conceptions. The rights and interests of Man can best be safeguarded when it is *his* personality which is that which counts the most in international law, rather than that of a fictitious creation like the state.

3.6 Conclusion

The words of Plato recalled at the beginning of this article hold much truth to them: international law needs the ineluctable reality of the individual human being to grow as a system. Renard, as well, reminds us that the state is a fictitious creation–it did not always exist, and it may not always exist either.[78] Man, then, is the *only* true element in any and every social construction–law being no exception. So, the idea of linking Man with the wider legal order by giving him a full international legal personality–which would provide him the *locus standi* required to act unilaterally, essentially, as if he were a state in the present system –is not unreasonable.

What is particularly interesting about the theories surveyed here is that the scholars and theologians behind them saw true virtue in simplicity. Building a system based on the human being was, and remains, an obvious and relevant basis around which to order the discipline of international law. Indeed, the vaguely-based claims made by the naturalist about the nature of Man (in particular his social nature) are now readily supported by the modern sciences of sociology and biology. It behoves us, then, to follow this strand of thought and bring it into the present to see how it interacts with the contemporary societal context. It would be rash, considering that law is a social phenomenon, to take for granted the enduring validity of historical propositions espousing Man's centrality to international law. We must therefore strive to adequately understand certain key aspects of contemporary global society which will then allow us to sensibly examine the place of Man within them.

4. GLOBALIZATION AND ILP

Pluralitas non est ponenda sine necessitate.

William of Ockham

4.1 Introduction

Law as a mechanism of social ordering is inseparably liked to its social context and it cannot escape notice that our social context is undergoing one of the most fundamental changes since the dawn of Mankind. Alas, this transformation is still ongoing and scholars have yet to grapple effectively with the changes happening in modern human society. Our attempts thus far to adequately define globalization have resulted in academic chaos; a playing field littered with definitions with no clear consensus on the horizon. This places us in a difficult situation when thinking about ILP and the future of international law. How can we plan for the future when we do not lucidly understand our present social condition?

It is my assertion that globalization is trying to tell us something; it is urging us to embark on a particular theoretical path. Indeed, this path is one which has neither carried realistic benefits nor held much hope for adequate implementation before today. Globalization is highlighting Man's innate desire to engage in social intercourse. These desires coupled with new means to communicate are indeed urging international law to redefine itself as a practice centred on the human person rather than the state. This new social context is trying to inform the law that secondary legal personality is no longer an acceptable solution to the position of the individual at international law.

Due to the turbulent state of the discussion on globalization, I cannot simply refer to globalization as if it were a term with an established meaning. Indeed, so many interpretations exist that the term has become nearly meaningless *per se*. Therefore, I propose to boil down globalization to its most essential meaning as a social concept. We can then use this basic definition to helpfully inform upon the context in which international law must now operate.

4.2 Nature of Globalisation

We must begin this investigation by gaining a better understanding of how we employ the terminology: what can we mean by the term 'globalization'? We must first distinguish between big G 'Globalization' and little g 'globalization'. The term 'Globalization' refers to *theories* purporting to explain and systematize evolutions that have taken place in global intercourse.[79] On the other hand, with 'globalization' we purport only to acknowledge *objective* developments in global intercourse, that is to note what is actually occurring rather than to try and explain it.[80] Globalization is a notoriously vague term and likewise has a multiplicity of meanings.[81] Attempting to understand something with so many different interpretations emanating from so many different disciplines is no easy task. To make any sense out of the concept, we must be especially vigilant in understanding the interpretative context of Globalization theory.

4.2.1 Terminology and Dilemma

The author Mittelman cautions us that globalization may be both an '... objective and subjective phenomenon.'[82] This is a powerful hypothesis because it admits the possibility that globalization is as much a product of our theories about it as it is an independent development. This means that Globalization theories do not merely operate as the *explanans,* but get re-circulated into the globalization mix and in the process theories themselves help form and become part of the *explanandum*. We might therefore conclude that Globalization theorists are in part responsible for constructing the phenomena which they proclaim to study. From this we may further conclude that the vaguity which surrounds the definition of globalization is in part symptomatic of its social construction. Each new theory adds an element or aspect to the concept, further diversifying the potential meanings of the term and thus further hampering academia's quest for a consensual definition. Purportedly authoritative definitions are not hard to find in the literature and elsewhere, but there is no escaping from the fact that '... globalization theories draw on a variety of different and sometimes contradictory perspectives'[83] and '... there is no consensus on a common interpretation of the nature of globalization.'[84]

As lawyers, grappling with a concept seemingly immune from authoritative definition is a terrifying prospect. Clarity and certainty are principles held dear in legal science, but we must–occasionally–come to accept that these are only ideals which we strive for. Concretely understanding globalization is seemingly one of these times–or is it really? At this point I would like to posit that perhaps globalization is not overwhelmingly complicated or hopelessly indistinguishable, but rather that we are simply focusing on the wrong *aspects* in trying to understand it. We have put all the right ingredients into the pot, but we have become so absorbed by all the bits floating around in the broth that we have forgotten to turn on the heat. To come to any *useful* understanding of globalization we must turn up the gas; we have to boil it down to the essence. Coming up with one essential feature or aspect which can capture the most fundamental essence of globalization is critical if we are to escape our current definitional paralysis.

4.2.2 Theoretical Overview

In starting our investigation into the essence of globalization, we must briefly survey some of the theories currently circulating in the literature. Least helpful in our investigation are those theories which seek to enumerate quantitative factors as defining characteristics. Economist Bhalla tells us that globalization can be defined by five economic and two non-economic factors.[85] The five economic features are: (1) growth in global trade; (2) growth in Foreign Direct Investment (hereafter FDI) and capital flows; (3) growth in production and consumption; (4) competition on a global scale; and (5) liberalization of trade and investment policies. The two non-economic factors are: (1) the loss of national sovereignty and (2) increasing standardization of values and culture. Fellow economist van Liemt posits similarly, identifying three key features.[86] The first are factors which enable globalization (telecommunications and reliable transport); second, government policies that promote trade liberalization; and lastly, corporate strategies of internationalization. Bhalla and van Liemt give us a rather narrow perspective, but one which is also reassuring owing to the prominence of quantifiable aspects. Interestingly, however, we see difficulty in arriving at consensus within the already discrete field of economics. Indeed, Bhalla and van Liemt arrive at fundamentally oppositional roles for the state: Bhalla concluding that the state is becoming *emasculated* whilst van Liemt posits that state action is a principle *driver* of globalization.[87] In sum, heavily quantitative definitions such as these cannot serve as satisfactory accounts of globalization: they are too detailed-oriented and too focused on specific manifestations. Other accounts are somewhat more successful.

Moving away from economics, we find less emphasis on drawing black-and-white conclusions about globalization and its manifestations. Whilst Bhalla and van Liemt merely chose a side (the state as anachronistic vs. the state as globalizer), other authors provide us with a more nuanced analysis of the state's role in globalization. It is doubtless that economics play a dramatic role in how globalization plays out in practice, but economic indicia are best taken as merely symptoms of something else. Authors writing from the sociologic perspective come closer to identifying this larger trend. Kilminster, for instance, tells us that '... the transnational level ... [is] becoming increasingly autonomous, such that processes at the lower integrative levels (nation state, region, community, kinship) are in the present period becoming increasingly governed by the order of the higher level.'[88] The result of this shift is that decisions that can be taken at the state level are decreasing as the continental and global levels increase in size and complexity: the traditional divisions are breaking down. Political scientists Baylis and Smith give us a somewhat more concrete, effect-based definition, they note: '[b]y globalization we simply mean the process of increasing interconnectedness between societies such that events in one part of the world more and more have effects on peoples and societies far away.'[89]

4.2.3 *Objective Awareness*

So far we have been able to isolate a number of factors associated with globalisation, namely changes in global economic indicia, marked advancement in certain technological areas and a perceived change in the meaning and effect of certain erstwhile well-defined concepts (for example, the meanings of: 'local', 'national' and 'international'). Whilst these are all traditionally accepted hallmarks of globalization, none of these factors tells us anything significant about the *essence* of globalization. They fail to transcend symptomatic representation to present a root cause. Robertson, however, gets us one step close when he informs us succinctly that globalization '... refers both to the compression of the world and the intensification of consciousness of the world as a whole.'[90] Here he highlights a crucial point; by incorporating the idea of consciousness, he incorporates human psychology as a factor in globalization. Globalization, described by Micklethwait and Wooleridge as 'a series of waves'[91] is above all a gradual transformation taking place in the depths of human consciousness. Consciousness, however, has two very different meanings. The first is that of *objective awareness*. Awareness of the world–the figurative shrinking of our planet–is fairly easily understood. Technology is making distance progressively less relevant in the performance of social intercourse. Langhorne points to three stages of technological evolution in explaining this trend: (1) the application of the steam engine to land and sea travel, making it faster and more reliable; (2) the invention of the telegraph; and (3) the generalized use of modern computers.[92] This development provides new *opportunities* to trade and communicate, but this doesn't explain *why* we use these 'enablers' as we do. It only explains *how* we have made the world shrink, so to speak. Explaining the 'why' brings us to the second aspect of consciousness.

4.2.4 Subjective Awareness

Man's *subjective awareness* is far more interesting for our present purposes, and we shall deal with it properly in just a moment. For the time being, it should be understood that it is only by interrogating this subjective aspect of Man's psyche that we can come to some useful understanding of globalization. Theorizing, as many do, based on a collection of symptoms is no doubt comforting. This is because symptoms give the *illusion* of unquestionable legitimacy as they can be plainly seen, they can be studied, and they are above all quantifiable. However, enumerating and studying symptoms alone does not tell us the whole story. If globalization were nothing more than a simple causative process, it would be easily understood. Explaining the proximal cause of each distal element (for example, increasing FDI) would, in that case, lead to a satisfactory (proximal) understanding of the whole phenomena. This is not the case–globalization stubbornly remains vague and ill-defined despite all the concretely identifiable elements. It is tempting to stop at subjective awareness–the preceding section giving a clear and simple causative explanation rooted in Man's scientific advancements. This, however, fails utterly to answer the burning question: *why* have we taken these particular links and made the chain we have made. The problem with finding–or accepting - the essence of globalization is primarily that it is not quantifiable in a way that makes us–lawyers, political scientists, economists – comfortable.

The second aspect of consciousness, the subjective is, in part, the missing piece we have been searching for. Understanding globalization is infinitely simplified when we acknowledge that what we think, what is in our minds as sentient beings, is as–and very likely more-important to defining globalization than any economic or technological account. As we have seen, technological advancement has made communication simpler, faster and less costly, which in turn has diminished the relevance of physical distance. We now find ourselves in a world where distance plays less of a role in our management of social intercourse, which leads to increased trade, sharing of ideas and a gradual, generalized blurring of pre-globalization social divisions, like the state.[93] The common account of this evolution often portrays Man as a helpless bystander, but these changes did not occur in a vacuum: they are the result of Man's *will* and Man's *action*. A rational human being does not act on whim alone; he considers the situation to arrive at a logical course of action. Our escapades beyond the borders of our native village have nothing whatever to do with chance.

4.2.5 Interest: the Essence of Globalization

The key to understanding the seemingly unbreakable enigma posed by globalization is as simple as it is unquantifiable. The essence of globalization is nothing more complicated than understanding the concept of *interest*. There are two types of 'interest' at play in globalization, which we shall now examine. The first sort is a very narrowly focused interest, whilst the second is extremely broad. In endeavouring to appreciate the first type of interest, it is helpful to consider the *process* of scientific and technological advancement. It can be summarized as an interest in determining whether or not a particular theory can be made to work in practice. Consider, for example, the question of whether or not information can be transmitted as an electrical pulse over a wire (the scientific principle behind telegraphy). This sort of interest is extremely circumscribed; it is limited to verifying and elaborating a scientific hypothesis. The aim here is only whether or not something can be done, and if so, via which modality. It *does not* explain why Mankind accepted and widely adopted the telegraph–or any other invention-once it was proven to work or why we sought to use it in attaining particular ends. These answers are comprehended by the second facet of interest.

Indeed, as the patent rolls bear witness, many talented inventors find success in the laboratory only to have their inventions relegated to the dustbin of history. The reason why the telegraph, the telephone, and the internet saw success was because they satisfied a particular need: *the basic human interest to communicate with other human beings*. These technological tools simply gave a broader scope to Man's pre-existing social interests. Man's desire to communicate is the second, broader form of interest under examination here. Every manifestation of globalization can be traced back to Man's fundamental nature as a social animal. The 'communications revolution' has merely allowed Man to make the world his village; in it he does nothing different than he would with his fellow tribesmen: talk and trade. On this Brown informs us that '[p]roximity in space makes for solidarity because it is prerequisite to interaction. Nearness of dwelling unit or work position is known to favour interaction and friendship.'[94] The only appreciable difference is the scale on which social intercourse ('interaction') can now easily transpire. Technology has not changed us; it has unshackled us to pursue our basic human interests on a more dramatic scale. Globalization's revolutionary effect is merely an instrumental one. Our interests –what motivates us to take advantage of technology in this remarkable way–are the very same social interests which imbued our primitive ancestors nearly a quarter million years ago.[95] New opportunities to interact despite great distances has only livened us to new possibilities to connect, in one way or another, with our fellow Man. This foundation of Man's innate sociability can be found at the core of every symptom, idea, or manifestation ever classified under the rubric of 'globalization'.

4.3 Meaning of Interest-based Globalisation for ILP

Our investigation up until this point has been rather far reaching, so it might prove helpful to draw closer attention to certain elements which one should have in mind as we move forth. In the first section we looked at the effect of legal personality and sought to distil its core meaning for us as a socio-legal concept. In the second section we explored some historical conceptions of ILP to not only gain perspective, but to examine several past cases made for individual ILP and, indeed, touch on why they ultimately failed to meet their burden. On the subject of globalization, undoubtedly one of the most intriguing topics of our time, we have sought to render a concise core meaning, which we have construed as 'interest'.

It is worth noting here a fascinating realization that unveils itself when dealing with ill-defined concepts like globalization. It is interesting to consider a paradoxical phenomenon in which the most abstract conceptions often seem the most real to us. Consider, for instance, the measure of FDI in a given country. In truth, neither of these seemingly tangible concepts holds any eternal meaning *in se*. Conversely, certain concepts which are poorly suited to systematic assessment can, on final reckoning, allow us a more meaningful understanding than a competing easily quantifiable characteristic. It is for this reason that simple, human - centred characteristic like Man's sociability make for excellent analytical starting points as they are not unduly mired in abstraction or contorted by theoretic contingency. We can say this because to deny Man's sociability would be tantamount to denying Man's very existence given that sociability is a defining characteristic of Man. Sociability, therefore, can be considered a basal characteristic as free from abstraction as is realistically possible through the use of language (which is itself, of course, a contrivance of Man).

4.3.1 *The Problem with Abstraction*

In our present investigation–which is focused mainly on the most basic theoretical underpinnings of larger concepts - abstraction is a hindrance to understanding. By discussing international law, international legal personality, the state and international globalization from the perspective of the only *real* element present in all of them, and the one which links them inseparably–Man–we begin to see things in a new way. This view is of course not absolutely novel, but rather a way not traditionally focused on in modern (positivist) international law. The first thing we realize when placing Man at the centre of our legal conceptions is that the law is not always constructed to serve him. In the case of ILP, the law is set-up to serve *states*, not the Men who created them and live in them. We are thus faced with a legal abstraction (ILP) centred upon yet another legal abstraction (the state)! Let us consider for a moment the motto of this chapter - *pluralitas non est ponenda sine necessitate.* In light of this methodological dictum, it behoves us to consider a model that does away with these unnecessary abstractions and repositions Man as the foundation for our legal conceptions in a way which accords with globalized society's likely perception of what ILP should look like.

One of the fundamental obstacles faced by theoreticians until about twenty years ago was the dispersed and isolated nature of Man's inhabitation of the earth. Even with the advent of mass communication in the early 20th century, it provided only a one-way channel of communication–a type of communication unable to satisfy Man's desire for socialization. An international system based on states had the one great advantage that communications could be concentrated though certain officials who were empowered and given the necessary means to engage in a discourse with other state officials creating a sort of exceedingly circumscribed society. In thinking about the role of the state we must not underestimate the time-consuming and resource intensive nature of non-electronic communications.

Technical hurdles in communications created the *need* for abstraction; for the state as imagined entity to front for a small group of empowered individuals. The world was essentially divided up into more manageable chunks (states) with point- men representing them (politicians and sovereigns). These technical hurdles no long exist due to key innovations in our recent history (*e.g.*: modern computers, telecommunications, the internet, jet aircraft). Any honest academic must, at some point, humble himself before the facts and question the logic and suitability of societal structures cobbled together over thousands of years in contexts vastly different than our own. Moreover, we must consider the reaction of the global population-which is now more accustomed than ever to free and broad abilities to act socially - to a secondary place in international law (which is, recall, a social creation itself). At what point must we finally concede that the present international system no longer meets our needs, that a fundamental handicap to basic social intercourse has finally been lifted? We must, at the very least, concede that logic is not on our side in maintaining this shambolic arrangement of abstractions and legal fictions.

5. REAPPRAISING THE DOMINANT CONCEPTUAL APPROACH

For even though the United Nations is an organization of states, the Charter is written in the name of 'We the Peoples'...Ultimately, then, the United Nations exists for, and must serve, the needs and hopes of peoples everywhere[96]

Kofi Annan

5.1 Introduction

As we have just seen, interest-based Globalization effectively *combines* two inescapable realities for us as human beings living in a time defined by technology: the *means* to communicate and the *need* to communicate. If we were to re-invent our organizing systems–in other words, the law–how would it look? This is, I recognize, a potentially controversial question to pose. Some may consider it rather pointless as implementing the fruits of such an endeavour might well prove impossible. Yet others may object on the grounds that a critical analysis of the system we are currently beset with might lead to a weakening of our trust in it. In the author's opinion, both these and other objections of a similar character-namely aimed at dissuading a close scrutiny of the current positivist international legal system-are motivated primarily out of fear of what we might find.

We must recall, however, that scholar and practitioner alike have a responsibility to understand their subject as completely and from as many angles as possible. Theorizing about the law as we would approach an appeal *de novo*–from the very beginning-is an excellent way to determine what really matters to us. We are duty-bound in this regard as all human societies rely on the law for their communal wellbeing and determining precisely what is important to us as human beings living together is vital to our long-term survival–nothing less. Such an investigation is thus surely not in vein, as a clearer understanding of what we *ought* to focus on can help us better manage our present legal arrangements regardless of how sharply it diverges from a logical ideal and perhaps even illuminate us to new possibilities never before thought practical.

Reinventing the law in all its intricacy is clearly not within the ambit of this investigation. We shall concern ourselves here with what methodology *would* be best if we were able to just start over from scratch. In other words, we are aiming to define a broad framework upon which such a new system could be built (or, for that matter, transposed) which rectifies the many illogical aspects of the present positivist system. Marks, in one timely example, succinctly portrays the problem we face *interacting* with international law as it presently stands. She tells us that '... when we treat international law as a redemptive force that could save the world if only it were properly respected and enforced, we obscure the possibility that international legal norms may themselves have contributed to creating or sustaining the ills from which we are now to be saved.'[97] She continues that '[i]f all it would have taken to make the [2003] war in Iraq legal was a few more votes in the Security Council, then perhaps at least some of the energy that is going into affirming the illegality of the war should be turned on the question of whether there is something wrong with international law.' Clearly, are *motivations* for having an international legal system are not as plain as they could be.

5.2 The Problem with State-centricity

An important point must be made from the outset. The international legal order, *in se*, is not broken. The perceived failing of international law to come to, with consistency, just solutions to grave problems is not a failing of the law. The law need not be universally obeyed or entirely without substantive deficits to be considered functional. Indeed, arguably, the international legal order works as well as can be reasonably expected given its current structure. The problem is, rather, with the *subject* about whom it primarily concerns itself: the state. As we have already concluded, the state is an abstract creation of Man's imagination. It is without any independent life outside of our constructed reality–were we to stop believing in it, it would effectively cease to exist. It is thus extremely problematic to have at the centre of our legal order something which amounts to nothing more than a figment of our imagination. The universe of which Earth is part exists only because the planets which constitute it have mass, their substance that of rock and dirt. For international law to hold together, for gravity to work for us, we too need a substantive core - that of flesh and blood.

Whilst the issue of state-centrism is highly problematic from a decidedly notional point of view, it poses important analytical concerns as well. Marks points to three such concerns.[98] Firstly, that state-centrism leads to a preoccupation with state actors to the exclusion of non-state actors. Secondly, that state-centrism leads to an interpretative framework that gives undue weight to state sovereignty at the expense of human beings. Lastly, that states' acting as political antagonists tend to overshadow their basic character as legal beings and the concurrent responsibility to respect the law. While these and other practical criticisms of state-centricity are useful in identifying particular deficiencies in the dominant conceptual approach, they are of limited transformative utility. Whilst these factors may be viewed as *deficiencies* of the state-centric approach, they are in fact part and parcel of the statist concept. The state is *supposed* to be supreme, larger than life, the end-all and be-all of international law. It is to miss the point to chastise the state for merely conforming to its definition!

For better or for worse, state-centricity is here to stay for as long as we continue to rely on it as our conceptual foundation. Maccorquodale. tells us that '[i]f state sovereignty can no longer be a shield between the people and the international legal system, then the values of international society expressed in the Preamble of the UN Charter, being human rights, peace, justice, and a better standard of life, can be achieved.'[99] He later goes on to elaborate an 'inclusive international legal system' whereby both states and non-states have meaningful roles. To posit this, however, is to fall into the statist trap. The state as it is presently defined and understood in international law does not allow for a shared reign of any significance. Any intrusion by non-state actors into the state's domain has been at the sole discretion of the state – it is the community of states who get to decide the fate of other entities claim to (graduated) ILP.

The state is a fickle judge and the influence of non-state actors can be countered by various state actions including political denunciation, decisions of the Security Council (a form of collective state action), enactment of municipal laws, and the drafting of treaties aimed at restrictively regulating certain non-state activity. This already occurs with respect to certain non-state actors which are deemed a threat to the primacy of the state. Security Council Resolution 1373 (2001) effectively sought to regulate terrorist organizations, which are, of course, prominent non-state actors. (In thinking about the power of states *vis-à-vis* regulating access to ILP, consider for a moment the converse scenario. The community of states could just as easily have accepted al-Qa'ida as a legitimate international actor replete with functional legal personality similar to that of an international organization.) The ambit of 'peace and security' is limited only by the imagination of states and every non-state actor is a potential target of Resolution 1373-type regulation. The fact that this is uncommon merely points to the highly entrenched position of the statist concept and accordingly, the formidability an adversary must display to rouse concern on the part of states. The state-toped hierarchy is maintained despite the *illusion* of a diversified international plane.

Schreuer tells us that '... we should adjust our intellectual framework to a multi-layered reality consisting of a variety of authoritative structures ... [in which] what matters is not the formal status of a participant ... but its actual or preferable exercise of functions.'[100] Indeed, what Schreuer suggests conveys a noble sentiment, but attempting to implement such an idea would have devastating results for international law. Whilst an adjustment to our 'intellectual framework' is clearly in order, playing fast and loose with the formal status of participants is a sure recipe for disaster. Status and function are inseparably linked as function dictates status within the logical framework of a system. To change our focus from status to function would lead to chaos–our traditional indicators of status would be rendered meaningless as status is indeed *derived* from a qualitative appraisal of function. Even without the dead-end of the statist trap discussed above, the true implication of what Schreuer suggests is starting over from scratch. Indeed, it is impossible to simply 'adjust' our thinking to somehow shoehorn new participants meaningfully into the system: the system would cease to have internal coherence and it would implode. We must in a sense start anew with a level playing field which would abolish the formal hierarchal distinctions ingrained in positivist ILP and by doing so also re-define formal status.

In sum, all calls for mere adjustment or reform are, in actuality and practicality, calls for demolition and reconstruction. Any attempt to change the participatory composition of the international system must be in unqualified harmony with the positivist definition of the state. The only way to enlarge the *dramatis personæ* of international law is to abandon completely our present definition of the state. Somewhat ironically, it is not inconceivable that many of the positivist international lawyers who revel so openly in the perceived virtues of the state would keenly decry any such concept were it proposed today. A personified legal fiction so omnipotent that real persons, no less its very creators, are banished almost (or completely, depending on one's perspective) entirely from its realm is not an obvious fit with the sound legal reasoning often taken as synonymous with positivism, let alone with common sense. Indeed, it is only by completely parting with this anachronistic, illogical concept that international law can fulfil its essential function as law: assure the wellbeing of human beings.

5.3 A Philosophical Reorientation

Throughout this investigation, simplicity has been the goal in appraising both ILP and globalization. It is important to recognize that the world as we know it is merely a cycle of Man's creation and subsequent interpretation looped together and played over and over again. Everything we think or say, or think we know is invented by Man. The corollary of this is both empowering and bewildering. As unique creators of knowledge, we are on the one hand privileged to be able to reinvent what dissatisfies us, but on the other hand condemned to live in perpetual uncertainty over what approach is the most satisfactory to any given problem. On any issue there are at least as many possible interpretations as there are people to proffer them. It is for this exact reason that simplicity has been chosen as the cornerstone to this investigation. Elaborating some manner of 'first principles' capturing the essential elements of ILP, globalization and statehood–three concepts central to modern international law–is essential not only to having a *useful* understanding of the concepts themselves, but also the system of which they constitute critical components and which we depend on for our collective wellbeing.

The 'first principles' elaborated in this investigation fulfil this requirement for two reasons: (1) their applicability depends not on any political or theoretical affiliation, but merely on acknowledging Man as a social animal; and (2) they eschew purely effect-based considerations and focus instead on those which best capture the *meaning* attached to our use of the aforementioned concepts. To do otherwise would mire this investigation down in useless complexity which would undoubtedly stop us from gaining a better appreciation of what motivates us to elaborate these legal constructs in the first place. Only by having a clear idea of our core motivation can we elaborate concepts and erect systems which satisfy our needs. We must be wary of becoming blinded by the comforting certainty of the *status quo*: over time core motivations become lost as the levels of abstraction multiply. These steps away from the philosophical centre are, of course, necessary for the elaboration of socio-legal concepts in practice. However, we must remain ever conscious of this process of abstraction in the cause of elaboration and that it results in a dilution or masking of the original (core) motivations. What this means is that in simply using concepts to reach practical ends our perspective of that concept changes. When we build on core concepts they tend to get lost in the ensuing convolution, often to the point where they are unrecognizable, imperceptible or simply forgotten by the contemporary practitioner or theoretician. This socio-psychological dynamic poses perhaps the most serious peril to the usefulness of international law.

Experts and laymen alike are quick to highlight the failings of international law, but their criticism is usually directed at what they can see, what is obviously failing in their view. Take for instance the work of the UN Security Council–voting often results in inaction; yet the applicable voting system is made perfectly clear in Article 27 of UN Charter and as long as the relevant provisions are abided by, the result must be considered perfectly valid and legitimate. What must be understood is that a system needn't produce pleasing results to be considered functional–doing nothing at all is a perfectly valid option but is often unfairly derided as a prelude to irrelevance. If we are going to criticise the Security Council, we most definitely cannot point to its dysfunctionality. It is perfectly functional; its decisions are simply not in accordance with the wishes of many observes, and this is because its function is not necessarily what it should be or what many think it is. Indeed, the 'first principles' of the Security Council particularly are that the victors of the Second World War ought to have additional powers and *not* that all decisions must be taken in the interests of humanity. The Security Council can thus be considered as a particularly public example of sound UN 'first principles' becoming lost in abstraction to implement; 'We the Peoples' becoming 'We the Victors of a War'.

6. CONCLUSION

> There can be no law without human will. Individuals have always applied international law and individuals have always in the last resort been subject of international law either directly (as pirates, officers, etc.) or indirectly (as citizens of the State against which sanctions of one kind are applied).
>
> *Edvard Hambro*[101]

6.1 Introduction

Throughout this investigation we have engaged in a fairly weighty task: to examine key aspects of the modern international legal system and reduce them to their most essential elements. The aim of this exercise has been to gain a better understanding of what our central goals and motivations are for engaging in international legal discourse in the first place and how we can express these goals through a reworking of our idea of ILP. International law is no longer in its infancy–it has matured and in the process become more complex. One of the results of this natural and unavoidable process is that core values and motivations become the subject of abstraction as they are transformed into practice. It is, of course, impossible to implement an idea without engaging in abstraction, but in so doing one also risks eventually losing sight of the original motivation. It is my assertion that this is precisely what has happened in modern international law. Our basic legal assumptions like the concepts of state and ILP are sufficiently mature that few enquire whether or not they serve the original goals foundational to any legal order or even if they make sense–which, needless to say, the aforementioned concepts fall short on both counts.

6.2 The Broken Chain of Logic

Laws exist to help Man survive against the challenges posed his natural environment. Legal rules do this by regulating behaviour to facilitate cohabitation. As we saw in Section 2, de Groot, and others, correctly isolated this basic socio-legal truth. He considered that natural law was an automatic outflow of people living together in society. de Groot then proceeded to give the role of law a more abstractly valuative connotation, one which seemingly went beyond our simple day-to-day survival. He tells us that legal rules exist not because of the existence of God or religion, but rather as a necessity for *peaceful* cohabitation in society.[102] Even this seemingly straightforward proposition can be misleading if we do not look at it closely. Indeed, what we consider peaceful cohabitation is in itself an impulse driven by Man's instinct for *survival* - a mechanism which pushes Man to limit the threats which surround him. Law thus exists not for any abstract or value-laden concern, but rather simply to appease our instincts for survival. Law thus can be seen as merely a coincidental product of Man's physiological capability for complex and abstract thoughts, a characteristic which fundamentally distinguishes Man from other animals.

When law is looked at as simply a tool in our struggle for day-to-day survival, many of the possible questions which surround legal theory seem less complex. With a clear 'first principle', thinking about law's orientation with respect to the countless possible courses it can be steered in seems far less daunting. Prospective approaches need only be held against a simple test: on balance, is Man's survival and wellbeing helped or hindered? Interestingly–and perhaps tellingly-this is a question which cannot be satisfactorily posed–let alone answered–in the state-centric legal order.

6.2.1 State-centricity: A Terminal Problem for International Law

So long as the state dominates the concept of international legal personality–and is thus seen as the only eternally legitimate international actor-only issues implicating the state can satisfactorily be considered. Of course, issues vital to Man's survival and wellbeing can be included under the rubric of 'state concerns',[103] but this holds true for most anything as the 'state' is an abstraction invented by Man. Man can construe the concerns of his abstract creations any which way he likes–the only obstacle is arriving at a consensual definition of the concern; which is at its base a dilemma rooted more in psychology and sociology than in law. Issues of Man's survival and wellbeing *can* thus be concerns held by the state, but due to its constructed nature this is *not necessarily* so. Modern observes of international law run the risk of being led astray by the *illusion* of state concern for Man's wellbeing and into believing that the present system is geared toward the wellbeing of human beings. It is not: it is geared *solely* to the wellbeing and survival of states. States, in turn, may occasionally act in the interest of human beings but this is strictly by choice and in no way can be confounded with the fulfilment of a general duty to do so. Similarly, access to legal standing at international law rests, on final reckoning, with the community of states. Man is thus a sidebar in a system of his own design; his concerns merely sprinkled throughout a massive state-centric international bureaucracy. Man's wellbeing will *always* come in behind that of the state, as the state is still supreme at international law.

The test derived from the original and most basic function of law is thus inapplicable in the current system. State-centricity *prevents* law from performing its most fundamental goal, which is to ensure the wellbeing of human beings and survival of Mankind. State-centricity also hinders our ability to make logically sound decisions about the direction the law should take. We do not readily accept or recognize that elements of its fundamental purpose–Man's wellbeing-are present only as adjunct concerns within the abstract creation of the state. The state is thus responsible for breaking the chain of logic which starts at the fundamental purpose of law and ends ostensibly in our implementation of that purpose in as pure a fashion as possible: the core purposes of law remain true, it is our implementation which is flawed. In sum, the law can never accomplish its fundamental purpose so long as the state exists in its present form.

6.2.2 False Assumptions Lead to Chaos

When one begins with a false assumption, the outcome of everything built upon it becomes unreliable. Calculated actions do not produce the desired results because the situation upon which our deliberation is based is not as we *believe* it to be. No amount of effort can bring about reliable outcomes if our deliberations are based on misleading information. The idea that (positivist) international law exists to serve humanity is a thought which condemns those noble souls who truly believe this fallacious proposition to great and enduring frustration. A system designed to privilege the state will *never* result in the privileging of Man.

It is quite likely, in my estimation, that most people acquainted with international law know this to be the reality on some level or another. International law's conspicuous inability to produce consistent outcomes privileging seemingly elementary humanitarian considerations (*e.g.*: preventing and arresting genocide) signals to observers that something is amiss - if not what precisely the problem is. This, in turn, leads observers and practitioners alike to feel a sort of existential dread about international law. On one hand the international legal system often fails miserably in upholding values which we as a collective of human beings (ostensibly) hold dear, yet on the other hand we persist in believing in international law as a force for good, as mechanism with essentially *social* values and goals no matter how often the objective evidence contradicts this.

Our angst about the failures of positivist international law and our delusion as to its true purpose and potential leads us to *fear change*. We wilfully abstain from changing the foundations of international law from the state to the human person because we persist in *falsely* believing in the ability of positivist international law to serve the interests of Man. Our false assumption about the veritable purpose of international law as it stands leads to a chaotic and incoherent international system in which observers often feel betrayed and practitioners often feel helpless to control. Fearful and demoralized people *do not* advocate for change; they merely cope, continue on with the *status quo* and hope for the best.

6.3 Possible Salvation through Globalization?

As we have seen earlier, the concept of the state is incapable of accepting change: monopoly on full international legal personality is fundamental to its definition. The state, however, can be seen as a *response* to organizational challenges posed by the great size and distance separating the people who compose the 'real' elements of the international legal system. Our desire to interact in meaningful and constructive ways is evidenced by the very fact that an international legal system is present today–it having been pieced together long before technology allowed us simple and effective means to communicate, collaborate and organize. Our interest in our fellow Man is to thank for the system we have now, but it must be recognized that it is adapted to a far different reality than that which we currently enjoy. A fine example of this can be seen in the changes which have recently taken place in the field of diplomacy.

When looking at the traditional role of the ambassador, we find that it was one marked by a high degree of responsibility and autonomy, where an ambassador was expected to regularly make important decisions based only on general instructions from the sending government.[104] Since the advent of modern communications, the case for ambassadorial autonomy has become much harder to make, and as a result ambassadors have seen their autonomy steadily decrease.[105] The role of the ambassador was defined by a *practical problem* which plagued sovereigns for millennia; yet as the circumstances changed, so has the role played by the ambassador. It is only natural that changes like this should take place as the operative context changes over time.

6.3.1 Is a Popular Revolt on the Horizon?

The ultimate lesson to be drawn from globalization is that its technological element allows for organization on a larger scale than ever before. This whole phenomenon, in turn, has as its very foundation Man's innate interest in interacting with other human beings: in other words, a social and biologically-based force which is universal amongst Man, unalterable and now newly awoken. This genuinely new ability to organize ourselves efficiently to the lowest levels of societal stratification signals a fitting opportunity to move away from the state-centric international legal system and towards one built upon Man and his wellbeing. The populations of a globalized world are increasingly conditioned to expect opportunities to participate and are increasingly well informed about international law and dramatic events occurring all over the world. Human beings are increasingly aware of each other, they are continually reminded that a wider social world exists, that they are part of it and that it is composed people much like themselves. It will thus become ever more difficult to justify to these masses of sensitized people that an international system based on the state is the correct and best course of action. This, all the while, as the traditional hard boundaries associated with the state continue to erode from the inside out. As this wearing away continues, fuelled by cheap technology, populations will eventually rebel against the idea of their international standing being dictated by a state-centric theory who's principle actor (the state) is *visibly* sliding further toward (perceived and actual) irrelevance. At some point international law and international lawyers will be faced with a chilling question: do we really want 6.6 billion people rallying against us?

Let us be clear, my purpose in signalling this opportunity (and concern) is not one born out of *naïve* utopianism–it is rather an exercise in buttressing intellectual honesty within the field of international law. Law must formally put Man on an equal footing with any other legal entity populating the international sphere. This is so even if the immediate practical benefits are not apparent. As a philosophical and psychological readjustment for international law and for international lawyers, it is fundamental to re-align the international system with the 'first principles' of law: safeguarding the wellbeing of Mankind. By repositioning Man at the centre of all our legal notions, we would be forced to refer to the interests of humanity in making legal decisions. Our system would be put back on track, aligned with the 'first principles' of law: the state would surrender its place to the human being. If preventing war, alleviating starvation, arresting genocides, etc., are activities we deem worthy of effort–no doubt because of their human impacts–then we should just admit this in our foundational theories. The populations of states likely agree with this, even if their governments do not–which is precisely the type of discord which is highlighted and heightened by the organizational and informational effects of globalization. Indeed, a clear theoretical motivation for international law–serving Mankind and the interests of humanity–would make the international legal process simpler and more predictable and above all one with popular support.

As it concerns practitioners, it would be some accomplishment in itself to gain a broad acceptance not that better alternatives exist, but that the dominant positivist conceptual approach has serious logical inconsistencies. Intriguing as alternative approaches may be to academics, change is improbable if we continue to focus our practical efforts on merely 'fixing' the present system. It is the most insidious form of self-delusion, given the fundamental flaws of the present system, to tolerate and encourage sincere effort to 'revise' the state-centric system to better serve the interests of humanity.

It might be, and quite understandably, incomprehensible to many that our current system with all the assorted references to Man and Mankind could really be indifferent to the plights faced daily by the entirety of humanity. This is however the reality. We have inherited a system cobbled together to serve a different reality than our own, with a different demographic than our own – one before modern communications where state monopolization of ILP was essentially the default outcome. Through the process of abstraction and with the progression of time, we have lost sight of law's 'first principles'; we have allowed a default outcome to become a panacea of false virtue. In sum, academic and practitioner alike must admit that the current system is faulty and *irreparable*.

Instigating this type of change is the true challenge here. The first step is, of course, opening one's mind to different foundational concepts of international law. Indeed, it is perhaps more important –and more realistic–to frame the solution not in terms of adopting any particular alternative, but rather to earnestly admit that the positivist state-centric system must eventually be abandoned. Doing this, interestingly enough, is less a problem for the lawyer as it is one for psychologists. It is a particularly futile endeavour to make the case for an alternative when ones audience (mainstream international lawyers) is too fearful–consumed simply hoping things don't get any worse - to seriously consider change. In this regard, it would be especially interesting to see psychologists enter the discussion and offer advice on presenting (conceivably) radical sounding ideas in a manner tuned toward minimizing anxiety. If the legal reasoning behind abolishment of state-centrism is sound–which I believe it is–then we must consider that perhaps the problem in gaining wide acceptance lies in the *packaging* of these ideas; something psychologists can help refine.

Were we to accomplish this intellectual *glasnost*, Man's instincts–his interest in other human beings–would likely accomplish something similar in international law as Adam Smith's 'invisible hand' does for the economy. This new system would clearly have to dispense entirely with the concept of the state due to its inalterable definition.[106] The new system, in turn, would have to be built with as little abstraction away from our 'first principle' of Man's survival and wellbeing as possible. The only way to accomplish this is to weigh every decision in that system's elaboration and subsequent alternation against that 'first principle' test. A first step in this journey is perhaps simply acknowledging that Man built the legal system in the first place and we are not helpless in the face of it; what we put up between us and the law we can take down.

Notes

1. I. Seidl-Hohenveldern and G. Loibl, *Das Recht der Internationalen Organisationen einschließlich der Supranationalen Gemeinschaften* (2000), 48.
2. H. Schermers and N. Blokker, *International Institutional Law* (2003), 985.
3. For example, a swath of land may possess an uncontroverted physical existence and yet not be considered a state at international law.
4. Indeed, it is possible to have a workable system which is in fact fundamentally flawed. However, doing so is wildly inefficient as one must work remedially to counter the effect of structural (that is, theoretical) flaws at the lower levels of abstraction. Flaws at the lower levels of the systemic structure result in unexpected outcomes which, if the desired outcome is to be eventually achieved, must be worked around. This results in wasted effort, unclear motivations, unsatisfactory results and ultimately a developmentally *limited* system.
5. *Edwards v. Attorney-General for Canada*, [1930] AC 124 (PC) at 136.
6. *Reference re Same-Sex Marriage*, [2004] 3 SCR 698, 2004 SCC 79 at para. 22.
7. *Ibid.*, at para. 23.
8. *infra*. Subsection 4.2.
9. P. Malanczuk, *Akehurst's Modern Introduction to International Law* (1997), 91.
10. Statute of the International Court of Justice, Art. 35.
11. Charter of the United Nations, Art. 4(1).
12. See Malanczuk, *supra* note 9, at 92.
13. *Ibid.*, at 92.
14. M. Shaw, *International Law* (2003), 176.
15. *Ibid.*, at 177.
16. *Ibid.*
17. Surely an entity cannot ascribe what it does not have.
18. *Convention for the Protection of Human Rights and Fundamental Freedoms*, ETS 5, Protocol 11.
19. P. Menon, 'The Legal Personality of individuals', (1994) 6 *Sri Lanka J. Int'l L.* 127, at 129.
20. *Ibid.*
21. Statute of the International Tribunal for the Prosecution of Persons Responsible for Serious Violations of International Humanitarian Law Committed in the Territory of the Former Yugoslavia since 1991, UN Doc. S/25704, at 36, annex (1993) and S/25704/Add.1 (1993), adopted by Security Council on 25 May 1993, UN Doc. S/RES/827 (1993).
22. Resolution 827, UN Doc. S/RES/827 (1993).

23. Though conditioned on the acceptance of that participation by the community of states.
24. S. Vago and A. Nelson, *Law and Society: Canadian Edition* (2004), 31.
25. R. Cuzzort, *Humanity and Modern Sociological Thought* (1969), 175.
26. R. Brown, *Social Psychology* (1965), 5-6.
27. See Vago and Nelson, *supra* note 24, at 17.
28. R. Pound, *An Introduction to the Philosophy of Law* (1922), 98-9.
29. See Vago and Nelson, *supra* note 24, at 16.
30. Translation from Latin: All law is created for the benefit of Man.
31. Sara M. Pons-Sanz, Norse-Derived Vocabulary in Late Old English Texts. Wulfstan's Works, a Case Study (2007), 80.
32. Black's Law Dictionary at 1255 (4th ed. 1951).
33. *e.g.*: Declaring war against ones neighbour for trespassing through your garden.
34. See Malanczuk, *supra* note 9, at 11.
35. See, *e.g.*, *Customs Régime Between Germany and Austria* (Advisory Opinion), PCIJ Rep Series A/B No 41, at 26; and *SS Lotus case* (*France v. Turkey*), PCIJ Rep Series A No 10, at 153/5.
36. See, *e.g.*, Declaration on Principles of International Law concerning Friendly Relations and Co-operation among States in accordance with the Charter of the United Nations, UN Doc. A/5217 (1970), at 124.
37. See, *e.g.*, Shaw, *supra* note 14, at 189 et seq.
38. L. Oppenheim, *International Law: A Treatise* (1912), 19.
39. Reparation for Injuries Suffered in the Service of the United Nations, Advisory Opinion, Advisory Opinion of 11 April 1949, [1949] ICJ Rep. 174 at 180.
40. See Schermers and Blokker, *supra* note 2, at 993.
41. H. Lauterpacht, 'The Subjects of the Law of Nations', (1948) 64 *L. Q. Rev.* at 112.
42. See Malanczuk, *supra* note 9, at 100.
43. R. Higgins, 'Conceptual Thinking About The Individual In International Law', in Richard Falk *et al.* (eds.), *International Law: A Contemporary Perspective* (1985), 476, at 478.
44. See Malanczuk, *supra* note 9, at 15.
45. *Ibid.*
46. L. Chipman, 'Grotius and the Derivation of Natural Law', (1983) *Bull. Austl. Soc. Leg. Phil.* 66, at 68.

47. M. Korowicz, 'The Problem of the International Personality of Individuals', (1956) 50 *Am. J. Int'l L.* 533, at 534; *Cf.* de Groot's definition of the state: *Est autem civitas coetus perfectus liberorum hominum juris fruendi et communis utilitatis causa sociatus.* De Jure Belli ac Pacis, L. I, Chapter I & XIV.

48. See Menon, *supra* note 19, at 151.

49. T. Hobbes, *De Cive (Imperium)* (1647) Chapter XIV; See Korowicz is note 47, at 534.

50. S. Pufendorf, *De jure naturae et gentium libri octo* (1688) Vol. II, Chapter III; See Korowicz is note 47, at 533.

51. See Menon, *supra* note 19, at 129.

52. *Ibid.*

53. See Malanczuk, *supra* note 9, at 16.

54. B.B.Röben, 'The Method Behind Bluntschli's 'Modern' International Law', (2002) 4 *J. Hist. Int'l L.* 249, at 249.

55. *Ibid.*, at 249.

56. *Ibid.*, at 249/62.

57. *Ibid.*, at 249-50.

58. *Ibid.*, at 265.

59. *Ibid.*

60. G. Manner, 'The Object Theory of the Individual in International Law', (1952) 46 *Am. J. Int'l L.* 428, at 449.

61. P. Heilborn, *Das System des Völkerrechts* (1896), at 84.

62. F. De Martens, *Traité de droit international* (1883), Vol. I, at 428/42.

63. *e.g.*: Malanczuk analogizing the position of animals as objects in municipal law to that of individuals in international law. See Malanczuk, *supra* note 9, at 91.

64. Cf. Section 2.2.1.

65. L. le Fur, *La théorie du droit naturel depuis le XVIIIe siècle et la doctrine moderne* (1928), 92.

66. A. Verdross, 'Règles générals du droit international de la paix' (1929) 30 *Hague Recueil* 347/9.

67. L. Oppenheim (ed.), *Collected Papers of John Westlake* (1914), at 78.

68. J. Nijman, *The Concept of International Legal Personality : An Inquiry Into the History and Theory of International Law* (2004), 197.

69. T. Zeldin, *France 1848-1954* (1973), Vol. I, at 593-94.

70. See Nijman is note 68, at 198.

71. *Ibid.*, at 199.

72. *Ibid.*, at 198.

73. *Ibid.*, at 199.

74. *Ibid.*, at 203.

75. N. Politis, *Les Nouvelles Tendances du Droit International* (1927), 73.

76. *Ibid.*, at 72-3.

77. *Ibid.*, at 78-9.

78. G. Renard, *La Théorie de L'Institution* (1930), 543-4.

79. V. Kumar, 'A Critical Methodology of Globalization: Politics of the 21st Century?', (2003) 10 *Ind. J. Global Legal Stud.* 87, at 88.

80. *Ibid.*

81. *Ibid.*

82. J. Mittelman, 'How Does Globalization Really Work?', in James Mittelman. (ed.), *Globalization: Critical Reflections* (1996), 229, at 230.

83. J. Grugel and W. Hout, 'Regions, Regionalism, and the South', in J. Grugel and W. Hout (eds.), *Regionalism Across the North-South Divide: State Strategies and Globalization* (1999), at 5.

84. S. Krishna-Hensel, 'Globalization and the International System, in S. Krishna-Hensel (ed.), *The New Millennium* (2000), at 5.

85. A. Bhalla, 'Introduction', in A. Bhalla (ed.), *Globalization, Growth and Marginalization* (1998), at 1-6.

86. G. van Liemt, 'Labour in the Global Economy: Challenges, Adjustment and Policy Responses in the EU', in O. Memedovic et al. (eds.), *Globalization of Labour Markets: Challenges, Adjustment and Policy Response in the European Union and Less Developed Countries* (1998), at 237.

87 88. See Kumar is note 79, at 102.

89. R. Kilminster, 'Globalization as an Emergent Concept', in A. Scott (ed.), *The Limits of Globalization: Cases and Arguments* (1997), at 257.

90. J. Baylis and S. Smith, 'Introduction', in J. Baylis and S. Smith (eds.), *The Globalization of World Politics: An Introduction to International Relations* (1997), at 7.

91. R. Robertson, *Globalization: Social Theory and Global Culture* (1992), 8.

92. J. Micklethwait and A. Wooldridge, *A Future Perfect: The Challenge and Hidden Promise of Globalization* (2000), at xviii.

93. R. Langhorne, *The Coming of Globalization: Its Evolution and Contemporary Consequences* (2001), at 2.

94. It should be noted that the state can be both globalizer and victim of globalization's blurring effect. By encouraging the economic aspects of globalization, states participate in advancing their own erosion.

95. See Brown, *supra* note 26, at 79.